Wellington and the Lines of Torres Vedras

The Defence of Lisbon during the Peninsular War, 1807–1814

Mark S. Thompson

Helion & Company

Helion & Company Limited
Unit 8 Amherst Business Centre
Budbrooke Road
Warwick
CV34 5WE
England
Tel. 01926 499619
Email: info@helion.co.uk
Website: www.helion.co.uk
Twitter: @helionbooks
Visit our blog at http://blog.helion.co.uk/

Published by Helion & Company 2021
Designed and typeset by Mach 3 Solutions Ltd (www.mach3solutions.co.uk)
Cover designed by Paul Hewitt, Battlefield Design (www.battlefield-design.co.uk)

ISBN 978-1-914059-85-8

British Library Cataloguing-in-Publication Data.
A catalogue record for this book is available from the British Library.

For details of other military history titles published by Helion & Company Limited,
contact the above address, or visit our website: http://www.helion.co.uk

We always welcome receiving book proposals from prospective authors.

Contents

Foreword

The Lines of Torres Vedras, whose purpose was to prevent the French conquest of Lisbon and the subsequent control of Europe's best Atlantic Ocean natural harbour, were never tested to their limit. The French invading troops of *l'Armée de Portugal*, under the command of *Maréchal* Masséna, bearing direct orders from Napoleon, stopped in front of the Lines, and only made weak attempts to test the fortifications which had been built so close to the objective of the French campaign.

What were the Lines of Torres Vedras?

In a notable short definition of a complex system, Professor Donald D. Horward wrote:

> The roads approaching the Lines were cut and barricaded; valleys were blocked with abatis; trenches were dug and hills scarped; rocky slopes were blasted into perpendicular precipices; trees obstructing the field of fire were felled; bridges were mined; and rivers were dammed and flooded. To facilitate the rapid movement of troops and communications, lateral roads (some of stone) were constructed, the Royal Navy established a telegraph system along the Lines, gunboats were anchored in the Tagus to cover the flanks, and construction workers, numbering in the thousands, were conscripted from as far away as fifty miles. By October 1810 the Lines included 126 redoubts and 249 guns manned by 29,750 men, supplemented by Wellington's entire field army of 60,000 men[1], ready to plug any gaps created by an enemy attack. It was unquestionably a novel scheme. If successful, Portugal would be saved; if a failure, Wellington's army would be driven into the sea, captured, or forced to take refuge on ships of the Royal Navy, leaving British foreign policy in a shambles.[2]

However, the Lines of Torres Vedras were much more than a strong defensive position. Indeed, they were the cornerstone of a strategic vision.

In 1810, Portugal was still recovering from the two previous French invasions (1807–1808 and 1809), which had brought violence and misery to

---

1   Professor Horward is considering here the combined strength of the Allied army, 60,000 men, adding together the figures of both the British and the Portuguese in equal proportions.
2   Donald D. Horward, 'Wellington and the Defence of Portugal', *The International History Review*, Vol.11, 1989, pp.44–45.

Portugal, and was preparing for the announced third invasion designed to be the *coup de grâce* to take control of a rebellious country that had resisted the Emperor's will, with the ultimate aim to finally drive the British leopard into the sea. For the British, the fate of Moore's army at La Coruña, in the winter of 1808–1809, was never to be repeated; for the Portuguese, the defence of Lisbon was a question of survival.

The Anglo-Portuguese Allied army, under the command of Viscount Wellington, was composed of a relatively small British army, which was the only British field army available for immediate use, and the Portuguese army, under the command of *Marechal* William Carr Beresford. The latter army had been reorganised and disciplined from 1809 onwards, with considerable support from the British nation, and by 1810 it was in the process of recovering its operational capability, which was a vital pillar of the British strategy.

Neither army was capable of defending Portugal on its own, let alone survive the onslaught of the huge masses of the French armies, which had gathered hundreds of thousands of troops under the French flag in occupied Spain. Nevertheless, together they could make a stand and attempt to reverse the trend witnessed all over continental Europe – the domination of Napoleon.

The defeat of Wellington's irreplaceable army, together with the potential loss of a foothold in continental Europe would have been fatal for the overall strategy to defeat Napoleon. Built to protect the Allied army, the Lines of Torres Vedras were the only defensive position capable of stopping a large French army advancing deep into hostile territory, having been designed to destroy the enemy's energy and morale, due to the lack of supplies. Masséna was to become isolated, for never having been a master of the terrain, he ended up 'surrounded' by the Allied army and also the Portuguese militia which incessantly harassed his army's rear and lines of communication with Spain.

In one of the most useful books ever written on leadership, Sun Tzu, states that 'to fight and conquer in all your battles is not supreme excellence; supreme excellence consists in breaking the enemy's resistance without fighting.'[3]

Much more recently, Liddell Hart wrote in his 'Indirect Approach' thesis, that '[T]he foundation of the British success [in the Peninsular War] lay in Wellington's shrewd calculation of the economic factor – the limited French means of subsistence – and his construction of the lines of Torres Vedras. His strategy was essentially that of indirect approach to a military-economic object and objective.'[4]

The Lines of Torres Vedras were a major example in military history of the principles of 'winning without fighting' and the 'Indirect Approach'. The Lines played a pivotal role in Wellington's strategic plan and were the cornerstone of the Allied victory over the French in the Peninsular War.

---

3   Sun Tzu, *Art of War* (New York: Barnes & Noble Classics, 2003), p.43.
4   Basil Liddell Hart, *Strategy: The Indirect Approach* (London: Faber & Faber, 1967), p.146.

Nevertheless, as the victory was achieved without fighting with no notable short-term decisive results, the Lines of Torres Vedras lack the same distinction as well-known victories in battles such as Talavera (1809), Bussaco (1810), Albuera (1811), Salamanca (1812), and Vittoria (1813).

The whole concept of the Lines of Torres Vedras was a masterpiece. A masterpiece of ingenuity, deception, secrecy, planning, and execution, not to mention the sheer hard work. A masterpiece which further strengthened the bonds between the Allied armies that had been forged during the heavy fighting on the ridge of Bussaco. A masterpiece that helped to bring about positive consequences with regards both the enemy, and also at home – in London, Lisbon, and Rio de Janeiro.

The planning, preparation, construction, and defence of the Lines were the responsibility of many actors: ranging from the decision of the Commander-in-Chief to the support given to him by D. Miguel Pereira Forjaz in the Regency; from the leadership of the officers of the Royal Engineers to the work of the Portuguese militias and peasantry; and also, from the occupation of the position by the Allied forces through to the support provided by the Royal Navy on the river Tagus.

The work of Dr Mark Thompson is a real gem in terms of the recognition of all these actors.

Based on a profound research of British, Portuguese, and French sources, this is an indispensable book for understanding the political difficulties of Wellington in his relationship with London and Lisbon, as well as the details of the making of the Lines.

The author gives the reader the benefit of his years of research and expertise on the topic of the Lines and has written a book which represents a masterful source of precious and enduring information. Those who think that all that is known has already been written on the subject will be pleasantly surprised to learn even more based on the further revelations brought to light in Dr Thompson's excellent book, which also serves as an excellent guide for those who plan to visit the Lines.

Major-general (Portuguese Army, retd) Rui Moura

Acknowledgements

This book is the result of an interest in military engineering that goes back 15 years and a request over 10 years ago by the Waterloo Association to prepare a talk on the Lines of Torres Vedras for the 200th anniversary of their construction. This interest led me to an amazing evening at the House of Lords in 2010 where a Portuguese government delegation visited specifically to discuss fostering relations to support the Lines of Torres Vedras. The formation of the Friends of the Lines of Torres Vedras followed, and it still retains links with the British government and has the Duke of Wellington as its patron.

Three people stand out for their work to develop an interest in the Lines, both in the general public and at governmental level. In Portugal, Clive Gilbert has worked tirelessly for many years to preserve the Lines and raise their profile. For his work he was awarded an MBE in 2017. Colonel (retd) Gerald Napier RE has played a similar role based in the UK encouraging interest in both countries. The bicentenary has triggered an explosion of interest in Portugal and there are many new books on the subject, the best being, *Coronel* (retd) Francisco de Sousa Lobo's, *A Defesa de Lisboa*, published in 2015.[1]

The Portuguese government and the local municipalities should also be thanked for their care of the many locations and their decision to make them National Monuments, which will help in their preservation. In 2014, 20 October was declared the *Dia Nacional das Linhas de Torres*. I would particularly like to thank the President of Torres Vedras, Carlos Bernardes and Councillor Ana Umbelino for their kindness during several meetings and visits.[2]

Many people have helped me in this journey, and I would like to recognise their support (in no particular order). This is my second book published by Helion and I would like to thank *From Reason to Revolution* commissioning editor Andrew Bamford, and Rob Griffith for his excellent copy-editing skills. The cover image comes from the easel of Chris Collingwood, who was commissioned by the Royal Engineers to paint this work to commemorate the 200th anniversary of the building of the Lines. I am grateful for his

---

1   Francisco de Sousa Lobo, *A Defesa de Lisboa 1809–1814* (Lisboa: Tribuna, 2015).
2   Carlos Bernardes tragically died in May 2021.

permission to use it. Please visit his website and see his superb paintings and prints: www.collingwoodhistoricart.com.

There are several people in Portugal who have provided the time and their knowledge freely. These include *Dra* Isabel Luna, Carlos Cunha and *Capitão de Fragata* (retd) Rui Sa Leal who helped particularly with Torres Vedras and telegraphs. *Major General* (retd) Rui Moura and *Coronel* José Paulo Berger have assisted with excellent advice and access to the military archives. I must also say a huge thank you to Rui for reading the manuscript, offering improvements, and writing the Foreword.

I would like to say 'nearer home', but since one lives in Australia and one in Hawaii it is maybe not correct, but it certainly feels like they are neighbours. Over many years I have received support and guidance from Rory Muir and Bob Burnham on all things Napoleonic and I greatly value access to their vast knowledge. Anthony Grey and Kenton White have willingly provided information from their knowledge of Masséna's third invasion and Zack White has helped in many ways including looking at the Wellington Archives to save me a 1,000 kilometre round trip. His enthusiasm to take Wellington on-line during the COVID pandemic should also be recognised; it has helped to keep many of us sane.

Finally, an unsung hero. My thanks to Kim McSweeney at Mach 3 Solutions (the typesetter) who has patiently and professionally led me through the process of getting the maps ready for publication.

Mark S. Thompson, April 2021

A Note About the Map of the Lines

When I started to draw a map of the Lines, I used the large map in John Jones' *Sieges*[1] and the even larger map held in The National Archives (TNA: MR1-523). What quickly became apparent was that neither was geographically accurate. The forts were generally in the right place, but the terrain was not drawn accurately.

My next step was to obtain modern topographical data, which was obtained from the www.opentopography.org website. This allowed me to build an accurate contour map of the area with GPS co-ordinates. Having done this, the exact position of known forts was added to the map using their correct GPS coordinates. Forts that no longer exist were then placed in their position based on their historical position (e.g. at Alhandra).

The biggest challenge was accurately placing the roads and in some cases the rivers. These were added using modern and historical maps with the most likely route used if there was no concensus. There is a huge difference in the roads shown on various maps, so there will always be some uncertainty about their position, particularly with the smaller routes.

A Note on Wellington's Dispatches

There are three versions of Gurwood's edited collection of Wellington's Dispatches. My primary source is the eight volume *New and Enlarged edition* of 1852. When citing from Wellington's Dispatches, I have included the details of the letter, including the date, but not the volume and page number. This allows readers to also use the original volumes 1–9 published between 1834–1837, or the revised 12 volume *New Edition* of 1837–1839, to look up most citations. The content of each of the versions is different. Fortunately, there is only one version of the Supplementary Despatches and volume and page number are used for these.

Place Names

In the book, I have used the modern national spelling of place names with the exception of Lisbon and Tagus, where I have retained the usual English spelling. I have not altered the spelling of places in quotations.

---

1   J.T.J. Jones, *Journal of the Sieges Carried out by the Army Under the Duke of Wellington*, 3rd Edition (London: John Weale, 1846).

Abbreviations Used

ACM	Arquivo Central da Marinha (Portugal)
AHM	Arquivo Histórico Militar (Portugal)
BD	Bibliotecas da Defesa (Portugal)
BL	British Library
BNP	Biblioteca Nacional de Portugal
REM	Royal Engineers Museum
TNA	The National Archives
WP	Wellington Papers, Southampton University

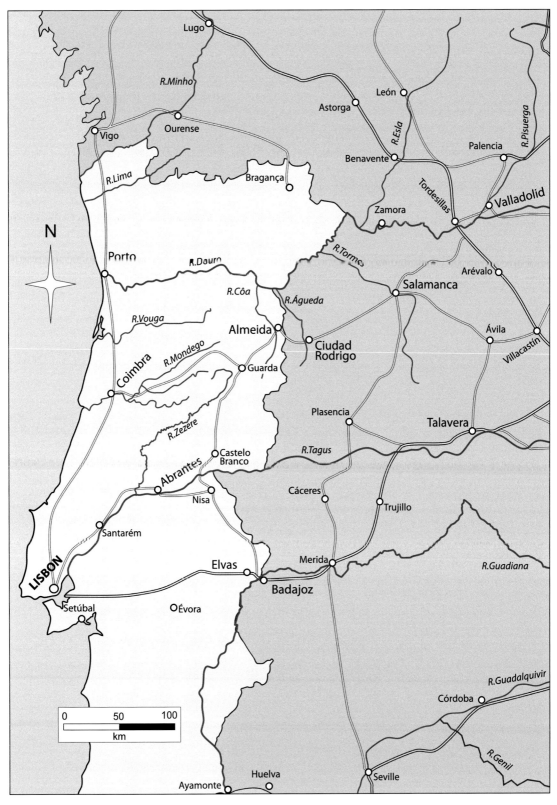

Portugal and Central Spain.

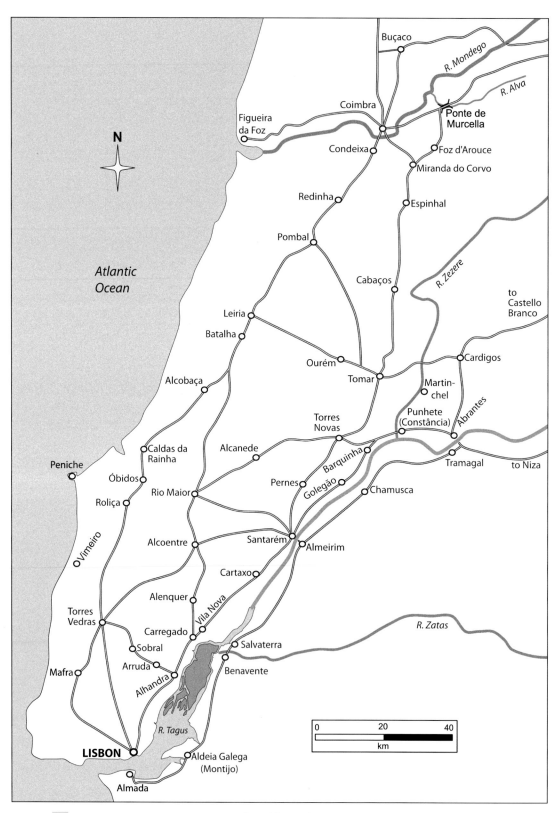

Central Portugal.

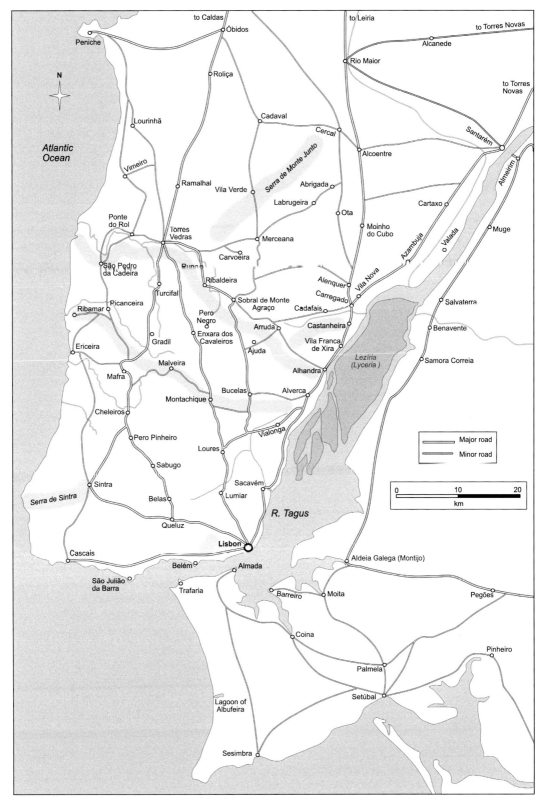

N

Atlantic
Ocean

to Caldas
Peniche
Óbidos
to Leiria
to Torres Novas
Alcanede
Rio Maior
Roliça
to Torres
Novas
Lourinhã
Cadaval
Santarém
Cercal
Vimeiro
Alcoentre
Ramalhal
Serra de Monte Junto
Abrigada
Vila Verde
Cartaxo
Labrugeira
Ponte
do Rol
Ota
Muge
Torres
Vedras
Merceana
Moinho
do Cubo
São Pedro
da Cadeira
Carvoeira
Ribaldeira
Alenquer
Vila Nova
Salvaterra
Turcifal
Sobral de Monte
Agraço
Carregado
Picanceira
Pero
Negro
Cadafais
Ribamar
Castanheira
Benavente
Arruda
Enxara dos
Cavaleiros
Ericeira
Gradil
Ajuda
Vila Franca
de Xira
Samora Correia
Malveira
Alhandra
Lezíria
(Lyceria)
Mafra
Bucelas
Alverca
Cheleiros
Montachique
Vialonga
Major road
Minor road
Pero Pinheiro
Loures
Sabugo
0   10   20
km
Sintra
Sacavém
Serra de Sintra
Belas
Lumiar
R. Tagus
Queluz
Cascais
Lisbon
Belém
Aldeia Galega (Montijo)
São Julião
da Barra
Almada
Trafaria
Barreiro
Moita
Pegões
Coina
Pinheiro
Palmela
Lagoon of
Albufeira
Setúbal
Sesimbra

Lisbon Peninsula.

1

Introduction

Wellington, writing to Charles Stuart, British Minister Plenipotentiary to Portugal on 6 October 1810, the day before the first of his troops arrived at the Lines of Torres Vedras, said, 'I believe that you and the government do not know where the Lines are. Those round Lisbon are not those in which I shall place the army, but those extending from Torres Vedras to the Tagus.'[1] It has been said that the French did not know about the Lines, but were the Portuguese government and the British Minister also ignorant of their existence? This is one of many questions that need answering about the defence of Lisbon during the Peninsular War.

Britain and Portugal have been allies for a very long time; over 600 years. In 1385, King Richard II supported King João I of Portugal against a Castilian invasion. At the Battle of Aljubarrota on 14 August 1385, a Portuguese army, 7,000 strong, of which 700 were English, defeated a combined Spanish and French army of 20,000. This friendship was formalised by the Treaty of Windsor in 1386. King João married Phillipa of Lancaster, the daughter of John of Gaunt. Over this long period there have been high and low points but the relationship between the two countries is still strong today.

The Lines of Torres Vedras were one physical example of this strong bond and at the start of the nineteenth century showed a British willingness to support Portugal against foreign aggressors. Even before the Peninsular War started, there had been a British force in Portugal in 1797 to deter a Spanish invasion which was supported by the French.[2] The British presence would have been a strong disincentive for any advance on Lisbon. This threat of invasion was to try to force Portugal to close its ports to British trade; the same cause that led to the eventual French invasion in 1807.

The bicentenary of the Napoleonic wars had led to an increased interest in military history and Portugal has shown great perseverance in preserving and protecting the Lines of Torres Vedras and developing the tourist

---

1   John Gurwood (ed.), *Dispatches of the Duke of Wellington. New and Enlarged Edition* (London: John Murray, 1852), Wellington to Stuart, Rio Maior, 6 October 1810. This is the edition referenced unless specifically stated otherwise.

2   John Fortescue, *History of the British Army* (London: Macmillan, 1899–1930), Vol.4, part 2, pp.601–602.

potential. The remaining forts that make up the first and second Lines are spread over six local municipalities and these organisations have worked together to obtain funding and provide a consistent plan for their future. Many have been cleared and preserved; there are now several 'Interpretation Centres'; signposts to the major forts; route guides for visitors and many new publications on the subject. The book on the Lines of Torres Vedras by *Coronel* Francisco de Sousa Lobo will remain the definitive work for many years to come.

Two other major events have shown the commitment to the future of the Lines. Firstly, the Portuguese government has declared 20 October as 'Lines of Torres Vedras Day' and this is remembered annually with various events. More importantly, the Lines are now recognised as a national monument and are protected from future damage or development.

It is now nearly 200 years since John Jones published his work on the building of the Lines, in 1829.[3] At the time, the publishing was delayed due to the civil war in Portugal and the view that the information could be of strategic value. The last book on the Lines published in English was nearly 20 years ago and there has been a great deal of new information found since then.[4] Much of the new research is by Portuguese historians and not easily accessible to the English-speaking market. There has also been a comprehensive study of the activities of the French chief engineer Vincent during his time in Portugal.[5]

Many people reading about the Lines see a carefully planned and organised engineering project lasting over a year. The truth is a bit different. From a fairly simple outline the development grew organically over three years with enhancements and adjustments continuing well past the date when the Lines were occupied.

This book will bring up to date the study of the Lines and the various people, British, Portuguese and French who contributed to the development of the defensive system that withstood the best of Napoleon's marshals.

The need for the defence of Lisbon

Portugal was a seafaring nation. It had territories all over the world and had been one of the great economic powerhouses in Europe. By the end of the eighteenth century, its power was past its peak, but it still obtained great wealth from overseas territories, particularly from Brazil. The Tagus estuary was lined with forts to defend Lisbon and the trade which entered the river, but once away from the coast Portuguese fleets were vulnerable to other

---

3   J.T.J. Jones, *Memoranda Relative to the Lines Thrown Up to Cover Lisbon in 1810* (London: Private circulation, 1829). This was also published later as volume three of Jones' third edition of *Journal of the Sieges...* in 1846.

4   Ian Fletcher, *The Lines of Torres Vedras, 1809–11* (London: Osprey, 2003). Also, John Grehan, *The Lines of Torres Vedras* (Staplehurst: Spellmount, 2000).

5   A. Vincente, *Le Génie Français au Portugal Sous L'Empire* (Lisbonne: Estado-Maior do Exercito, 1984).

seafaring nations as it was no longer able to compete with powerful navies such as those of France or Britain.

Portugal tried very hard to remain neutral as war flared across Europe, but this was impossible. France wanted an economic blockade of Britain and there were to be no exemptions, especially from countries seen as Britain's allies. The first attempt at enforcing the closure of Portuguese ports at the end of the eighteenth century was not successful but by 1807, Napoleon's patience had ended. His plan for invading Britain had been abandoned and economic warfare was now his main weapon. The Portuguese Regent was given an ultimatum, to enact the blockade or be deposed. Unfortunately for João, the Prince Regent, there was similar pressure being applied by the British government. If Portugal sided with the French, Britain would take or destroy the Portuguese navy and disrupt the trade with South America. This would have been catastrophic to the Portuguese economy.

The French *Général de division* Jean Andoche Junot, with Spanish permission, crossed Spain into Portugal, arriving at Lisbon on 30 November 1807.[6] Just before his arrival, the Portuguese Royal Family along with thousands of citizens, had sailed for Brazil with a strong Royal Navy escort. The Regent had given orders for the army and population not to resist the invasion hoping to spare his country the worst of the ravages that a French invasion entailed. It did not work, but it was his only hope. France now held the largest city in Portugal which again appeared to show the futility of resisting Napoleonic France.[7]

The French invasion of Portugal marked the start of the Peninsular War, which continued for the next seven years until the abdication of Napoleon in 1814. Whilst Junot consolidated his hold on Portugal, Napoleon saw another opportunity in Spain where the Royal Family were in public disagreement. Inviting them to Bayonne in 1808, Napoleon forced the Spanish king and his son to abdicate in favour of Napoleon's brother, Joseph. This caused open revolt in Spain and with the similar insurrection against French rule in Portugal, the whole Iberian Peninsula was soon in open revolt and both nations sent emissaries to Britain seeking support.

Junot was now placed in a difficult position. Whilst there was no organised regular military resistance, there was armed civilian rebellion across the country; he had limited forces to maintain order and there was little chance of reinforcements being sent. His challenge was how to defend Lisbon and Portugal against internal and external forces. This was a challenge that over the next three years, France, then Portugal, then Britain had to face.

---

6   For his efforts, Junot was given the title Duc d'Abrantès.
7   Lisbon was not the capital city, which moved to Rio de Janeiro with the Prince Regent.

2

The French Occupation of Portugal, 1807–1808

Junot's route through Portugal in November 1807 was over poor roads and this caused the dispersion of his invading army. Had the Portuguese resisted, he would have found himself in serious trouble. The chief engineer with Junot's invading army was *Colonel* Charles Humbert Marie Vincent. He was given the challenge of determining how to defend Portugal. His initial problem was a lack of information, and his first task was to improve French knowledge of the country. In January 1808, he reported on the documents he had obtained from *General* Louis-François Carlet, Marquis de la Rozière, the Chief-of-Staff of the Portuguese army.[1] This information was extensive and included plans of the major fortresses and maps of the coast and country.[2]

Vincent sent French and Portuguese officers to survey the main fortresses and roads across the kingdom. In a matter of months, there were reports on most major towns in the kingdom from Bragança in the north to Faro in the south. There were reports on most border fortresses including Elvas, Almeida, Campo Maior, Juromenha and Ouguela.[3] There were also reports on the main routes to Lisbon from Almeida, Elvas, Castelo Branco and Lagos. In March 1808, Vincent wrote a report, 'Military considerations on the land and sea borders of Portugal'.[4] The bulk of the report was on the defences in the vicinity of Lisbon. Vincent also ordered the production of a map of the whole kingdom. The *Carta Militar*, as it is generally known, was used by the Allies extensively throughout the war. It is less clear how widely it was used by the French. The principal Portuguese engineer involved in the production of the map was *Major* Lourenço Homem da Cunha d'Eça. It was published under his name in 1808.[5]

---

1   De la Rozière was a Royalist French émigré working for the Portuguese army.
2   Vicente, *Génie Français*, pp.203–210.
3   Vicente, *Génie Français*, map facing p.170, reports, pp.151–167.
4   Simão José da Luz Soriano, *História da Guerra Civil e do Estabelecimento do Governo Parlamentar em Portugal* (Lisboa: Imprensa Nacional, 1893), Vol.5, part II, pp.57–63.
5   *Carta Militar das Principais Estradas de Portugal*, also known as the Eloy (engraver) map.

Also, in January 1808, Portuguese engineer, *Tenente Coronel* Carlos Frederico Bernardo de Caula was ordered to undertake a formal survey of the area between Lisbon and Peniche.[6] Two other Portuguese officers were ordered to assist, *Major* José Maria das Neves Costa and *Capitão* Joaquim Norbert Xavier de Brito.[7] The purpose of this survey was to determine the best points for defending Lisbon. Neves Costa had been employed for several years in the department of the Inspector General of the Borders and Maritime Coasts and he had previously mapped the Alentejo. This work commenced but had not progressed far when the French were removed from Portugal. These officers will return to our story later.

As it became clearer that there might be an attack on Lisbon, Vincent began looking at the area around the city. His report dated 28 June 1808, recognised that 'the port of Lisbon may be attacked at the same time by sea and land'.[8] His observations for defending against an attack from the sea required the strengthening and arming of the existing forts on the river and assumed support from the Russian naval squadron that was trapped in the Tagus estuary and moored at Lisbon. Vincent made a number of recommendations to resist a land attack with a layered defence. The initial concern was controlling 'groups of insurgents' rather than regular forces. The French were having difficulty putting down the various uprisings and Vincent noted that his suggestion to start the outer defences on the left bank of the Tagus might not be possible 'if the tranquillity of Lisbon does not admit of detaching [troops] from thence.'

The proposed outer line of defence on the right (northern) bank of the Tagus, about 120 kilometres from Lisbon, would run from Punhete, where the Zêzere and Tagus rivers meet, to the west through Tomar and Leiria. The Tagus below Punhete was considered impassable.[9] The second defensive line, about 80 kilometres from Lisbon, would run from Santarém to Peniche, 'where the ground being studied and reconnoitred beforehand, would probably afford powerful means of repelling an attack'. Vincent continued, 'Not far from thence would also be found the excellent position of Alenquer and Torres Vedras, the right of which would be extended to the Tagus, the left to the sea'. This was close to Wellington's original proposal for the outer defences of the Lines of Torres Vedras.[10]

6   André Filipe Vitor Melícias, *As Linhas de Torres Vedras, Construção e Impactos Locais* (Torres Vedras: CMTV, 2008), p.129.

7   Geraldo, José Custódio Madaleno, José Maria Das Neves Costa e as Linhas de Torres Vedras, *Revista Militar*, No. 2495, December 2009. Available online at: <https://www.revistamilitar. pt/artigo/530>, accessed 9 September 2019.

8   C.W. Vane, Lord Londonderry (ed.), *Correspondence, Despatches and other Papers of Viscount Castlereagh, Second Marquess of Londonderry, Edited by his Brother, Charles William Vane, Marquess of Londonderry*, Second Series (London: Shoberl, 1851), June 28, 1808, Vol.6, pp.376–381. The following quotes by Vincent come from this report. The original report, in French, was published in Wellington (ed.), *Supplementary Despatches of the Duke of Wellington* (London: John Murray, 1858–1872), Vol.6, p.145–148.

9   Punhete is now called Constância.

10   Sir Arthur Wellesley was not made Viscount Wellington until August 1809. I will use the name Wellington throughout to avoid confusion.

The final defensive line if 'the army should be reduced to the necessity of retiring from the position of Alenquer and Torres Vedras' would be 'in front of the town a fine position, the right supported by the rivulet of Sacavém, the left by the heights of Bellas' [Belas]. Lisbon is extremely hilly and there have been defences around the city for hundreds of years. Vincent recommended strengthening them, which is what the Portuguese did after Junot was evicted. Vincent also recognised, the danger from the south bank of the Tagus opposite Lisbon: 'we must reasonably apprehend that he [the enemy] would direct his troops and artillery to the occupation of the heights of Almada, from whence he could do infinite mischief to the town and to the ships: it is, therefore, indispensably necessary to provide against this danger by securing a good position to cover Almada and to ensure its defence'.

Vincent's report to Junot, barely a month before Wellington landed in Portugal, shows a good understanding of the challenges in defending Lisbon. Some of the recommendations are similar to what was done by the Portuguese and British in 1809–1810. The only major difference is that Wellington needed a place where his army could be evacuated by the Royal Navy. The French, if forced to withdraw, intended to fight their way north to Almeida.

Vincent wrote a number of other reports around July 1808, describing the terrain and how best to defend it. One was written after he was sent north on the rumour of an allied landing on the Mondego river, near Coimbra. His report described the terrain north of Lisbon and described the chain of hills from Montejunto to Cape Roca (Sintra). He then described the position mentioned in his report above, between Alenquer and Torres Vedras, which would be held prior to a retreat to the city defences.[11] He noted the strength of the positions at Sobral de Monte Agraço, Runa, Montachique (Cabeço de Montachique) and Bucelas. He also noted the main routes from Torres Vedras to Mafra and Montachique and the route along the banks of the Tagus through Castanheira (do Ribatejo) and Sacavém. Vincent clearly understood the options for defending Lisbon from an invading army.

Events changed so quickly that the French never had an opportunity to create defensive barriers, but as mentioned above, they were generally planning for an attack by armed civilians, rather than a regular army. Wellington's landing and the rapid victories at Roliça and Vimeiro in August 1808 forced the French back towards Lisbon. It is a surprise that having recognised the strength of the positions around Torres Vedras, no attempt was made to use them to resist the advance of the British army. Lieutenant General Sir John Moore noted when he passed through the area at that time:

> The country we marched through these two days is exceedingly strong and difficult; and if the French have 12,000 or 15,000 men, it is odd they did not attempt to stop us instead of fighting a battle [Vimeiro] on the 21st. Had they determined to make a defensive campaign they must have kept us out of Lisbon for a considerable time and obliged us to gain every mile at considerable loss.[12]

11   Soriano, *História*, Vol.5, part II, pp.63–74. Also, another report, pp.74–81.
12   J.F. Maurice, *The Diary of Sir John Moore* (London: Arnold, 1904), Vol.2, p.260.

After the battle of Vimeiro, command of the British army transferred to Sir Hew Dalrymple. Following a representation from the French, a ceasefire was agreed whilst negotiations to remove the French from Portugal were discussed. Whilst this armistice between the armies was negotiated, Wellington was based around Torres Vedras and got his first sight of the imposing hills north of Lisbon and the potential they held for its defence.

The armistice between the armies was quickly turned into an agreement to evacuate Junot's French army from Portugal. The Convention of Cintra (Sintra) was deeply unpopular at the time and the commanders of the British army were recalled for an enquiry leaving Sir John Moore in command. Wellington escaped any criticism, and the following April was back in Lisbon as commander of the Allied forces.

3

The Portuguese Defence of Lisbon, 1808–1810

Sir John Moore's advance into Spain in late 1808 led to the damaging retreat to La Coruña and the loss of his life at the Battle of Corunna on 16 January 1809. The British army was evacuated and there was no clarity on when, or if, allied reinforcements would return to Portugal. A small British force had been left at Lisbon under Lieutenant General Sir John Craddock, but it was too small to achieve anything, including defending Lisbon. The Portuguese were left with the need to plan for the defence of their country not knowing what support they would get from Britain.

Defences around the city of Lisbon were not a new idea. There have been settlements in the area for 3,000 years and evidence of fortification for over 2,000 years. The original city fortifications were improved by the Romans and the Moors with further improvements when it once again became a Christian city in 1147. Significant improvements were made by King D. Fernando from 1375 and some portions of these walls were still in existence in 1809, although they were not designed to withstand cannon fire. Significant upgrades were carried out to the city walls in 1640, following independence from Spain and coastal batteries were established along the Tagus estuary, reflecting the importance of sea trade to the city.[1] At the start of the nineteenth century, there was a need to enhance the land-based defences for the city. The conflict had made this an urgent requirement for whoever held Lisbon.

Following the withdrawal of the French in October 1808, the Portuguese government considered the options they had for the defence of the country. On 13 December 1808, the Minister of War issued a decree which effectively put the whole country on a war footing.[2] All citizens were expected to play a part in defending the country from future invasions:

---

1   Helena Rua, 'Historical and Territorial Analysis. A Contribution to the Study of the Defence of the City of Lisbon: The Peninsular War', *Computer Applications to Archaeology* (CAA), 2009, Williamsburg, USA, p.2.

2   *Gazeta de Lisboa*, no. 50, 13 December 1808.

I order that the entire nation will resort to weapons to forcefully repel the wicked, sinister, and hateful intentions of their enemies. I order that the Portuguese nation, without exception of people, or class, would arm themselves … that all cities, towns and villages will cover the entrances and main roads with two, three or more traverses.[3]

Near Lisbon, defences were ordered to be constructed at Torres Vedras, Mafra and Vila Franca de Xira with military governors being appointed to complete the tasks. Work did not start immediately, but by the spring of 1809 the construction had commenced. The Portuguese historian, André Melícias commented:

> The decree of 11 December 1808 thus established a concept of defence based on regional fortified positions, where civilians, militia and ordenança [Civilian levy] would act, supporting the regular army in its actions. These positions, which in the case of the villages of Torres Vedras and Mafra, may have been the origin of some [earlier] fortifications which were later built on as the 'Lines of Torres Vedras' defensive system.[4]

The terrain of the Lisbon peninsula has some key features. The most northerly point was the range of hills running north-east to south-west, with Montejunto at the northern end. This range of hills was effectively impassable to armies, so an attacking force had to make the decision to advance to the western (coastal) or eastern (Tagus) side. An advance could be made on both sides, but this would leave each force at risk of an attack by a concentrated defending army. The Montejunto range of hills became lower around Runa before rising again to form the Serra de Sintra on the Atlantic coast many miles to the south. South of Runa were ranges of hills running roughly east to west that blocked most of the Lisbon peninsula. If these were occupied in force, they would make excellent defensive positions, as had been identified by all who had looked at the terrain.

The outer defensive line of hills had three major crossing points, where the main roads to the south pass, at Torres Vedras, Sobral de Monte Agraço and by the Tagus at Alhandra. Several kilometres behind this range of hills, is a second line which has four main crossing points at Mafra, Montachique, Bucelas and Alverca (do Ribatejo). Whilst there were many smaller crossing points, any major force with wheeled vehicles would have to use these routes.

By the date that the Portuguese decree was published, Neves Costa had already written to the Portuguese Secretary of War and asked for permission to continue the survey work ordered by the French.[5] Permission was given and Neves Costa, Caula and Brito started work again in November 1808, although Caula was quickly reassigned as governor of Vila Franca de Xira.

---

3   *Gazeta de Lisboa*, no. 50, 13 December 1808, author's translation.
4   Melícias, *Torres Vedras*, p.48. Note. This book says 11 December, but the decree in *Gazeta de Lisboa* was dated 13 December 1808. Author's translation.
5   Geraldo, *Revista Militar*, No.2495.

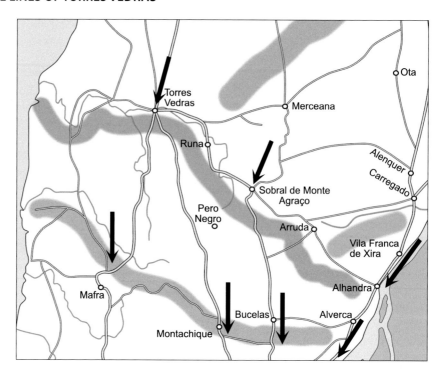

Routes to Lisbon.

The survey was completed in February 1809 and the report was delivered to the Portuguese government on 6 June 1809.

Neves Costa's report was a detailed description of the possible defensive positions to the north of Lisbon.[6] It followed the outline of Vincent's earlier report, describing the terrain, the main communication routes and its suitability for defence, rather than making specific recommendations for the location of defensive structures. In his own words:

> Let us therefore examine the natural positions that can be taken to prevent the enemy's march, whatever their direction, by the various roads in these lands … leaving to the genius and talent of the generals the combination of these partial positions, to form the particular defence system … it was not my duty to determine any particular system of defence … [it was for the generals] to choose the most suitable for forming the said system [of defence].[7]

Neves Costa was proposing a system, where the defending forces remained mobile and used the terrain to slow down the enemy's advance, rather than using fortifications to stop them. Attached to Neves Costa's report was a detailed map of the area which showed all the potential defensive positions. Each position was categorised into one of three grades signifying the strength of the position. There were several points where the defensive positions identified by Neves Costa were used by Wellington as part of the Lines of

---

6   José Maria das Neves Costa, *Memoria Militar Respectiva ao Terreno ao Norte de Lisboa* (Lisboa: Revistas das Sciencias Militares, 1888).

7   Neves Costa, *Memoria Militar*, p.4 and Note (b), author's translation.

Torres Vedras. There are also many positions identified by Neves Costa that were not used. Neves Costa commented that he was not recommending that all the positions identified in his report should be occupied or fortified, that would depend on the plan of defence and the actions of the enemy, and that is why it had to be left to the generals to determine what was required. We will come back to Neves Costa's report when we look at the British plans for the defences. Melícias observed:

> Although starting from principles of observation similar to those put into practice in Vincent's report, and having several points in common with it, the work of Neves Costa had a greater detail in the study of the terrain and indicated positions, revealing a greater contact with the very ground, which Vincent could not have arranged. We can infer from the study of the two plans, that the idea that both authors had, of taking advantage of the terrain surrounding Lisbon for defensive purposes suggests a logic similar to that at the centre of the [plan for the] Lines of Torres Vedras. However, they point to a different tactic from that adopted by Wellington, since Vincent suggested a defence that adopted a 'long' defensive movement, taking advantage of successive natural defensive lines, and Neves Costa's only seems to point to the fortification of some key points, not to the perspective of the construction of a line that potentially served as a barrier to the enemy everywhere, but [just] to constitute points of support and protection in manoeuvres; that is, to reinforce the defence and not to constitute it.[8]

By the time Neves Costa had submitted his full written report, Wellington had been in the country six weeks, had thrown Soult out of Portugal's second city, Porto, and was now planning an advance into Spain. The issue of the defence of Lisbon was no longer the immediate priority, although work associated with the Portuguese decree of 13 December 1808 continued.

Neves Costa was not the only Portuguese engineer proposing defences to the north of Lisbon. *Major* Lourenço Homem da Cunha d'Eça submitted his report on 20 March 1809, before Neves Costa's had been completed. At this time, he was the military governor at Sacavém. His primary recommendations were broadly the same as the other reports; the defences 'should pass through the heights of Mafra, Cabeça [Cabeço de Montachique] and Bucellas [Bucelas], with the right leaning on the Tagus at the town of Alhandra, the left at Ericeira and the centre at Bucellas and Cabeça'.[9] The defending force would be divided into five districts and move as required to react to any enemy advance. He also recommended signal stations using lanterns that could pass messages night or day. D'Eça recognised that once a position was taken or outflanked, the whole of the defensive line would need to retreat to the next defensive line. Like Neves Costa, his proposals were based on defence by mobile forces rather than extensive fixed positions.

Whilst Neves Costa and d'Eça had concentrated on defences to the north of Lisbon, there were separate Portuguese plans to upgrade the defences around the city itself. The Portuguese engineer, *Marechal de Campo* José de Morais

---

8   Melícias, *Torres Vedras*, p.38, author's translation.
9   Soriano, *História*, Vol.5, part II, pp.5–10, author's translation.

Antas Machado developed detailed plans for defences on the outskirts of the city.[10] His proposal recommended the construction of a number of defensive positions, but also suggested reinforcing many stone buildings that were in, and near Lisbon. All the main roads would be blocked with ditches and traverses; troops and artillery would move as required to face any attackers. The original plan recommended constructing 12 redoubts containing 79 cannon and four howitzers.[11] Machado's plans assumed that there would be resistance to an invasion further from the city and his defences would be the last resort.[12] Machado's proposals to construct these defences were approved, but it is not clear when the construction work started.

The British engineer, Captain Stephen Chapman arrived in Portugal on 4 March 1809, and took temporary command of the Royal Engineers in Portugal. Clearly, the defence of the kingdom was high on the priorities of the local commanders. Lieutenant General Sir John Craddock was the senior British officer in Portugal, with Major General William Carr Beresford who took over command of the Portuguese army on 19 March 1809 and was appointed *Marechal do Exército* (Commander of Army). Both were in Lisbon. Chapman noted:

> … in consequence of the commands of Lieutenant General Sir John Craddock, I have directed Captain [Henry] Goldfinch and Lieutenant [Alexander] Thomson to proceed to Porto with all possible despatch … to put the city in such a state of defence as circumstances will permit. Lieutenants [Rice] Jones and [Frank] Stanway are gone into the interior for the purpose of ascertaining whether gun boats can act with effect up the Tagus upon the flanks of an army as far as Santarem, and whether carronades in ships launches will be beneficial as far up as Abrantes. I have also directed Lieutenant Jones to examine the Zêzere where it joins the Tagus, and to proceed from there by Thomar [Tomar] as far as Leyria [Leiria] and to report to me in writing on his return, the result of his observations upon these positions. Lisbon is to be placed immediately in a state of defence and a project has been presented to General Beresford by the Portuguese Chief Engineer [Machado] for that purpose; which plan as well as the choices for the redoubts and batteries have been submitted for my opinion; I have therefore been employed upon the examination of the several points upon the ground and I hope to make a beginning to the works immediately; the several officers therefore of the corps now at Lisbon are actively employed correcting the plans and sketching on the ground … This service is to be performed under the direction of Lieutenant General Beresford and the expense to be defrayed by the Regency.[13]

As happened on several occasions, the overall command of tasks appeared to be directed through British engineer officers, who often were junior to

---

10   Soriano, *História*, Vol.5, part II, pp.49–55. This proposal is dated 12 May 1809. Sousa Lobo, *Defesa*, p.175, refers to an earlier report, by Machado, which was delivered on 14 February 1809.

11   Soriano, *História*, Vol.5, part II, p.56.

12   Melícias, *Torres Vedras*, p.29.

13   TNA: WO55/958, Chapman to Morse, Lisbon, 22 March 1809.

their Portuguese engineer counterparts. This issue of rank was resolved by passing orders through senior army officers, even though the junior engineer officer was making all the decisions. In this case a Portuguese *marechal de campo* (major general) was theoretically being directed by a British captain, with the orders being relayed through *Marechal do Exército* Beresford. This cannot have helped Portuguese morale or the smooth running of tasks when there were officers from both nations present. It must be noted, that at this time, the quality of the Portuguese army was unknown to the British and the same would be true of the Portuguese engineers. At the time of the letter above, Beresford and Chapman had only been in the country two weeks.[14] The despatch of Captain Goldfinch to Porto also demonstrates an unwillingness to leave things to the Portuguese at this time. The role of the Portuguese engineers has been minimised in English accounts and there is understandable frustration amongst Portuguese military and historians about this lack of recognition. Sousa Lobo commented on the complete lack of mention of the city defences in Jones' book on the Lines of Torres Vedras and the similar lack of recognition of Neves Costa. He added:

> The fortification works in Lisbon were documented and were carried out under the direction of Portuguese engineers … The work was under the responsibility of the Portuguese engineer commander, *Marechal-de-Campo* José de Morais Antas Machado, and the technical director, Lieutenant Colonel Fletcher, although delegated to Captain Goldfinch, who reported to Marshal Beresford, commander of the Portuguese Army[15]

This is not strictly true as Jones did mention them but in a way that suggested little work was done and there was no Royal Engineer involvement. Both of these points were incorrect.[16] There was no change in the situation after Lieutenant Colonel Richard Fletcher arrived on 2 April 1809, to take command of the Royal Engineers, keeping Chapman as his second-in-command. Fletcher noted the following day 'arrangements are making for entrenched positions in front of Lisbon. The outer line is, I fear, very extensive but I have not been over the ground'.[17] Similar concerns had been expressed three months earlier. Major General John Randoll Mackenzie, who was briefly the British commanding officer in Lisbon before he was replaced by John Craddock noted:

> Took a ride this day with Sir John Craddock, to look at the position of Bellas [Belas]. It is a very strong part of the great line, for the defence of Lisbon, and is generally considered the left point, the right being at Sacavém. But without

---

14   Even later when the skill and competence of the Portuguese engineers had been established, there was still a reluctance to employ Portuguese and British officers together. There are a number of letters where Portuguese engineers have been asked for, but it was specified that they must be captains or majors, so that there was no issue about command.

15   Sousa Lobo, *Defesa*, p.175. The comment refers to a slightly later period, after 2 April 1809, when Fletcher arrived in Portugal. Before that, Chapman was the senior engineer.

16   Jones, *Sieges*, Vol.3, pp.14–15.

17   TNA: WO55/958, Fletcher to Morse, 3 April 1809.

examining more minutely than one day's ride would permit, I cannot help thinking the line would be incomplete without a part towards Cintra [Sintra]. This line would take at least twenty-five thousand men to defend it properly.[18]

Mackenzie's opinion had not changed in March 1809:

The part of the great position our little army at present occupies, reaches from Sacavém to Lumiar, crowning a chain of hills, and covered for above half way by the Sacavém river. Our advanced posts are on the other side of the Sacavém reaching from Louras [Loures] by Cabeca de Montachiga [Cabeço de Montachique], to Freixial, Bucellas [Bucelas], and some smaller posts on to Alhandra & Alverca on the Tagus. What we have already taken up is too extensive for our numbers, so that all to the left of Lumiar is unoccupied. The very essential post of Bellas, the command of the Mafra & Cintra roads etc. It would take at least thirty thousand men to occupy the whole.[19]

Fletcher sent another update home on 9 April 1809:

Positions are to be taken in front of the town, but I feel they are too extensive to be defended by the present British force, and on the discipline and firmness of the Portuguese, but little reliance can be placed; they are now deserting by whole regiments. The tract of country to be enclosed within the positions, will, I should imagine, be quite insufficient to subsist the inhabitants of this populous city, and therefore once completely invested they must soon be compelled to surrender as I do not conceive they could bring any considerable supplies by water when an enemy possesses the left bank of the Tagus.[20]

Fletcher had a point; with only perimeter defences around the city, there was little space for the population, and any refugees. He was also right to be concerned about defending the position with only Craddock's several thousand British troops and no regular Portuguese troops to rely on. His updates home continued:

The Portuguese are doing little or nothing to their entrenchments immediately covering the town of Lisbon. Sir John Craddock considers the fortifying and defending this line as exclusively a concern of their own. Upon an extent of six miles, they have now a hundred and sixty-nine men employed though I have urged in the strongest way the necessity of having at least some thousands constantly at work if they mean to fortify it. I have twice seen their Minister at War who promises great things; but I confess I have but little confidence as any good effects from his exertions. I have Lieutenant Wedekind in Lisbon to assist the Portuguese engineers.[21]

---

18   BL: ADD39201, Mackenzie diary, 25 January 1809.
19   BL: ADD39201, Mackenzie diary, 26 March 1809.
20   TNA: WO55/958, Fletcher to Morse, 9 April 1809.
21   TNA: WO55/958, Fletcher to Morse, 13 April 1809.

Ten days later, Fletcher was still reporting little progress. He noted that he had instructed Lieutenant Charles Wedekind (from the King's German Legion engineers, who operated as part of the Royal Engineers) to apply directly, in writing, to the Portuguese Secretary of War for workmen.[22] A year later, Royal Engineer Captain Goldfinch was still complaining that he had only about 100 workers and 'that it was impossible to complete the task'.[23]

Of interest, is Craddock's view that the defence of the city was for the Portuguese to progress. This lack of clarity about responsibilities continued for some time and the involvement of the Royal Engineer officers in the city defences clearly continued. On 4 May 1809, Fletcher, who had joined the British army that was moving north towards Porto, complained that:

> General Beresford has contrived to have Chapman ordered to Lisbon as having first received his (the [Portuguese] generals) ideas about the positions for covering the town[24] … and to report on the practicability of defending both banks of the Tagus by detachable independent works. He is also to visit Palmela and Setuval [Setúbal], to give his opinions of the strength and local importance of the towns, and of the general state and utility of the works.[25]

Despite the British reticence, the defences around the city were constructed. Machado's original 12 redoubts were built as were another 21 positions, making 33 in total.[26]

Returning to Lisbon with Chapman, was Lieutenant Anthony Emmett RE, who recorded in his diary that he had been ordered to 'examine the ground from Belem to St Julian's for covering the embarkation of the army, should that be necessary'.[27] Peniche had also been reviewed as a point of embarkation but Rear Admiral George Berkeley, commander of the Lisbon station, was firmly against it, as weather conditions could make it impossible for ships to operate in the area.[28] This was many months before Wellington's memorandum of 20 October 1809, but he was clearly collecting information about the defence of Portugal and the embarkation of his army.

As Fletcher was with Wellington's army, there were less comments on the activities in Lisbon. However, we do know that one of the first tasks Chapman carried out was a reconnaissance of the fords on the river Tagus below Abrantes.[29] Lieutenant Rice Jones in early June, noted that Chapman was still in Lisbon where 'they are fortifying it upon some large scale'.[30]

---

22   TNA: WO55/958, Fletcher to Morse, 24 April 1809.

23   Sousa Lobo, *Defesa*, p.175. Letter dated 31 March 1810.

24   TNA: WO55/958, Fletcher to Rowley, Coimbra, 4 May 1809. The order for Chapman to return to Lisbon came from Wellington, Gurwood, *Dispatches*, Wellington to Villiers, Coimbra, 7 May 1809.

25   TNA: WO55/958, Fletcher to Morse, Coimbra, 4 May 1809.

26   Sousa Lobo, *Defesa*, pp.174-183. See also Appendix II, p.203.

27   Royal Engineers Museum (REM): 4601-57-1, Emmet's journal, 4 May 1809.

28   BL: ADD39201, Mackenzie noted on 17 March 1809 that Berkeley had refused to send a victualler to Peniche, 'alleging it unsafe'.

29   TNA: WO55/1561/5, Report on the fords below Abrantes on the Tagus, May 1809.

30   Henry Shore, 'An Engineer Officer in the Peninsula', *Royal Engineers Journal*, Vol.16, No.3, September 1912, p.171.

Chapman's focus over the coming weeks appeared to be on potential points of embarkation.

The issue of too few workmen continued. Wellington, writing to Beresford in June 1809, mentioned a letter he had received from Fletcher, reporting that work on the defences at Lisbon had stopped. Pointedly, he stated that if the work had stopped due to a lack of workmen, then he wanted the Royal Engineer officers in Lisbon sent back to the army.[31] The tone suggests that Wellington expected Beresford to resolve the issue.

At some point Chapman was called back to the army from Lisbon, as he wrote a report from Trujillo, dated, 18 August 1809, describing the options for defending the left bank of the Tagus (Almada to Trafaria) and an embarkation point on the right bank (between Belém and Oeiras). His view at this time was that both areas were too extensive for a rear-guard to defend.[32] Work on the city defences appeared to slow from the summer of 1809 until the spring of 1810. There is no mention in Royal Engineer correspondence between Chapman's report of 18 August and 25 December 1809, during which period, work had begun on the Lines of Torres Vedras. On that date, Fletcher reported to Wellington: 'Goldfinch is employed in assisting the Portuguese engineers in the defences of Lisbon as requested by Marshal Beresford and on which I have desired him to prepare a detailed report.'[33]

Goldfinch, like almost all the other Royal Engineer officers, had been ordered to Lisbon at the end of October 1809. It is not known when he was ordered to join the work on the defences of Lisbon, but Rice Jones reported him working on the task in a letter dated, 16 December 1809.[34] Goldfinch's report was dated 24 January 1810, and ran to 16 pages.[35] He proposed splitting the city into six districts with layered defences and described his ideas in detail. He noted 'it is impossible on paper, to give a correct idea of so extensive a position and the importance of its different defences, otherwise than by an accurate drawing, which I have not been able to procure; to prepare one of such a city is a work of considerable time.' To make rapid progress, Goldfinch emphasised that it would be a major project:

> The first step, would be, the appointment to each district, of five or six officers of engineers, or in want of sufficient numbers ... officers selected from the artillery and regiments of the line, who from inclination and activity shall be found best capable of serving in such a capacity: ... each district, ... must be immediately furnished with the labourers sufficient to commence every proposed work, that does not too far, interfere with public convenience or individual property ... in

---

31   Gurwood, *Dispatches*, Wellington to Beresford, Abrantes, 22 June 1809.

32   TNA: WO55/1561/6, Report dated 18 August 1809.

33   Wellington, *Supplementary Despatches*, Fletcher to Wellington, Lisbon, 25 December, Vol.3, p.457.

34   Henry Shore (ed.), *An Engineer Officer under Wellington in the Peninsula* [Rice Jones] (Cambridge: Ken Trotman, 2005), p.47.

35   REM: 2001-149-2, Report upon the works required and general system of defence for the city of Lisbon. The Portuguese archives contain many letters from Goldfinch to Machado reporting on the progress of the defences, AHM: PT-AHM-DIV-3-01-04-14.

short, everything, that did not seriously interrupt public roads or destroy the dwellings or valuable property … Advantage must then be taken of the sensation such an event [a new French invasion] will certainly produce in the capital, to call for the exertions of every individual capable of working … [the] arrangement for tools and materials will rest with the commanding engineer in each district; the public stores are certainly not equal to such a supply, requisitions must therefore be made, by those in authority, for the articles required, … It is probable that not less than 10 or 12,000 workmen would be required …which considering the population is not a very large proportion.

He noted that because of the differing terrain, it would be difficult to accurately estimate the time and resource required. He estimated up to 60 redoubts may be required and at the rate of 200 men completing a redoubt in 30 days, 12,000 men would be needed to complete the task in 30 days. In his conclusion, Goldfinch recognised the scale of work he was proposing but argued:

If the magnitude of works suggested be objected to, it should be observed, that the extent of the line is proportionally great, as well as the resources of the capital and I am of opinion, that less would not answer the purpose of a protracted siege, nor would it guard against the known system of the enemy, to disregard the sacrifice of men to carry his point.

The final number of defensive positions was nearer 30, so Goldfinch's arguments were not accepted. It is difficult to see how 12,000 workers could be collected when the work previously carried out had struggled to obtain 200. His expectation was that a new invasion would concentrate the minds of the Portuguese authorities to assign the necessary resources. At this time there was a great concern that there could be a French invasion in the spring of 1810, in which case urgent building work would be required. It seems likely that Beresford reacted on receiving Goldfinch's report, but not in the way that Goldfinch proposed. Five days after the report was issued, Machado reported to the Portuguese Secretary for Foreign Affairs, War and Marine, Dom Miguel Pereira Forjaz, that he had received orders from Beresford to resume work on the defences.[36] Goldfinch continued to write making suggestions on the key places to be defended, but lack of manpower remained the major problem. In terms of the design, Goldfinch made attempts to standardise the forts, specifying the heights of the parapets (walls), the use of embrasures rather than barbettes for the artillery and the design of powder magazines.[37]

The complex command relationship would not have helped, with Machado having to write to Beresford or Forjaz for instructions and Goldfinch giving instructions 'by order of Beresford' either directly, or through his British engineer superior, Fletcher.[38] A later letter from Goldfinch, makes it clear that his extensive proposal had not been accepted:

---

36   Sousa Lobo, *Defesa*, p.176.
37   Sousa Lobo, *Defesa*, pp.175–182.
38   Sousa Lobo, *Defesa*, p.175.

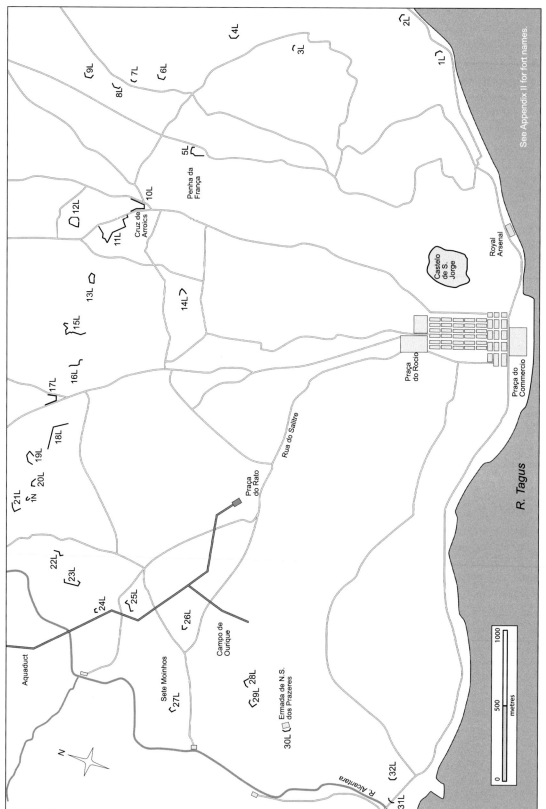

See Appendix II for fort names.

Lisbon City Defences 1810. (Also see Appendix II)

2L

4L

1L

3L

9L

7L

8L

6L

5L

Penha da França

12L

10L

Cruz de Arroics

11L

Castelo de S. Jorge

Royal Arsenal

13L

14L

15L

Praça do Rocio

Praça do Commercio

17L

16L

Rua do Salitre

R. Tagus

18L

19L

21L

20L

1N

Praça do Rato

22L

23L

24L

25L

26L

Campo de Ourique

Aquaduct

Sete Moinhos

27L

29L 28L

30L Ermada de N.S. dos Prazeres

R. Alcantara

32L

31L

N

1000

500

metres

0

32

I have this morning received your instructions dated 2nd inst., desiring me to state to Brigadier General Roza [José António da Rosa, Commander of the Portuguese artillery] the designation and number of guns that will be required for the defence of Lisbon. I feel it necessary to defer this statement until I learn, with what I am to make it out. Whether upon the scale suggested in my report of 24 January, or merely for the alterations pointed out by Marshal Beresford, in the existing works. In the first case, 200 guns of more or less, half, heavy and half, light, would be required. In the latter, few if any, saving some field pieces for the traverses of the roads that are not yet sufficiently defended. I have already sent to Marshal [Marechal de Campo] Machado, chief of the Portuguese engineers, sketches with descriptions, of the greater part of the alterations proposed, and shall, in the course of next week, complete the whole. Within these few days, the 100 workmen employed on this service, by order of the Portuguese government, have been doubled. As well as I can judge, from the progress hitherto made, the alterations will employ these 200 men for three months to come. This service is certainly the first that requires attention, because the batteries in their present open state, would be immediately run-in-upon by an enemy and their guns, at least, would then be rendered useless. I confess and believe it my duty to state to you, that the more I see of Lisbon, the more I feel strengthened in the opinion expressed in the report before alluded to, that nothing short of the multiplied lines of well entrenched batteries on every side, together with the other means therein suggested, can make this place defensible against a very superior force and that to carry such a project into effect, is impracticable without something like the means and assistance pointed out in the report. You are best acquainted with the nature of the services now carrying on in this neighbourhood and can judge how far the numerous artillery are thereby exposed or likely to fall into the hands of an enemy … I cannot avoid expressing my doubts, whether the existing works when altered and improved, will suffice to hold such an enemy in check many hours.[39]

Of greater concern, must have been the continued low number of workmen. Goldfinch's estimate of three months to complete the initial alterations was far too long when, at this time, the expectation was that the French invasion could start at any moment. Six weeks later on 22 May 1810, Goldfinch stated that the number of workers had not increased, and bad weather had further delayed progress with the defences.[40] It is difficult to understand why so little progress was being made. One possibility was that work on the Lines of Torres Vedras was being prioritised, but that does not seem likely as separate resources were being used for the two projects. There was a common complaint throughout the construction of the various defences both around Lisbon and wider, including the Lines, the city defences, São Julião (da Barra),[41] Setúbal, Abrantes and Peniche, that there was never enough workers and those ordered, often did not turn up. The Allied expectation was that the French would now arrive during the summer and if they had kept to that timescale, the Lisbon defences would not have been ready. Perhaps

---

39   REM: 5501-59-15, Goldfinch to Fletcher, Lisbon, 4 April 1810.
40   REM: 5501-59-15, Goldfinch to Fletcher, Lisbon, 22 May 1810.
41   Called St Julian's in most English accounts.

Goldfinch was correct in his report of 24 January 1810, that it would need the French to cross the border before the Portuguese authorities would give the work the priority it required. At that point there might not be time to complete the work.

Goldfinch's involvement appears to end in July 1810, when he was assigned to the army on the frontier. By this time, the design and scale of the defensive work was decided. Fletcher had written to Wellington on 25 June 1810, indicating that 'as the Portuguese engineers now possess drawings … to finish the redoubts … it seems unnecessary to detain Captain Goldfinch any longer', although Fletcher suggested that Goldfinch should first visit the Bayona islands off Vigo which were being considered as an offshore base for allied troops.[42] Machado would have remained in charge of the construction work. There is no reason why the city defences could not have been designed and built by the Portuguese alone. Goldfinch and Fletcher were competent, but so were the Portuguese engineers. This was most likely to keep a single chain of command over the various works. If the Portuguese and British had worked independently on different projects, there would have been inevitable clashes for scarce resources.

The additional time given to the allies by the slow advance of the French, meant that the Lines of Torres Vedras could be strengthened to a point where they were impregnable to Masséna's army. The city defences were never attacked. However, that does not mean they were not necessary. Had the French been stronger and / or Wellington defeated, the city defences would have slowed the French advance. However, in either of these scenarios, the British would probably have evacuated Portugal, the Portuguese would not have resisted the inevitable defeat and would have come to terms with the French.

---

42   Wellington, *Supplementary Despatches*, Vol.6, p.538.

4

The Threat to Portugal in 1810

Wellington could not have been clearer in his opinion that Lisbon could be defended and that its defence was his priority. Before returning to the Peninsula in April 1809, Wellington wrote a 'Memorandum on the Defence of Portugal', laying out his thoughts on the coming campaign. His opening sentence was: 'I have always been of the opinion that Portugal might be defended, whatever the result of the contest in Spain.' He continued, 'even if Spain should have been conquered, the French would not have been able to overrun Portugal with a force smaller than 100,000 men'.[1] Wellington retained this opinion through the next two years, even when many around him doubted the possibility. The immediate challenge for the British government was, that to succeed, the Portuguese army needed to be reformed, armed and paid. Many senior Portuguese officers had gone to Brazil with the Regent, and some troops were transferred into the French army with most of the rest being disbanded. A small number fled to England and eventually became the Loyal Lusitanian Legion.

Just before leaving for the Peninsula, on 14 April 1809, Wellington wrote to the Duke of Richmond, Lord Lieutenant of Ireland, expressing concern that the French could have taken Lisbon before he arrived. He thought that they would move a force to the south of the Tagus and push the British fleet out of the Tagus estuary, 'If they should not make this detachment, I have no doubt that Lisbon may be, and will be defended'.[2]

On his first day in Lisbon, 23 April 1809, Wellington wrote to Beresford and Craddock mentioning the defence of Lisbon and the Tagus to both officers.[3] There were two French armies threatening Portugal. *Maréchal* Soult, after the battle of Corunna, moved into northern Portugal and had taken Porto. To the east, *Maréchal* Victor was at Mérida and could make an advance along the northern or southern banks of the Tagus. Wellington, however, saw the removal of the French from Porto as his first priority. This was both a political and practical decision. Porto was the country's second

---

1   Gurwood, *Dispatches*, Memorandum on the Defence of Portugal, London, 7 March 1809.
2   Gurwood, *Dispatches*, Wellington to Richmond, Portsmouth, 14 April 1809.
3   Gurwood, *Dispatches*, Wellington to Craddock, Lisbon, 23 April 1809 and Wellington to Beresford, Lisbon, 23 April 1809.

city and the Portuguese government wanted it recovered. Secondly, this was an area with plentiful supplies and Wellington did not want these to be left to the French. Thirdly, pushing Soult across the border would remove the invaders from the country which would be a major political boost for the allies and a loss of face for the French.

Moving swiftly north, Wellington ejected Soult from the city on 12 May 1809 and very nearly surrounded the retreating French, who realising the danger abandoned much of their equipment and escaped over mountainous tracks into northern Spain. The pursuit was hampered by supply problems and was a foretaste of his next operation. Wellington now moved his forces south having agreed to a joint operation with the Spanish commander, *Teniente General* Gregorio García de la Cuesta. The plan was to move on Madrid and force the French to abandon the capital city. Cuesta had agreed to provide supplies to Wellington's army. Joining forces near Talavera de la Reina, a battle was fought on 27–28 July 1809, which the allies narrowly won after two days of fighting.

The promised supplies did not arrive, and Wellington now found himself with a starving army and endangered by superior French forces, including the reorganised army of Soult, who was threatening his communications with Portugal. A rapid retreat back to the Portuguese frontier was made amongst mutual recriminations between the British and Spanish commanders. Wellington had no alternative to the retreat and at that time he did not know how far and how fast the French would pursue him, perhaps all the way to Lisbon. The realities of working with the Spanish forces in Spain in 1809 were not as Wellington had hoped and there was a renewed interest in the defence of Lisbon.

As mentioned above, Chapman, who had remained around Lisbon throughout the Porto and Talavera campaigns, wrote a report, detailing possible embarkation points north and south of the Tagus. The following days saw both Fletcher and Wellington making comments on the defence of Lisbon, suggesting that it was an important topic to them at that time. The news of the defeat of the Austrians at Wagram would have been received and the high hopes of the spring and summer had received a reality check. The expulsion of Soult from Porto in May and the expectation of a French defeat in July probably pushed the immediate defence of Lisbon and Portugal from the top of the priority list. The withdrawal after Talavera and the news of Wagram, will have pushed it back to the top. Wellington writing to Robert Stewart, Viscount Castlereagh, the Secretary of State for War, repeated his previous view that:

> … we ought to be able to hold Portugal, if the Portuguese army and militia are complete. The difficulty upon this sole question lies in the embarkation of the British army. There are so many entrances into Portugal, the whole country being frontier, that it would be very difficult to prevent the enemy from penetrating; and it is probable that we should be obliged to confine ourselves to the preservation of that which is most important, the capital.
>
> It is difficult, if not impossible, to bring the contest for the capital to extremities, and afterwards to embark the British army … Lisbon is so high up the Tagus

that no army that we could collect would be able at the same time to secure the navigation of the river by occupation of both banks, and the possession of the capital. One of these objects must I fear, be given up, and that which the Portuguese would give up would be navigation of the Tagus; and, of course, our means of embarkation. However, I have not entirely made up my mind upon this interesting point. I have a great deal of information upon it, but I should wish to have more before I can decide upon it.[4]

Wellington's final sentence makes it clear that the ability to defend Lisbon was not something he had decided in his brief visit in October 1809, but something he had been considering in detail for some time. Fletcher who was with Wellington, was less positive, saying that he thought:

The practicability of defending the Capital to the last extremity and of afterwards embarking the British troops, I confess I have always doubted. Sir Arthur Wellesley is naturally anxious to combine these two objects, but I believe that he now begins to feel that the doing so, would be certainly difficult if not altogether impossible.[5]

Fletcher continued, echoing Chapman's findings that the number of troops required for the defence of any embarkation point would be larger than the army could provide. He also pointed out that if the only other defences were those around the city of Lisbon itself, then starvation would quickly force the Portuguese to surrender. He observed that surrender would be a better option for the population than giving the French a reason to sack the city. To make an embarkation point near Lisbon feasible, there would need to be other defences further north to keep the French away from the city defences. Fletcher noted that Wellington intended to go to Lisbon soon 'to determine what steps can be taken'.

Events in Europe were also having an impact on Wellington's planning. The French victory at Wagram and the subsequent peace treaty with Austria meant that additional French troops could be sent to Portugal. In summer 1809, Napoleon's intention was to come to the Peninsula himself with 100,000 men to sort out the British problem. Fortunately for Wellington, sorting out a new empress and an heir to the French throne took priority. *Maréchal* Masséna was given the job and the size of the force allocated to him dropped significantly. It is interesting to note that Wellington's original view from March 1809, stated that the French would need 100,000 troops to conquer Portugal. Napoleon might have achieved it. Masséna with nearer 50,000 by the time he arrived at the Lines was destined to fail, before the invasion had started.

Wellington was also being constantly reminded that Britain could not afford to lose his army and that its safety was a priority. Robert Banks Jenkinson, Lord Liverpool, was acting as Secretary of State for War and the Colonies, following Castlereagh's resignation after his duel with Canning. He mentioned this in his letter on 20 October 1809, 'we should not be justified

---

4   Gurwood, *Dispatches*, Wellington to Castlereagh, Merida, 25 August 1809.
5   TNA: WO55/958, Fletcher to Morse, Merida, 28 August 1809.

from want of timely precaution, in sacrificing that army which forms the far greater part of our disposable force.'[6] Seven weeks later, another similarly worded letter arrived, telling Wellington that His Majesty:

> … cannot, however avoid noticing how large a proportion of the disposable force of this country is at present employed in the Peninsula, and how essential the return of that army must be to the security of his own dominions in the event of Spain and Portugal falling under the dominion of France.[7]

France could afford to lose an army; Britain could not. At this time, the disaster at Walcheren was unfolding and Britain's only two armies in the field were under serious threat.

Wellington, having remained with the army around Badajoz through the late summer of 1809, set off for Lisbon on 8 October 1809, arriving late on 10 October. With him were Colonel George Murray, his Quarter Master General (QMG) and his Chief Engineer, Lieutenant Colonel Richard Fletcher. It is probable that before he started his journey, he had received Castlereagh's reply to his letter of 28 August, mentioned above:

> As the return of the British army to Portugal will afford you an opportunity of turning your undivided attention to the defence of that Kingdom, I have to request that you will, as early as possible, transmit to me … a full report on that subject, stating your opinion of its defensibility, with what force, British and Portuguese, and at what annual expense … You will also state your opinion upon the practicability of embarking the British army in the Tagus … in the event of it being obliged to fall back … in the presence of a superior enemy.[8]

There is an unusual, urgent and directive tone to this letter. Writing to Castlereagh on 14 October 1809, Wellington commented, 'I have come down here to arrange finally for the defence of Portugal' not, the safe evacuation of the British troops.[9] A week later, Wellington wrote that he hoped 'to be better enabled to form a judgement on the points referred to in your Lordship's dispatch of the 14th of September, upon which I hope to be able to report in the course of a few days'.[10]

There are few details of where Wellington was over the next 'few days', before he wrote his memorandum to Fletcher. From his despatches, he appeared to stay in Lisbon through most of his visit, but there are gaps when he could have travelled further afield.[11] He made a visit to Sacavém and Castanheira on 16 October, but that was possible in a day.[12] Travelling to Torres Vedras or Sobral would have been challenging in a single day, but he

---

6   Wellington, *Supplementary Despatches*, Vol.6, pp.412–413.
7   Wellington, *Supplementary Despatches*, Liverpool to Wellington, 15 December 1809, Vol.6, pp.438–439.
8   Londonderry, *Castlereagh Correspondence*, Vol.7, pp.120–121.
9   Wellington, *Supplementary Despatches*, Vol.6, p.401.
10   Gurwood, *Dispatches*, Wellington to Castlereagh, Lisbon, 22 October 1809.
11   There are letters from Wellington in Lisbon, dated, 11, 12, 13, 15, 16 and 19 October 1809.
12   Shore, *Engineer Officer*, p.45.

had been to those places before. He may also have visited them and stayed overnight on the dates where there are no entries in his dispatches.[13] The locations of the engineer officers are also interesting. Rice Jones recorded being at São Julião on the 14 and 15 October, sketching then drawing up the ground.[14] Fletcher wrote on 15 October that he had been in the same area with Chapman, so all three engineer officers were looking at possible embarkation points. On 16 October, Fletcher accompanied Wellington to Sacavém and Castanheira. On 23 October, according to Rice Jones, Fletcher and Wellington travelled to Setúbal. There are few letters in the dispatches on 23 and none on 24 October.

Fletcher's letter of 15 October 1809 described the area around São Julião. This was a follow-up to Chapman's earlier reconnaissance described in his report of 18 August 1809.[15] Fletcher recorded they 'examined the ground between Belem and Fort St Julian's, with a view to discover the most proper situation for an entrenched position to cover the embarkation of the army.' The original intention, as surveyed by Chapman several weeks before, appeared to be to use the area around Paço d'Arcos, between Belém and São Julião. Fletcher's view was the same as Chapman's; it was far too large an area, which would require the whole of the army to defend and therefore could not be used as an embarkation point where a rear guard could defend the loading of the rest of the army. There was a risk that a fleet anchored off Paço d'Arcos might be within range of artillery on the southern bank of the Tagus. Fletcher continued:

> There is a bay about 400 yards broad to the eastward of, and immediately adjoining, Fort St Julian's. This appears favourable for beaching boats … a body of men might be covered from the view of an enemy, were the hill commanding the fort occupied by a strong field work … Its front should, I think, be of a regular figure … It would be well occupied by 1,200 or 1,500 men as long as this fort could be held, its fire, aided by that of the fort [São Julião] would render it impracticable for an enemy to attack the troops assembled for embarkation.[16]

Fletcher's proposal for an embarkation point was essentially what was done. Wellington understood the potential for defensive positions to the north of Lisbon but until an embarkation site had been identified, he could not finalise his plans. That would explain why the focus of the engineers with Wellington was on identifying an embarkation point. Once that was agreed, the defensive positions to the north of Lisbon could be confirmed. If the embarkation point was elsewhere, for example Peniche or Setúbal, then different defensive positions would have been required. When Fletcher recommended the bay at São Julião, he was aware that the Royal Navy had concerns; 'the bay itself may be considered by naval officers as objectionable,

---

13   14, 17 and 18 October 1809.
14   Shore, *Engineer Officer*, p.45.
15   TNA: WO55/1561/6, Report dated 18 August 1809.
16   Wellington, *Supplementary Despatches*, Vol.6, pp.403–405. Fletcher to Wellington, 15 October 1809.

and I am aware that the situation is not by any means all that could be wished. It appears to me, however, to be the only one in which 1,500 or 2,000 men could … cover the … army against a superior force.'[17] Jones also noted the concerns: 'even at that spot [São Julião], at intervals, such a sea rolls in for days together that no boat can with safety approach the shore.'[18] Before Wellington made his final decision on the embarkation point, based on the engineers' recommendations, he wrote to Rear Admiral Berkeley asking for his opinion. Wellington identified four options, Peniche, Paço d'Arcos, São Julião or Setúbal. Although the decision was made to use São Julião, the other options were not discarded.[19] Surveys and improvements to defences were made at Setúbal and Peniche for reasons that will become clear later.

Based on the information Wellington already had, and on the surveys carried out during the visit, he prepared his instructions for the defence of Lisbon. The engineer effort was expended on investigating embarkation points, which was clearly very important. Wellington does not say where he went, but that may be part of what appears to be a conscious decision on his part not to include detailed information of his plans in his letters home, due to his concern it would end up in the newspapers. There is almost no mention of the construction of the Lisbon defences in his correspondence through the end of 1809 and most of 1810.

On 20 October 1809, Fletcher received his instructions for the defence of Lisbon. These will be discussed in the following chapter.

On 21 September 1809, Castlereagh fought a duel with Foreign Secretary, George Canning and in the aftermath both resigned from the government. Castlereagh was replaced by Lord Liverpool and Wellington's reply to Castlereagh's letter of 14 September, on the defence of Lisbon was not written until 14 November 1809. Wellington explained his delay in responding, citing, the need to visit Lisbon, correspond with Berkeley on embarkation points and to make a visit to Sevilla. He maintained his opinion that in the current situation, Portugal could be defended, but noted that future defence would depend on the size of any French reinforcements and the continued resistance of the Spanish nation. Wellington added that the defence would require the British to support the expansion and training of 45,000 Portuguese soldiers, plus the militia. The Portuguese economy had collapsed mainly because of the loss of customs revenue, much of which now flowed into Great Britain and gave 'Portugal a claim for some assistance'.[20]

What is interesting is that in the letter Wellington provided no details on how he would defend Lisbon or embark his army if he was forced to leave Portugal. He also made no comment on the likely cost of the defences around Lisbon, which John Jones estimated to have been £200,000 by the end of the war.[21] Wellington did not want details of his proposals appearing in

---

17 Wellington, *Supplementary Despatches*, Vol.6, pp.403–405. Fletcher to Wellington, 15 October 1809.

18 Jones, *Sieges*, Vol.3, p.5.

19 Gurwood, *Dispatches*, Wellington to Berkeley, Lisbon, 26 October 1809.

20 Gurwood, *Dispatches*, Wellington to Liverpool, Badajoz, 14 November 1809, first letter.

21 Jones, *Memoranda*, p.108.

the British newspapers. On the same date, Wellington wrote a second letter to Liverpool, now confirmed as Secretary of State for War, answering the questions that Liverpool had raised in his letter of 20 October.[22] Wellington remained confident, 'I do not think they will succeed [in invading Portugal] with an army of 70,000 or even 80,000 men'.[23]

Clearly, the issue of withdrawing the British army and leaving Portugal to its fate was very sensitive and would remain so through 1810. Even more sensitive was the issue of whether it would be possible to embark any of the Portuguese army as well. Even discussing the matter was seen to be problematic as it would increase the fears of the Portuguese government that the eventuality was being seriously considered. Wellington writing to Liverpool in early 1810 commented:

> I have no doubt that some, possibly a large proportion, of the Portuguese troops will be desirous of withdrawing from Portugal at the time that this country shall be evacuated by the British army, but it is impossible to devise any mode by which information can be acquired, or any estimate formed, of the numbers which would be likely to go.[24]

A more mundane problem was also highlighted by Wellington, in the same letter; the Portuguese troops 'generally had a great objection to embarking in ships'. The provision of transports was in itself a major issue. Keeping sufficient tonnage in Lisbon to evacuate the British army was extremely expensive. The transport fleet was made up of over 250 ships amounting to 75,000 tons.[25] Wellington had already recommended that most horses should be abandoned, as the cost of retaining horse transports would quickly exceed the value of the horses. Wellington suggested that Portuguese vessels could be prepared to evacuate Portuguese troops but had two concerns. First, preparations could not be done in secret and second, anti-French civilians would be expecting to use local vessels to escape and would resist them being commandeered. Wellington's solution was to fortify Setúbal and Peniche to give secure locations for Portuguese soldiers and civilians to wait until they could be evacuated.

The option of retiring Portuguese troops to the Algarve was discounted as Wellington believed that any French attack would include an enemy column moving to the south of the Tagus, cutting off such a route. Another option that was considered was removing British or Portuguese troops to islands off the Atlantic coast. The Berlengas islands, off Peniche and the Bayona islands, off Vigo were considered.[26]

The issue of the security of the army and the embarkation point would not go away and Wellington had to repeat his thinking on a number of

---

22 Wellington, *Supplementary Despatches*, Vol.6, p.412.

23 Gurwood, *Dispatches*, Wellington to Liverpool, Badajoz, 14 November 1809, second letter. This is also in Wellington, *Supplementary Despatches*, dated, 19 November, Vol.6, p.423.

24 Gurwood, *Dispatches*, Wellington to Liverpool, Viseu, 31 January 1810.

25 Brian De Toy, *Wellington's Admiral: The life and career of George Berkeley, 1753–1818* (PhD Thesis, Florida State University, 1997), pp.498–500.

26 Wellington, *Supplementary Despatches*, Vol.6, p.467.

occasions. Writing to Charles Stuart, he stated 'Peniche and Setuval can be made use of only as places to receive those who may go to them by sea'.[27] He continued, that Peniche could not be used at it would be outside the line of Lisbon defences, the position of which was set by where the Tagus could be forded in the summer, that is, below Salvaterra de Magos (on the left bank). Moving the defensive line north would expose the army to being cut off from Lisbon. He confirmed that he intended to improve the defences at Peniche. The situation was the same for Setúbal, because the army would be concentrated on the north bank of the Tagus it would be impossible to keep communications open with that town. Again, Wellington explained that he intended to occupy Forts São Filipe and Outão at Setúbal, and Palmela castle. Wellington was much more concerned about keeping the Portuguese army away from the French if he was forced to embark, than he was about rich Portuguese civilians and their wealth.

On 13 March 1810, Liverpool wrote to Wellington, reporting that: 'a very considerable degree of alarm exists in this country respecting the safety of the British army in Portugal ... you would be excused for bringing away the army a little too soon than, by remaining in Portugal a little too long, exposing it to those risks from which no military operations can be wholly exempt.'[28]

So far, so good. Wellington will have understood the concern. However, Liverpool now continued in a way that suggested armchair generals were whispering in his ears: 'The chances of successful defence are considered here by all persons, military as well as civil, so *improbable* that I could not recommend any attempt at what may be called *desperate resistance* [present author's italics].'

The situation will then have been made worse by Liverpool questioning the decision to use São Julião rather than Peniche:

> The position at St Julian's and the means of getting out the Tagus must always be uncertain; and the position, if I am not misinformed, is one that could not be maintained long ... Peniche ... is represented to be so far an impregnable position, that, with proper precautions, it may be defended for weeks and even for months ... being able ... to embark the army in perfect safety.

Wellington will have been very unhappy with this letter. It was almost exactly a year since he had first written his memorandum on the defence of Portugal. It was four months since Wellington wrote to Liverpool explaining his proposals for the defence of Lisbon. To be fair, the British government was in a weak position. The impact of the disastrous Walcheren expedition was still being played out in Parliament and Wellington now commanded the only field army the British currently had; they could not afford to lose it. Liverpool was also broadly correct in the statement that all persons thought a successful defence was improbable. That view was shared by pretty much everyone in Wellington's army! Liverpool had good reason to be worried.

---

27   Gurwood, *Dispatches*, Wellington to Stuart, 10 March 1810.
28   Wellington, *Supplementary Despatches*, Vol.6, p.493.

Had Napoleon or Masséna turned up with 100,000 troops, Portugal could have been indefensible. Had a smaller French force turned up three months earlier, then defence would also have been very difficult. Wellington's response, three weeks later was measured:

> I am much obliged to you for the consideration you have given to our situation in this country … The great disadvantage under which I labor [sic] is, that Sir J. Moore gave an opinion that this country could not be defended … and although it is obvious that the country is in a very different situation … yet persons … entertain a prejudice against … any plans for opposing the enemy … and will not even consider them … My opinion is, that as long as we shall remain in a state of activity in Portugal, the contest must continue in Spain … If they [the French] should invade [Portugal] … and should not succeed in obliging us to evacuate … the more likely they are to suffer materially in Spain.[29]

Wellington then answered Liverpool's questions about Peniche. He started by saying:

> All the preparations for embarking and carrying away the army … are already made … and my intention is to embark as soon as I find a military necessity exists … and shall do everything in my power to avert the necessity of embarking at all … there is no intention or desire to attempt a desperate resistance … I have not mistaken the place of embarkation … I think you have received your information … from some of those persons who have never considered the subject and probably have never even looked at either place [São Julião or Peniche].

Wellington's composure slipped in the final paragraph: 'If government takes the opinions of others upon the situation of affairs here and entertain doubts upon the measures which I propose to adopt, then let them give me their instructions in detail and I will carry them strictly into execution.'

Liverpool's position appeared to have changed in his letter of 13 March 1810. He clearly said that 'the safety of the army is to be your first object'. On that basis, his argument to use Peniche may have been valid. Wellington was still operating on the basis that his primary objective was to save Portugal, unless the government gave clear directions to change his priorities. In a letter to Fletcher, the following day, Wellington was clearly sticking to his interpretation, but was recognising that the Government may make changes. There was a need to:

> … give some security to Setuval, Palmella and principally to Peniche. The object in respect of the first two, is to be able to hold them some time as places of refuge for the inhabitants of the country, who might wish, or to whom it might be desirable to evacuate the country. The object in occupying and improving the last mentioned place, is the same; but I think it not impossible that government may

---

29   Gurwood, *Dispatches*, Wellington to Liverpool, 2 April 1810.

be disposed to go a step farther in respect of Peniche and to make an arrangement for occupying it permanently.[30]

The letter concluded by ordering improvements to the defences at Peniche which were not as 'impregnable' as Liverpool had been told.

Wellington summed up his feelings in a letter to Berkeley, 'The government is terribly afraid that I shall get them, and myself, into a scrape. But what can be expected from men who are beaten in the House of Commons three times a week?'[31] In early 1810, Wellington was still a junior Lieutenant General with no big victories to his name, commanding Britain's only field army, against an enemy that almost everyone thought he could not beat. Wellington was also sending limited information home on his plans, so it is not really surprising that the government was nervous. The lack of detail being sent home would continue for many months, throughout the construction period of the defences.

---

30   Gurwood, *Dispatches*, Wellington to Fletcher, 3 April 1810.
31   Gurwood, *Dispatches*, Wellington to Berkeley, 7 April 1810.

5

Wellington's Memorandum

Wellington's orders for the defence of Lisbon were contained in a document entitled: 'Memorandum for Lieutenant Colonel Fletcher, Commanding Royal Engineer' and dated, Lisbon, 20 October 1809. This was the basis of the construction work that would continue for three years, although much of the work would be completed in the first year. It is worth having a detailed look at the contents of this memorandum as it does not contain what many people think.[1] The second paragraph contains the purpose of the memorandum: 'The great object in Portugal is the possession of Lisbon and the Tagus, and all our measures must be directed to this object. There is another also connected with that first object, to which we must likewise attend, viz., the embarkation of the British troops in case of reverse.'

As he had done several times previously, Wellington clarified that his purpose was the defence of Lisbon with a secondary requirement for a safe embarkation point for the British army. After this mention of the secondary purpose it is not mentioned again in the memorandum, which focusses on the defence of Lisbon. The memorandum also contained the first mention of a policy to deny all local resources to an invading army, the so-called scorched earth policy:

> They [the army] should stand in every position which the country could afford, such a length of time as would enable the people of the country to evacuate the towns and villages, carrying with them or destroying all articles of provisions and carriages, not necessary for the allied army

He expected simultaneous attacks north and south of the Tagus. Any plan had to ensure that an attack from the south of the Tagus was not able to cross the river behind the allied army, cutting it off from Lisbon. Wellington also considered a third route of attack through Castello Branco and assigned a force to protect this route.

The detail of the memorandum and his opening explanation showed that he expected the main attack would come down the right (northern) bank

---

1   See Appendix 1 for the full text of the memorandum.

of the river, 'the high road to Lisbon by the Tagus', possibly after a southern attack had crossed the Tagus at its lowest crossable point. His plan had the majority of the allied army being placed near the right bank of the river and slightly inland. The only exceptions were forces at Torres Vedras, Sobral and Arruda (dos Vinhos). This concentration of the forces on the eastern side of the Lisbon Peninsula is quite different from the final design of the Lines of Torres Vedras.

With the exception of Torres Vedras, all the troops and defences were at, or to the east of, Sobral. There was no expectation that a French attack would come down the Atlantic coast. The key outer positions proposed were at Torres Vedras, for 5,000 men; Sobral, for 4,000 men and Arruda, for 2,000 men, along with the yet-to-be decided defences at Castanheira. Wellington had no expectation of holding these outer positions if attacked. He wrote 'in case the enemy should succeed' and once any one of the positions was lost, the defenders would all have to withdraw to the next defensive positions at Mafra, Montachique, Bucelas and Alverca.

The bulk of the memorandum described where Wellington wanted defences built and many places where further examination was required. In addition, the memorandum described other tasks; the destruction of a number of key roads; the improvement of a different routes; the damming of rivers at Castanheira, Alhandra and Loures, and the destruction of bridges at Castanheira and Loures. The summary below describes the range of tasks and shows that building defensive positions was only part of the proposal.

Summary of Wellington's Memorandum, 20 October 1809

Task	Number
Build defences	16
Dam river	3
Scarp river banks	1
Examine road	4
Destroy road	5
Repair road	1
Destroy bridge	2
Construct signal stations	1
Prepare map	1

Wellington indicated that there was an urgency in starting these tasks:

> … it is necessary that different works should be constructed immediately, and that arrangements and preparations should be made for the construction of others. Accordingly, I beg Colonel Fletcher, as soon as possible, to review these several positions.

At this time, the position at Castanheira on the right bank of the Tagus, was seen as critical to the defences. This was the location that Wellington believed was below the lowest point that the river could be crossed and would be the pivot for the whole of the defences. Whilst Wellington was clear about several defensive positions such as those at Torres Vedras, Sobral, Arruda, Montachique and

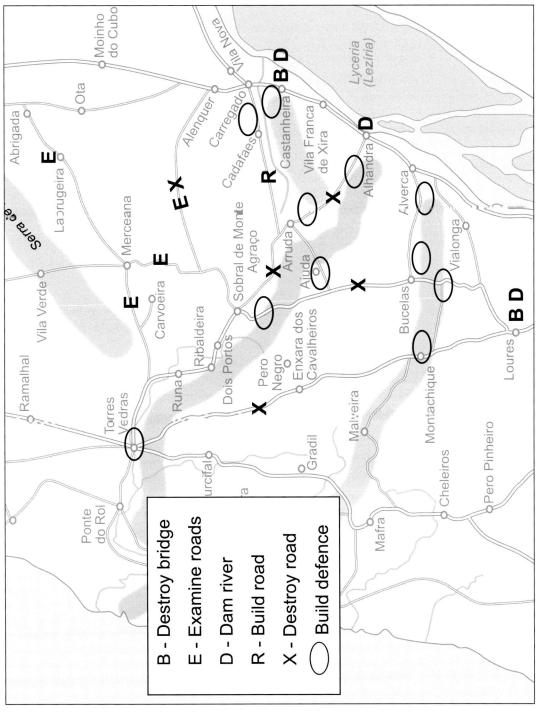

Wellington's Memorandum, 20 October 1809.

B - Destroy bridge
E - Examine roads
D - Dam river
R - Build road
X - Destroy road
◯ Build defence

Bucelas, he clearly did not have detailed knowledge of Castanheira, and the memorandum asked Fletcher to examine the area and suggest options. Why Castanheira was chosen would become the subject of dispute later.

When the forward defences were breached, the allied army would fall back to the main position on the Mafra, Montachique, Bucelas, Alverca line. These defensive positions were to be substantial including defences for 5,000 men at Montachique. At Bucelas and Alverca, Wellington asked for an examination of the ground and recommendations on the scale of defences to be built.

What is interesting is that although we know that Wellington was considering a number of places for the possible embarkation of the army and that São Julião was the preferred option, there was no mention of constructing any defences there, or a potential retreat to this position in the memorandum. As written, the memorandum did not consider the final withdrawal of the British army. This should have been a key component of Wellington's operational planning and it is surprising that there is no mention of it. There should have been some broad plan on how the army would retire from the second line of defences to the banks of the Tagus. Wellington would have expected to be present, to command the withdrawal, but accidents happened, and if he was injured there was no plan laid down and, in fact, no clear second in command. Moving a defeated army to the embarkation point, possibly through a city that would be in turmoil, with no clear plan, would have been disastrous. Was Wellington so sure that the defences would hold? If not, then why was there no plan?[2]

Fletcher's first action was to order the recall of almost all Royal Engineer officers to Lisbon. As the officers arrived in Lisbon, they were assigned to the priority tasks. This will be described in the next chapter. Only two engineer officers, Captain John Burgoyne and Lieutenant Anthony Emmett were omitted. There were ordered to remain with the army stationed near Badajoz.

Before leaving Wellington's plan for the defence of Lisbon, it is necessary to consider the controversy about who first thought of the idea to defend Lisbon in this way. There is a strong claim that the Portuguese engineer, José Maria das Neves Costa made similar proposals before Wellington wrote his memorandum of 20 October 1809 and because of that should be given the credit for the idea. Neves Costa was very unhappy that he had received no recognition and in 1812 applied to the Portuguese government for a pension for himself and Major Caula. His claim was referred to Wellington.[3]

There is no doubt that Neves Costa's report was in the hands of the Portuguese government in June 1809. There is no doubt that Beresford and Chapman had seen it. This leaves two questions to be answered. First, had Wellington seen Neves Costa's report before he wrote his memorandum? Second, if he had seen it, how much did he use it?

---

2   Dr Will Fletcher's latest research on the Quarter Master General's department has found some papers on planning a withdrawal to the embarkation point, but this information does not appear to have been communicated to his senior commanders.

3   There is a good summary of the situation in Kenton White, *The Key to Lisbon, The Third French Invasion of Portugal 1810-11* (Warwick: Helion, 2019), pp.64–67.

It is inconceivable that a recent survey carried out by an expert Portuguese engineer would not have been brought to the attention of Wellington. Since Wellington was extremely interested in how to defend Lisbon, it would have been negligent not to look at it. Wellington acknowledged in 1812 that he had seen Neves Costa's report and the associated map of the area. The answer to the second question is more difficult. Wellington, in the same letter, acknowledged:

> When I came to examine the ground, I found both so inaccurate, that I could place no reliance upon them and it is a fact that having trusted in one instance to the plan and the memoir, without reconnoitring the ground, I was obliged to make a second journey to Lisbon, in February 1810, and to destroy the works that had been commenced.[4]

Wellington's response was very dismissive and he appeared very unhappy about Neves Costa's claim that the whole idea was his, saying in the same letter: 'I solemnly protest against it being understood that Major Das Neves [sic] or Colonel Caula, either formed the plan, or conceived the idea of the system which was carried into execution for the safety of Lisbon under my direction.'

As discussed above, Neves Costa's report provided a detailed description of the area to the north of Lisbon. Wellington's complaint about them being 'so inaccurate that I could place no reliance on them' appears unfair. The defensive potential of this area of country was well understood by every military man who looked at it, so Neves Costa claiming it was his idea is not justifiable either. Wellington had seen Vincent's report on the defence of Lisbon and an earlier report by Lieutenant General Sir Charles Stuart from his time in Lisbon in 1799.[5] Also, the Royal Engineer who was on Stuart's expedition, Captain Lieutenant Frederick Mulcaster, sent copies all his papers to Fletcher in March 1809. These included reports on the defence of Lisbon and the left and right banks of the Tagus.[6]

However, the detail contained in Neves Costa's report will have been very useful to anyone looking to build defences in that region. The British officers, including Wellington, did not have the detailed local knowledge that Neves Costa had. Neves Costa did not envisage an extensive series of defences being built over these hills. His proposal was for mobile troops using the terrain to slow down any advance on Lisbon. His expectation was that the commander of the defending army would choose positions from the several descriptions provided by him. Neves Costa, appeared, like many allied officers, to make the mistake of assuming the defending army would occupy the defensive positions and there would be few troops left to move to face a direct attack. He wrote:

---

4   Gurwood, *Dispatches*, Wellington to Forjaz, 24 April 1812.

5   William F. P. Napier, *History of the War in the Peninsula and in the South of France from the Year 1807 to the year 1814* (London: T & W Boone, 1828-1834), Vol.3, p.255.

6   TNA: WO55/1561/10.

... it is hardly possible to defend these positions if we follow the system of guarding them in order to stop the enemy everywhere. The movements that would result from such a dispersion of the armed forces, supposed to be inferior to the attacker, would not be counterbalanced by the natural advantages of these positions.

None of these will avoid being forced or outflanked [quickly], and it is in the nature of the defence of similar lines of positions that [when] one of those which is won by the enemy, will render unusable all others of the same line, which the defending troops will be obliged to abandon before being attacked, or risk being cut off, in case they continue to defend them.

In my view, the defence system which seems most appropriate in these circumstances, the one, of which skilled generals have taken great advantages and which has certainly admired the results of the modern tactics of the French, is that of an active [mobile] defence ... The exact and detailed knowledge of the terrain is the basis and provides the data necessary for the complete execution of the system I am advising.[7]

This was not what Wellington was proposing in October 1809 or what was in place in October 1810. The use of Neves Costa's report by Wellington is well described by Melícias in his recent book:

Wellington's plan was likely to have taken advantage of Neves Costa's reconnaissance and military report, it was not simply an appropriation of those elements, but rather a use of a work already done, an act that reveals above all intelligence and capacity of resource management. Wellington's use of Neves Costa's work would even be in keeping with the latter's aim, which stated that it was not his job to propose a particular defence system, but to make available the necessary material for the generals to do. This seems to have happened, and such a hypothetical use is no more reprehensible than the hypothetical use by Neves Costa of the works already developed by Vincent in the elaboration of the topographical chart and the report of which he seems to later claim for usurpation.[8]

Other Portuguese historians take a different view. Geraldo wrote:

Perhaps here lies the main difference between the two plans. José Maria Das Neves Costa conceived studies and works primarily for the defence of the capital, while Wellington, in his plan for the defence of Portugal, placed 'firstly, the construction of fortifications to protect the embarkation place; and, secondly, a number of field fortifications to block the four main passages through the hills north of Lisbon.'[9]

---

7   Neves Costa, *Memoria Militar*, pp.30–31, author's translation.
8   Melícias, *Torres Vedras*, p.44, author's translation.
9   Geraldo, *Revista Militar*, No. 2495, quoting A.H. Norris, R.W. Bremner, *As Linhas de Torres Vedras: As três primeiras linhas e as fortificações ao Sul do Tejo* (Torres Vedras: Câmara Municipal de Torres Vedras, Museu Municipal Lionel Trindade, 2001), p.13, author's translation.

Sousa Lobo also inferred that Wellington's priority was the embarkation of the British army, not the defence of Lisbon.[10] As previously stated above, this was not what Wellington wrote. In his Memorandum of 20 October 1809, he said: 'The great object in Portugal is the possession of Lisbon and the Tagus, and all our measures must have been directed to this object. There is another also connected with the first object, to which we must likewise attend, the embarkation of the British troops in case of reverse.'[11]

The order of the two statements above is significant. Wellington clearly stated that possession of Lisbon was his primary objective and embarkation was an option, only in case of defeat. Wellington repeatedly wrote that his priority was the defence of Lisbon, and his actions support this view. Building a hugely expensive system comprising over 150 forts, with many new roads and other types of defence was not a public relations exercise to fool the Portuguese into thinking that his primary aim was not to run for his ships.

The final point to consider is the placement of the right of the defensive line at Castanheira. In Wellington's letter of April 1812, quoted above, he clearly lays the blame for the selection of Castanheira on Neves Costa. This was the position selected by Wellington in his memorandum and Wellington infers it was due to the recommendation in Neves Costa's report. After a second visit by Wellington in February 1810, the decision was made to destroy the defences already constructed there and move the right of the line back to Alhandra. Castanheira was judged to be too far forward and vulnerable to being outflanked. The riverbank was also much wider there than at Alhandra.

One of Neves Costa's main arguments for saying that Wellington must have seen his report is because Wellington identified Castanheira for the Tagus end of the defensive line and then later changed it to Alhandra. Neves Costa's report recommended Castanheira. Therefore, either Wellington made the same mistake, or he had seen Neves Costa's report. On this point, they appear to be in agreement. Wellington says he picked Castanheira because he had never been there, and Neves Costa had recommended it. There is one potential flaw in Wellington's argument. The Royal Engineer, Lieutenant Rice Jones, who was Fletcher's adjutant, said Wellington did go to Castanheira with Fletcher on 16 October 1809.[12] In that case, blaming Neves Costa for the error is unreasonable. Even if Wellington did not go there on 16 October, Fletcher and several of his senior engineers did a few days later and spent several days surveying the area. Construction work did not start until 8 January 1810.[13] Issues with using Castanheira should have been picked up much earlier. If they were, and no decision was made until Wellington personally rode over the ground in February, then it suggests that Wellington did not have much confidence in his engineers. The decision to select Castanheira and then reject it was made by Wellington and his

---

10 Sousa Lobo, *Defesa*, p.175.
11 Gurwood, *Dispatches,* Memorandum for Lieut. Col. Fletcher, 20 October 1809.
12 Shore, *Engineer Officer*, p.45.
13 Jones, *Sieges*, Vol.3, p.120.

engineers, even if Neves Costa had also proposed it as a possible defensive point. The reasons that Castanheira was rejected will be covered later.

When all the argument is over, some things remain clear. It was Wellington who ordered the construction of the Lines. It was Wellington who pushed to get the money and resources to build the Lines. The construction of the Lines was managed by British, German and Portuguese engineer officers. The lines were built by Portuguese militia and civilians. The Portuguese government could not have achieved this by themselves. And, finally, Neves Costa's detailed report will have helped to support the decision making of the officers who designed and built the Lines. Whilst Neves Costa did not work directly on the construction of the Lines, he did carry out other work in 1810 including surveying and repair work on roads around Caldas and Leiria and a survey of crossings on the lower parts of the Zêzere.[14]

At this time the British Royal Engineers were a very small, officer only corps. The total number of officers never exceeded 260 and in 1809, there were only about 180. Of this number, there were about 30 in the Iberian Peninsula. The engineering rank and file, what we now call sappers, did not really exist. There was a sister corps to the Royal Engineers, called the Royal Military Artificers (RMA), which provided workmen for engineering tasks, but they were generally not available for duties with field armies. The RMA had been established and expanded as a garrison only workforce and were released begrudgingly, in tiny numbers, to serve with the army. The Royal Engineer officers did not want the responsibility of commanding 'sappers' and the RMA tradesmen were not trained for field operations. This unacceptable situation did not change until 1812 when the School of Military Engineering was formed and the first trained sappers did not arrive in the Peninsula until 1813. The artificers available to support the engineers on the defence of Lisbon never exceeded 20 men and were generally in administrative or supervisory positions.

Working alongside the Royal Engineers were the engineers of the Portuguese army. Their numbers were also small, probably less than 100 at this time, with the requirement to provide officers for overseas stations. The reorganisation of 1812 set the corps establishment at 72. These officers were used differently, due to the different organisation of the British and Portuguese armies. The Royal Engineers were not part of the British army (being part of the Board of Ordnance) and were not allowed to take up staff positions or governorships. The Portuguese officers were part of the army, so many were utilised on the staff or as military governors at fortresses or major towns. This meant there were fewer available for military engineering tasks.[15] However a number were involved in the construction of the Lines in addition to their work on the Lisbon city defences.

Having identified the officers, who were to oversee the construction, the next task was to identify the workforce. Wellington wanted his army,

---

14   M Monteiro (ed.), *The Lines of Torres Vedras; A Defence System to the North of Lisbon* (Lisbon: PILT, 2011), pp.155–156.

15   Mark S. Thompson, 'The Portuguese Engineers in the Peninsular War', in Andrew Bamford (ed.), *Command and Leadership, 1721–1815* (Warwick: Helion, 2019), pp.44–67.

including the recently trained Portuguese units, monitoring the actions of the French near the border. Other Portuguese army units were in training and using them as labourers was inappropriate. The initial decision was to allocate militia units to provide the manpower. Fletcher's initial requests for resources were met from the Torres Vedras and Figueira da Foz Militia regiments.[16] Wellington issued the order on 26 October 1809 for 600 men to be sent to Torres Vedras, 500 to Sobral and 800 to São Julião.[17] A small number of Royal Military Artificers were present and a similar small number of tradesmen volunteers from the British infantry regiments in Lisbon. This was the available workforce.

Work on the Lines of Torres Vedras was now ready to begin, by 'turning those vast mountains into one stupendous and impregnable citadel' as Napier boasted.[18]

---

16   REM: 5501-59-18, Fletcher to Jones, 5 July 1810.
17   Gurwood, *Dispatches,* Wellington to Beresford, Lisbon, 26 October 1809.
18   Napier, *Peninsular War*, Vol.3, p.255.

6

Construction of the Lines, November 1809 to July 1810

A major difficulty that Wellington faced in early 1810 was that he did not know how much time he would have to build the defences. In 1809, *Maréchal* Soult had invaded Portugal from the north in February. Admittedly, Soult knew there would be little organised resistance and he was under direct orders from Napoleon to proceed quickly. The situation the French faced in 1810, would be very different as there was an army waiting to meet the invaders. In late 1809, Napoleon was planning to come himself, with an army of 100,000, so a rapid campaign, led by the Emperor was possible. What Napoleon could do, which his marshals could not, was ensure total subservience to his orders and full support from every marshal.

The allies needed to move quickly whilst there was a possibility that Napoleon would lead the invasion. Once command was delegated to Masséna, the cautious approach by the French gave the allies longer than first thought. The work over this period of nearly one year, can be broken into three periods. Between November 1809 and February 1810, the work was concentrated at the four key locations of São Julião, Castanheira, Sobral and Torres Vedras. Between February and July 1810, the work was extended to cover the other areas mentioned in Wellington's memorandum. Between July and October 1810, as more time became available, the works were extended to the west and into what became the first line. Work on additional defences continued after the forts were occupied in October 1810.

Whilst Fletcher waited for his engineers to arrive, orders were placed for basic building materials for the forts; 19,000 palisades and 10,000 fascines, some to be sent to Torres Vedras and Sobral with the remainder held in Lisbon to be delivered as required. The palisades would be used to make an impenetrable barrier in the ditches and the fascines to strengthen the earthwork parapets. Wellington informed Fletcher that his decision to hold the main stock at Lisbon was to make the whole length of the Tagus available for collecting material.[1]

---

1   Gurwood, *Dispatches*, Wellington to Murray, Commissary General, 31 October 1809.

The first location where work started, was one not described in Wellington's memorandum. This was the embarkation point at São Julião.[2] The fort of São Julião da Barra was one of the key defensive positions on the river Tagus. Its construction had started around 1550, so it was already 250 years old when the Napoleonic Wars began. Forts including Santo António da Barra (Cascais), São Lourenço do Bugio, São Vicente de Belém and, on the southern bank, Torre Velha da Caparica, controlled the entrance into the port of Lisbon.

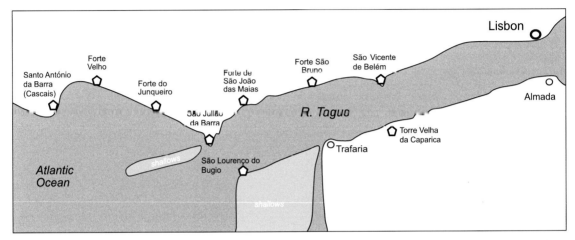

Forts on River Tagus at Lisbon.

The primary purpose of São Julião was to protect the entrance into the Tagus estuary, but after having been twice successfully captured, extensive land defences were added. The work was extended many times in the following years to become a formidable defensive position against attacks from the land or the sea.[3] By 1660, the land defences of the fort looked like Vauban on steroids. Much of these outer, land-based defences had been removed by 1809, but still left a substantial fortress.

The work was assigned to a Kings German Legion (KGL) engineer, Captain Charles Wedekind. The KGL were integrated into the British military and Wedekind reported to Fletcher. It is likely that his first task was starting on the proposals made by Fletcher after his visit on 15 October. Fletcher had identified a hill in front of the fort which 'if occupied by a strong field work' would protect the fort and cover the embarkation point. This hill had been previously covered by the seventeenth century fortifications.[4] He continued that the flanks of the field work would be protected by the fort and 'its rear should have a weak profile to prevent an enemy finding immediate cover against artillery if he should succeed in taking it.' He believed that with a garrison of 1,500 to 2,000 men it could protect the embarking troops from

2   Jones, *Sieges*, p.18, stated that work started on 3 November 1809. Mark S. Thompson (ed.), *The Peninsular War Diary of Edmund Mulcaster RE* (Sunderland: Amazon CreateSpace, 2015), p.69, says that Wedekind was already there on 31 October and work had started on the new redoubt.

3   Fort of São Julião da Barra, *Fortalezas.org*, <http://fortalezas.org/index.php?ct=fortaleza&id_fortaleza=674>, accessed 16 November 2019.

4   Wellington, *Supplementary Despatches*, Vol.6, p.401.

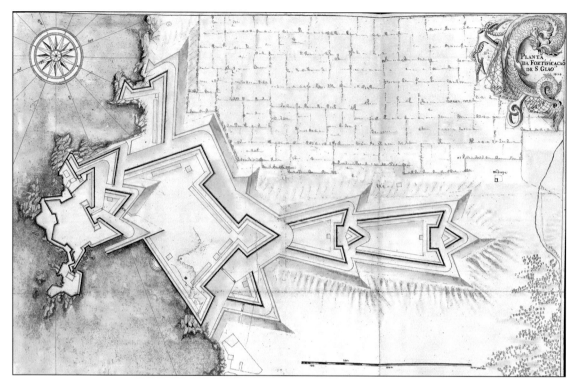

São Julião da Barra in 1660.
(Public Domain)

a superior enemy force and with covering fire from the fort most, if not all, of the garrison could withdraw. He finished by recommending that all sea-facing artillery in the fort should be removed, so the French could not fire on the fleet when they eventually took the fort after the embarkation had been completed. All other guns in the fort and the field work should be spiked or otherwise disabled before they were abandoned. The redoubt in front of São Julião would eventually be numbered Fort 98, named Forte Algueirão, and would be the most powerful fort on the Lines. It was the only one armed with 24-pounder cannon, so that it would be able to out-range any French field artillery or guns they had captured. The French would have to bring a siege train to take the redoubt.

Also included in the first pieces of work near this location were repairs to fort São Lourenço do Bugio, which was located on a rock in the middle of the Tagus estuary. Rear Admiral Berkeley had informed Wellington that the fort was in need of repairs.[5] Berkeley had an interest in the security of the estuary at Lisbon and would provide sailors and marines to man some of the forts on the coast.[6] In December 1809, Wellington wrote to Berkeley, informing him that he had asked the Portuguese government to introduce a registration system for all boats on all rivers 'but particularly the Tagus'.[7] The primary purpose was to ensure that all boats were removed in the event of an invasion.

---

5   Gurwood, *Dispatches*, Wellington to Berkeley, Badajoz, 20 November 1809.

6   Gurwood, *Dispatches*, Wellington to Berkeley, Coimbra, 8 May 1809. Wellington approving the issue of supplies to them.

7   Gurwood, *Dispatches*, Wellington to Berkeley, Badajoz, 19 December 1809.

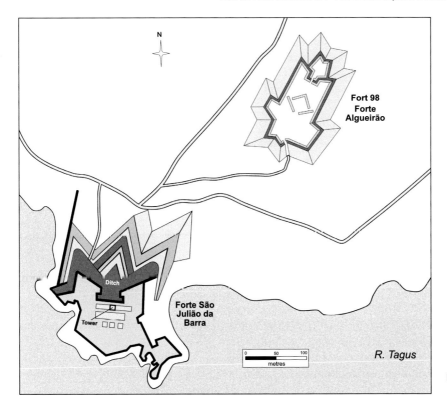

Fort of São Julião da Barra and
Fort 98.

Work commenced at the other two primary locations: at Sobral on 4 November and Torres Vedras on 8 November 1809. For the next two months, these were the only three places where building work was underway, the labour force was the two militia regiments, about 2,000 strong. The reason why the work at Castanheira was delayed until the first weeks of 1810 was because Fletcher had not yet fully examined the area and made his recommendations. This did not happen until late December 1809. There was probably less urgency as the bulk of Wellington's army would be concentrated on the banks of the Tagus, at least until some defences were built there.

The Royal Engineer, Captain Edmund Mulcaster, who would play a major role in the construction of the Lines, reported on the situation soon after the work commenced:

The following is to be the distribution of the officers:

Fletcher, Chapman, Goldfinch, [Rice] Jones – General superintendence – we shall be looked into enough.

Baron Wedekind – Hornwork at St Julian's.

Mulcaster, Thomson – Torres Vedras.

Ross, Forster – Sobral.

Williams, Stanway – Royal Surveyors.

Mudge, Hamilton[8] – Lisbon, [the engineer headquarters and drawing of plans]

---

8   Hamilton had been badly wounded at the taking of Porto in May 1809 and was unable to carry out any field duties. He continued to work in the engineers' office until he died in May 1810.

> [We] first made a plan of a tolerable position at Castanheira which is to be taken up by part of the army if they come here before the French. There are to be also various redoubts at Montachique and other places. But of course, you will not mention this to anyone, all being a most profound secret. Williams occupies Ross' post till he comes. Stanway is here [at Torres Vedras] to survey this place.[9]

Mulcaster also recorded that there was a Portuguese engineer officer with him, so there was a Portuguese presence from the earliest days in the building of the Lines. The lack of confidence between the engineers of the two nations was apparent here as well. Mulcaster commented:

> I have an old captain of Portuguese Engineers here under my orders. He complained to Thomson that I don't tell him my plans. I must treat him with more confidence in the future … There is [also] a Major at Sobral under their orders (that is of Williams and Forster)[10] We don't treat our allies with much respect.

The Portuguese officer was *Capitão* Luiz Máximo Jorge de Bellegarde. He was about 38 years old. Did that really seem old to 22-year-old Mulcaster? It is suggested that Bellegarde was present due to his expertise as a hydraulics engineer. He was there to build the dams on the Rio Sizandro.[11] Mulcaster had arrived in Lisbon on 30 October and rode to Castanheira, with fellow engineer, Forster, on 1 November 1809. The next day Fletcher and Chapman arrived, and the day after, three more engineers.[12] Mulcaster was involved in the survey work at Castanheira from 2 to 5 November before riding to Torres Vedras on 6 November 1809. He recorded on 7 November: 'Rode in the morning with the Colonel and Chapman over the position, found the works already marked out with the exception of the detached redoubts which we however traced.'[13]

The first working party of 50 men arrived on the morning of 8 November and were put to work. The number had increased to 100 by the end of the day and 400 by the following morning, which Mulcaster expected to be the usual number in future. Burgoyne described the construction methods used at Torres Vedras:

> The works at Torres Vedras were chiefly excavated in rock, the upper part of the exterior slope lined with sodwork [i.e., earth]. The interior slope with fascines made of fir; 10 feet long and one foot in diameter; having about six strong picket bindings about 4 feet long and from 1½ to 2½ inches in diameter. They were rough, but for the service excellent and likely to last very long.[14]

---

9   REM: 4601-74, Mulcaster to Burgoyne, Torres Vedras, 12 November 1809.
10   Captain John Williams; Lieutenants Alexander Thomson and William Forster RE.
11   This information was provided to me by *Coronel* José Paulo Berger, Portuguese army.
12   Captain Williams, Lieutenants Stanway and Thomson.
13   Thompson, *Mulcaster Diary*, p.70.
14   REM: 4201-68, Notebook, p.46.

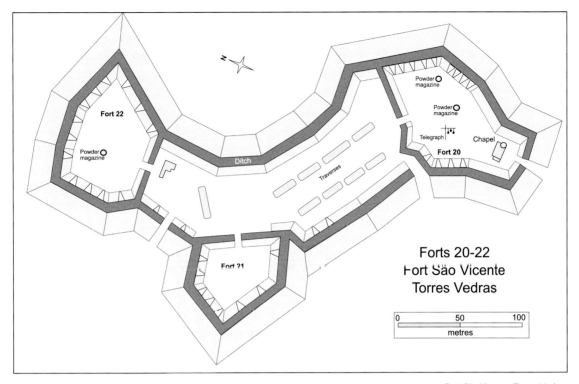

Fort São Vicente, Torres Vedras.

The speed with which the arrangements had been made led to some complications. The militia soldiers and the volunteers from the army were to be paid for their work. However, there was no process in place, nor staff to organise the finances. The engineer officers found themselves responsible for making and recording the payments to the workers and of course, were personally responsible for any mistakes in the payments. They were not happy! Mulcaster commented, 'Settled pay lists ... after some trouble. NB Always to begin with general correct lists ... Underwent for the first time the inexpressible delight of being paymaster.'[15] The engineer resource was very small and having to prepare and dispense payments to hundreds of militia was a hugely time-consuming task. Mulcaster noted his daily routine: 'Rise at 5:30, breakfast at 6:15, parade at 7:00, on the works till 12:00, examine the check list till 1:30, on the works till 5:00, dine at 6:00, employed the evening in correcting pay lists etc.'[16] Until civilian clerks were appointed, payment of the labourers would take up a lot of engineer time.

Between 25 December and 24 February, Fletcher wrote four extensive reports making recommendations on how to defend the Lisbon peninsula. Below, are descriptions of the key points in these reports.

15   Thompson, *Mulcaster Diary*, p.70.
16   REM: 4601-74, Mulcaster to Burgoyne, Torres Vedras, 12 November 1809.

Fletcher's Report of 25 December 1809[17]

In this first report, Fletcher examined the country round Mafra:

> The position at Mafra is undoubtedly very important, and, were it possible to approach it only by the road from Torres Vedras, would be exceedingly strong; but this strength will naturally induce an enemy to attempt the flanks and … these are, I fear, our most vulnerable points.
>
> The country in this part of Portugal, though chiefly composed of a succession of strong hills, is not of that decided mountainous character … infantry may pass with ease almost anywhere. The importance of the different positions … is very much increased or lessened by the difficulty … of turning them with artillery, and these very much depend on the season of the year.[18]

Fletcher covered an extensive area in this reconnaissance. On the route from Torres Vedras to Mafra he identified defensive positions at Serra da Vila, Turcifal and Azueira before the heights of the Serra de Chipre, which he noted as 'excessively strong'. Here he suggested the construction of four redoubts 'were it not multiplying the works too much'. These became Forts 78–81. A defensive position for troops was proposed between Codeçal and Murgeira and redoubts to defend the roads from Ribamar to Mafra and also the road that runs from Codeçal to the main Montachique to Mafra road to the east of Mafra. Around Mafra, he recommended 11 fortified positions, 5,000 men and 21 guns (Forts 74–77, 82–87) but noted that these would not be sufficient to stop a major French attack along this line.[19]

Fletcher made a number of comments showing his concern about positions being outflanked and noted on the Atlantic coast there was a road from Ericeira to Sintra, that was used all year by carts. Two forts, 95 and 96 were built to block this route. Fletcher also noted that there were roads to Ericeira from the north which connected to Ponte do Rol through Encarnação and further north again from Ponte do Rol to Peniche. This meant there was a coastal route from north of Torres Vedras to Sintra. Fletcher commented 'the Governor of Mafra … [is] of the opinion … any of these roads would be easily passed with light artillery, unless after continued rains'.[20] Forts 89-94 would cover the area to the north of Ericeira.

Fletcher now turned his attention to the area between Mafra at Montachique and noted that there were several smaller roads that could be used to turn the main positions at these two towns. No specific recommendations were made at this time in this report but there were multiple forts built in this area (Forts 62–73). At Montachique, Fletcher recommended forts to block the roads to Torres Vedras and Mafra (Forts 52–61) and from Freixal towards

---

17   Wellington, *Supplementary Despatches*, Vol.6, pp.451–458.
18   Wellington, *Supplementary Despatches*, Vol.6, p.452.
19   Wellington, *Supplementary Despatches*, Vol.6, p.453.
20   Wellington, *Supplementary Despatches*, Vol.6, p.454.

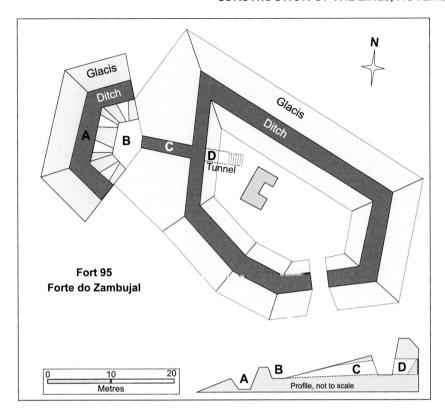

Fort 95, Forte do Zambujal.

Loures (Forts 49–51). For this area he recommended 16 fortified positions, requiring 3,200 men and 25 guns.[21]

Fletcher continued moving east and looked at the Bucelas area. He reported he was waiting for detailed drawings of the area to be completed. He noted the strength of the Bucelas pass for defence, as it 'affords excellent placement for guns.' The valley sides were so steep that the forts built there did not need a garrison (of infantry), just guns; no frontal assault was expected. At Loures, he recommended destroying the bridge on the main road and damming the river, pointing out that the dams would need to be defended.

The letter concluded with a round-up of the general situation on the construction work. He wrote that he needed to make recommendations for defences between Runa and Torres Vedras to stop an attack from Merceana. He also commented 'it would also be desirable to have something to check him [the French] on the hill south of Runa or between Ribaldero [sic Ribaldera] and Enxara dos Cavaleiros'. This was not done before the French arrived in front of the Lines. At São Julião, Fletcher reported being 'seriously uneasy' about the works at Oeiras. The ground was rockier than expected and this was slowing down the building work. Of greater concern was the lack of workers: 'The number of men, notwithstanding my repeated applications, does not increase … Goldfinch mentioning that with the militia now at St Julian's (about 400), the above works would not be completed in less than

---

21   Wellington, *Supplementary Despatches*, Vol.6, p.455.

three months.' He continued: 'Our number at Sobral has never yet amounted to more than half what I asked for and is now much less than that proportion.'

The requested numbers were 800 at São Julião and 500 at Sobral. Fletcher ended his letter saying he was now proceeding to Castanheira and the work would start as soon as the militia arrived. The problem with the supply of workmen would not recede during the building of the Lines.

Fletcher's Report of 31 December 1809[22]

Fletcher now moved on to consider the defences at Castanheira. There was two kilometres between the riverbank and the heights to the west, which rose quickly to over 100 metres. Being flat, the river plain needed a considerable barrier to stop the movement of enemy troops, particularly their cavalry. A river barrier met these criteria. The next significant river was 20 kilometres to the south at Sacavém. Wellington wanted the barrier to be as far north as possible to make access to the Arruda valley difficult and primarily to be the highest point on the river where it could not be crossed. The first two requirements in Wellington's memorandum of 20 October 1809 were:

> 1st. He will examine particularly the effect of damming up the mouth of the Castanheira river; how far it will render that river a barrier, and to what extent it will fill.
>
> 2nd. He will calculate the labor [sic] required for that work, and the time it will take, as well as the means of destroying the bridge over the river, and of constructing such redoubts as might be necessary on the plain, and on the hill on the left of the road, effectually to defend the plain. He will state particularly what means should be prepared for these works. He will also consider of the means and time required, and the effect which might be produced by scarping the banks of the river.[23]

Wellington had also explained his requirements in letters dated 4 and 13 December 1809.[24] Fletcher's letter above of 25 December began: 'I beg, however, first to mention, that as to the plan of the defence for the plain near Castanheira, I was certainly influenced by what I understood to be the bias of your Lordship's opinion, to which it is no less my inclination than my duty to pay every attention.'

This suggests that Fletcher had concerns about Castanheira even before he had completed a detailed survey; concerns that proved correct. Fletcher's letter of 31 December first considered the possibility of scarping the riverbank. Wellington wanted there to be no cover on the riverbank from the fire of the defenders. This meant cutting away the bank into a slope. Fletcher's proposal needed 1,000 workmen for three and a half days and required elevated forts

---

22   Wellington, *Supplementary Despatches*, Vol.6, pp.459–462.
23   REM: 5501-59-1, points 1 and 2.
24   Fletcher's letter to Wellington of 4 December and Wellington's to Fletcher of 13 December 1809, sadly, are not in the Wellington archives. Thanks to Zack White for checking.

to be within 60 yards of the riverbank, which was probably impracticable. Fletcher continued, commenting that the locals said the mouth of the river was impassable due to the water and mud. He persuaded a boy to make the attempt 'which he did with tolerable ease … the boy did not sink so high as his waist.' Fletcher concluded 'that the Castanheira river at low water, when the Tagus is low, is not, at any point … a serious impediment.' A heavily laden soldier crossing the river mouth would have had much greater difficulty and for cavalry or artillery it would still be impossible. Fletcher was being pessimistic.

The letter considered the construction of a dam to make the river more difficult to cross. Due to the wide range of water levels between wet and dry periods, Fletcher insisted that a sluice gate would be necessary to stop the dam being swept away in wet weather. He also stated that it would require workmen with expertise in dam building 'of whom there must be many in Lisbon.' His final point was that the terrain around Castanheira provided significant cover for the invaders due to numerous drains and sunken roads crossing the area. The enemy could approach close to the proposed defensive positions without being seen.

Wellington's letter of 13 December had asked for the defensive positions to be concealed, if possible, Fletcher reported that this would be difficult on the plain without moving large volumes of soil. In terms of redoubts, Wellington had asked for one from the main ford (the road bridge would be destroyed) and another at the junction of the 'river of Castanheira' (Rio Grande da Pipa or Vala do Carregado) and the Tagus. Use would be made of the many drains that had been cut to transfer water into the Tagus and Fletcher suggested some could be extended right across the plain. He particularly mentioned a large trench, with an embankment, 600–900 yards from the river which could 'with a moderate degree of labour … be turned into a good parapet'. At least two redoubts were proposed for the heights opposite the position.

It is not obvious why Wellington wanted the defences to be concealed. Any surprise gained from the first approach would be very limited. Possibly this was more about concealing them from the population. If major defensive works were seen at Castanheira, it might have led people to look for construction work elsewhere and the likelihood that the French would hear about them quicker. The engineer, Captain George Ross commented:

> In a former letter I told you all I knew of what was going on here in our way, being at liberty to do so … I could not repeat it now, being one of the confidential agents. This much I think I can tell you as it is known to [those] who have the curiosity to wish to know what we are doing here. That a cordon of Portuguese sentries say *noã* [sic *não*] *pode* [can not] to the rash intruder who presumes to look at our mysterious works.[25]

---

25   REM: 4501-86, Ross to Dalrymple, Carregado, 28 January 1810.

Ross was almost certainly working at Castanheira at this time. He was originally assigned to Sobral, but his letter above was written from Carregado, just north of Castanheira and many miles from Sobral.[26]

As in his previous letter, Fletcher complained about the availability of workmen, reporting that the number at São Julião on 28 December had dropped to 300, there had been no increase at Sobral and none had yet arrived at Castanheira. There was no complaint about Torres Vedras, where Mulcaster wrote:

> My entrenchments are getting on, but not so rapidly as I had hoped, for I have met with a large proportion of rock and hard gravel, and have a month's work in store, that is completely to finish and give myself a week over. I wish you could see my entrenchments. Unlucky dogs that ever have to attack them if they are defended by Englishmen.[27]

Fletcher's Report of 11 January 1810[28]

Fletcher's third letter concerned the defences between Torres Vedras and Sobral. He repeated his concern from his letter of 25 December about the weaknesses of the area. An enemy coming from Merceana to the north, would join the main road between Torres Vedras and Sobral near Runa. A fortified position here would control the road from the north but also any movement east or west on the Torres Vedras to Sobral road. Fletcher suggested one or two redoubts between Runa and Torres Vedras to block any approach to the key point of Torres Vedras. This would be Fort 26 and later 149. He acknowledged that these were not a priority at the moment, particularly whilst workmen were scarce.

Fletcher's biggest concern was that a force approaching Runa from the north would continue on the minor, but passable roads, through Ribaldeira or Zibreira da Fé and breach the first defensive positions. Once at Enxara dos Cavaleiros, the enemy would re-join the main road to Lisbon through Montachique or they could move west to Enxara do Bispo and then head south to Malveira, again avoiding the main defences at Montachique and Mafra. He suggested two forts at Enxara dos Cavaleiros that would block the routes from the north and west. These were: 28, Forte Pequeno da Enxara, and 29, Forte Grande da Enxara.

The remainder of the letter gave a progress update of the work at Torres Vedras and Sobral. At Torres Vedras, he remarked that the 'works first proposed' were nearly completed. Number one (Forts 20, 21 and 22, São Vicente) would hold 2,500 men and 19 guns. Number two (Fort 24, Reduto da Forca) was for 500 men and eight guns. Number three (Fort 23, Reduto dos Olheiros) would hold 300 men and six guns. The castle (Fort 27, Castelo

---

26   Shore, *Engineer Officer*, p.49 says that the Quinta da Condessa da Lousa was selected as the quarters for the engineers at Carregado.

27   REM: 4601-74, Mulcaster to Burgoyne, 2 January 1810.

28   Wellington, *Supplementary Despatches*, Vol.6, pp.469–472.

de Torres Vedras) would hold 300 men and seven guns. Number four, (Fort 25, Forte de São João) would hold 200 men and two guns.[29] Fletcher suggested that up to three additional works could be built to the right of the town. He again mentioned the possibility that the French could outflank the defences by staying close to the coast and moving from Ponte do Rol to Ericeira. To block this route defences would be needed at Ponte do Rol and São Pedro da Cadeira.

At Sobral, the four main forts (Forts 14, Forte do Alqueidão, 15, Forte do Machado, 16, Forte do Trinta and 17, Forte do Simplício) were being completed. He suggested three other positions for redoubts; one covering the road to Sapataria and two covering the road towards Montachique.

Fletcher ended with a worker update. 700 militia had arrived at Castanheira and had started constructing the communication trenches (on 8 January 1810 according to Jones).[30] He continued, 'I am sorry to say that the men at Sobral amounted two days since to only 160, and the day before only 180', one third of the required number. Progress was being severely affected.

Mulcaster's diary indicated that work at Torres Vedras was not as advanced as Fletcher suggested. On 9 January, he recorded 'went with Colonel and settled for the battery and blockhouse at the old convent' (Fort 25). Three days later he records 'began work … at the chateau' (Fort 27). The work there was not finished until 3 February 1810.[31] However, the main fort at Torres Vedras was complete and a week later, some of the militia were moved to Sobral.

Wellington's Letters of 12 January 1810

Crossing in the post with Fletcher's letter of 11 January 1810, were two from Wellington replying to Fletcher's letters of 25 and 31 December. In the first letter, Wellington clearly agreed with Fletcher's concern for the western end of the defences:

> The left of the line between the Tagus and the sea is certainly the most important to *us* [emphasis in original], the English, and I have always been apprehensive that we should experience great difficulty in defending it. Upon the whole line, I consider the defence of the two ravines in front of Ericeira and of that between Ericeira and Corvoiera [sic Carvoeira] to be the most important of any.[32]

Wellington did not want to be cut off from the coast and the Royal Navy. He explained that his intention was to have a moveable force based at Sobral that could react to any threat to the west but was also available for any threat to the east. Wellington continued:

---

29 Fletcher's report suggests faster progress than recorded in Sousa Lobo's, *A Defesa*, p.200, which records only São Vicente (Forts 20, 21 & 22) were complete by January 1810.

30 Jones, *Sieges*, Vol.3, p.120.

31 Thompson, *Mulcaster*, pp.78, 81.

32 Wellington, *Supplementary Despatches*, Vol.6, p.474.

> I wish you therefore, to construct all the works which you have proposed for the
> defence of these positions [Mafra and Montachique], beginning with those on the
> left for the ravines of Ericeira and Corvoiera, and taking them up afterwards in
> the order of their relative importance in your own opinion.

It would be another month before the work started on the left, the work at Mafra and Montachique starting at the same time. Wellington was showing an unusual amount of trust in a subordinate in letting Fletcher choose the order of construction.

Wellington's second letter was in response to Fletcher's report on Castanheira.[33] Wellington ordered Fletcher to scarp the bank of the river to remove any cover for the attackers. He also ordered construction of the dam with a sluice and asked Fletcher to 'make all your preparatory arrangements and to execute that work as soon as you may think proper.' Further, he ordered construction work to begin on the redoubt at the junction of the rivers and the 'concealed' redoubts on the hill. Wellington deferred other decisions about additional defences on the plain until he 'had another opportunity of looking at the ground.' From his letters, Fletcher, was not sure about the position at Castanheira and neither was Wellington.

As Fletcher had confirmed, work at Torres Vedras was nearing completion. Mulcaster wrote on 18 January 1810, from Ponte do Rol, that he was 'beginning new works between St Pedro [São Pedro da Cadeira] and the sea.' Fletcher's and Wellington's concern about being outflanked using the coastal routes is again seen in this decision. Whilst many miles north of Ericeira, these defences were covering the road that led to that town and would provide additional blocking of this route. Mulcaster's responsibilities had grown from Torres Vedras to the whole area to the sea. Like many of his fellow engineers, he was not very happy about being kept working on the defences, especially when there was an expectation that the army may be engaged. It was still assumed that a French invasion would occur early in 1810. Writing to his engineer friend Burgoyne, he moaned:

> I am still doomed to a three week further residence in this vile place [Torres
> Vedras]. But who can see or suspect rocky ground under firm clay … I fear that
> after this concern is finished, I shall come in for some of the redoubts which are
> to be scattered like hail over the country … [The] Portuguese Militia here, are on
> finishing, to go to Sobral where for want of men they [are] very little advanced.[34]

Mulcaster was right; many more redoubts were to follow. On 8 February 1810, he noted starting a new redoubt, possibly Fort 26, Forte da Ordasqueira. This was one of the positions that Fletcher had recommended to cover the road from Torres Vedras to Runa.

---

33   Wellington, *Supplementary Despatches*, Vol.6, p.473.
34   REM: 4601-74, Mulcaster to Burgoyne, 24 January 1810.

Wellington's Visit

On 4 February 1810, Wellington arrived back in the Lisbon area. He left Viseu on 1 February, reaching Óbidos on 4 February and Torres Vedras the next day.[35] Mulcaster wrote in his diary on 5 February 1810, that: 'The Colonel [Fletcher] set out very early for Peniche to meet his Lordship who arrived [at Torres Vedras] late in the evening.' Mulcaster then stated that 'Wellington rode round the works [at Torres Vedras] and afterwards set off for Mafra.'[36] Wellington wrote despatches from Mafra on 7 February, Lisbon on the 9th and Vila Franca [de Xira] on the 10th before heading north again via Santarém and Tomar. Rice Jones' diary said Wellington and Fletcher visited São Julião on 9 February 1810, which makes sense. Wellington would have wanted to see the defences at the embarkation point.[37]

Wellington, continuing his pattern of providing limited information to the government (and the British newspapers), described the purpose of his journey in a single sentence: 'I have come to this part of the country to view the progress of the works which I had ordered to be constructed when here in October.'[38]

There does not appear to be any written update to the original plan, but there was a decision to scrap the defences at Castanheira and move them further south to the next defensive position at Alhandra. The original memorandum of 20 October 1809 had ordered defences at both Alhandra and Alverca, slightly further to the south, so this decision was concentrating the defences. Moving back to Alhandra exposed the routes inland from Carregado to Torres Vedras via Arruda, Sobral and Runa, but the risks of this movement by the enemy had already been considered in the original memorandum and the subsequent reports by Fletcher.

Neves Costa described Castanheira as follows:

> The first position that may serve to defend this road is formed by the small heights that lie north of Castanheira, where the Carregado or Couraça bridge can be broken, to which come the roads to the Capital on the North of the Tagus from most of the kingdom. From these heights a part of the valley of Cadafais is protected, where the road to Carregado from Arruda and Sobral de Monte Agraço goes and also protects the plain that lies between Castanheira and the Tagus.
>
> This position, however, has more importance ... that it desires us to defend the right side of the Arruda Valley, which can be linked to the defence of other positions inland and along the Tagus ... these heights are not difficult to reach and require the help of art for their defence, and because between them and the Tagus [there is] an extensive plain where the enemy will seek to penetrate to outflank us. To avoid this, Ribeiro de Cuarteira [Rio Grande Pipa] forms a natural channel there, flooded by the flood tides and covered with mud on the ebb, which makes it impassable. Our cavalry and artillery, backed by the boats positioned in

---

35   Dates taken from the location of Wellington's dispatches.
36   Thompson, *Mulcaster*, p.81.
37   Shore, *Engineer Officer*, p.51.
38   Gurwood, *Dispatches*, Wellington to Liverpool, Lisbon 9 February 1810.

the Tagus and by some of the redoubts built on this plain, could advantageously serve to reinforce this position.[39]

Neves Costa identified that the main advantage of the Castanheira position was the river barrier and its ability to block the valleys to the west which could be used to outflank the main route down the riverbank. He identified four other defensive positions on the river at Póvoa de Santa Iria, Vila Franca de Xira, Alhandra and Alverca do Ribatejo, stating that the Vila Franca position was the most important. Burgoyne commented on the decision to abandon Castanheira:

> … at length, his Lordship was persuaded by Colonel Fletcher, to give it up for the following reasons: It was above two miles in extent, the right half of which was on the plain between the Lisbon road and the Tagus behind a small river which it was intended to dam and place works on, flanking each other; a chain of heights began on the left of the road extending westward, their summits were to have been crowned with redoubts, the left was on a steep ravine; the objections, were first, the difficulty of the damming concern, muddy bottom, heavy winter torrents etc; next, the enemy had good cover within 600 yards of the front and could play with your [sic] left from very high ground covering their operation of turning it; the small river also turned in among the heights on the left, separating the position and rendering the communication difficult; the heights were apparently, all rock, a very serious objection to making works.[40]

Fletcher and, eventually, Wellington, felt that the risks of not making the plain fully defensible outweighed the benefits of blocking the valleys to the west. The alternative position had also been identified by Neves Costa. The main benefit of Alhandra was that the riverbank was much narrower than at Castanheira, about 500 metres rather than 2–3 kilometres. Alhandra also had heights rising quickly to the west meaning the route along the riverbank was within short cannon range from the defensive positions on these hills.

The first mention of this change comes in Mulcaster's diary on 13 February 1810. He noted 'Castanheira given up and Mafra and Ericeira to be begun with those workmen.'[41] He expanded the following day in a letter:

> Chapman tells me he [Wellington] appeared extremely satisfied and pleased at the forward state in which he found everything and most perfectly satisfied everywhere. He has given up Castanheira, the works are filled in and Ross and Stanway begin immediately at Mafra and I believe [Rice] Jones at Ericeira on the coast [to the] left of Mafra. I have another eight weeks job in a new redoubt as I believe I before told you I give up every hope of ever seeing the army till it falls back this far, as I believe Arruda, Alhandra and Monte Chique [sic] are still in store.

---

39   Neves Costa, *Memoria Militar*, p.22, author's translation.
40   REM: 4201-68, Burgoyne papers, Notebook, pp.45–46.
41   Thompson, *Mulcaster*, p.82.

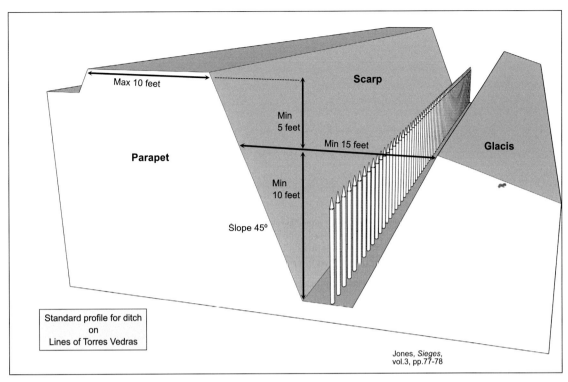

Standard dimensions of ditch on Lines of Torres Vedras.

He continued:

> We have desperately bad weather this week. My slopes suffer a little but not more than must be always expected in hasty field works … All agree that this post is taken up in a masterly style; of the execution [I] must say nothing and if these storms continue the less I say the better till the damages are repaired.

The weather at the start of February had been particularly bad. Between 1 and 14 February, Mulcaster had noted rain on nine days with work being completely stopped on one day. The redoubts were earthworks and repair after wet weather would be a constant drain on the limited resources. The issue of secrecy was again raised in this letter. We can assume that the officers were being ordered to be discrete. 'You will [perceive?] that there are many secrets of state in this letter, but I submit everything to your well known discretion.'[42]

The decision to abandon Castanheira allowed work to start on the next priorities. The first was at Ericeira, which was the area that most concerned Fletcher and Wellington. The second was around Mafra using Fletcher's recommendations contained in his letter of 25 December 1809. Based on the authority which Wellington had granted Fletcher to decide on priorities, the two westernmost areas were selected. Fletcher probably surmised that the bulk of the defending army would stay near the Tagus, so the western

---

42   REM: 4601-74, Mulcaster to Burgoyne, Torres Vedras, 14 February 1810.

extremity was the area most in need of defences as it might take time for supporting troops to arrive. Also, no survey work had yet been carried out at Alhandra, this would need to be completed before recommendations could be made on the defences there. What is really interesting is the latitude that Fletcher was being given to make decisions. This level of authority was not something that Wellington usually gave to his subordinates.

Fletcher's Report of 24 February 1810[43]

Fletcher now investigated, in detail, the ground between Mafra and Montachique. He had described the area in his letter of 25 December 1809 but made no specific recommendations. His view was that 'I do not find it will be possible to command the several roads falling in from the northwards … with less than 13 redoubts, which would require 3,000 men.' He continued that due to the rocky nature of the ground, troops to support the redoubts would be 'absolutely necessary.' The recommendation from Fletcher appears to closely match what was constructed, with redoubts 62–73 covering this area. Another recommendation was made to 'throw up three redoubts to command the three principal roads leading across the ravine in the rear of Encarnação by Ribamor [Ribamar], Marvão and Pecaneira [Picanceira]. Six redoubts were eventually built in this area, 89–94. Fletcher noted that he had sent a request to *Marechal* Beresford to provide the necessary guns and ammunition for the proposed redoubts. Fletcher also noted that he would order work to be started on a military road across the Serra de Serves, connecting to the road at Vialonga.

From all the reports of Fletcher and his officers, one thing was clear, decisions on the defensive positions were being made by visiting the ground in each location. The officers may have had access to Neves Costa's report, but they were not relying on it.

Fletcher's letter also gave an update on the number of defenders required to occupy the three main forts at São Julião, Sobral and Torres Vedras 'at the rate of two men to a yard, as decided by your Lordship'. The numbers were 3,300 at São Julião, 2,500 at Sobral and 3,800 at Torres Vedras including 600 to occupy strong buildings in the town. He noted that 37 guns had arrived at Alhandra (presumably shipped up the Tagus from Lisbon) and they would be split between Torres Vedras and Sobral.

Fletcher reported that the works on the Serra do Chipre (Forts 78–81); at Murgeira (Forts 82–87) and below Ericeira (Forts 95–97) had all commenced. These were under the control of Captain George Ross RE, who would remain here for some time. By April 1810, he had 'commenced twenty-three redoubts.'[44]

---

43 Wellington, *Supplementary Despatches*, Vol.6, pp.487–488. The letters from Wellington to Fletcher, 18 February 1810 and Fletcher to Wellington, 19 February are not in the Wellington papers. Thanks to Zack White for checking.
44 REM: 4501-86, Ross to Dalrymple, 25 April 1810.

In Fletcher's letter, there was the first mention of using civilians for the construction work, with Fletcher saying he was employing 'peasantry at six vingtems [sic] per day.'[45] Mulcaster also mentioned requesting *ordenanças* to work at Ponte do Rol and Ericeira.[46] There was still a major concern that the French would arrive before the defences were ready, Fletcher commenting 'should the contest come to extremities very soon, I am conscious the system proposed will not be easily completed.' The lack of workmen was not helping the situation.

Surprisingly, work at Montachique did not start until March. This had been approved in Wellington's letter of 12 January 1810. Rice Jones had stated that the construction work under Mulcaster started on 19 February 1810.[47] Mulcaster's diary makes no mention of Montachique until 25 March 1810 and noted that the 8th Militia Company marched for Montachique on 26 March. He did not make his first visit until 27 March 1810, marking out the first redoubts on 28 March 1810.[48] This is five weeks later than Rice Jones recorded.

Mulcaster's area of responsibility had grown again. He still retained responsibility for work around Torres Vedras; he was also overseeing the work at Ponte do Rol being carried out by Lieutenant Alexander Thomson RE; he had recently started the redoubts at Enxara dos Cavaleiros, and was now being asked to start nine redoubts around Montachique. He was still responsible for the payment of the workers and the number was steadily growing. It was not until 16 April that clerks were found to organise paying the workmen. On top of this construction work, he was also having to repair the damage caused by the winter storms. He noted on 2 March, that the escarp of the new work at Torres Vedras was tumbling in. After more heavy rain, he complained:

Same agreeable showers with the additional charms of hail and lightning, a dash of the latter falling near the hide [magazine] in the new work infusing a sulphurous smell, set them [the workmen] to the route calling on all the Saints of Paradise. During a fine interval in the afternoon, the gents not working, rode to see the destruction of the left salient and … the sloped dry wall has been unable to resist the fury of the storm found it in a most perfect breach, the stones in falling, having broken the palisading.

Two days later: 'Rainy morning, wind violent. Found on going up, innumerable breaches in all directions not excepting the unfortunate Castle wall. All the valley a complete sheet of water. Did not work.[49]

Five days later the damage was still being repaired. The weather continued to be very wet for most of the month and into April. On 26 March, he wrote: 'Rode afterwards to Torres [Vedras] where I found the damage not much

---

45   Six vintens was about 8 pence; this was later increased to 10 vintens. Daily pay for a British soldier was one shilling (12 pence), but roughly ¾ was taken in deductions for food and equipment. Bob Burnham & Ron McGuigan, *British Army Against Napoleon, Facts, Lists, and Trivia* (Barnsley: Frontline, 2010), p.197.

46   Thompson, *Mulcaster*, p.87. Fletcher may have meant *ordenanças* rather than civilians.

47   Jones, *Sieges*, Vol.3, p.18.

48   Thompson, *Mulcaster*, p.89.

49   Thompson, *Mulcaster*, p.86.

short of the great storm. From thence to Ponte do Rol; Thomson getting on famously, also a little annoyed by the heavy rain.'[50]

The work at Ponte do Rol (Forts 30–32) had started around 27 February, with Thomson and the '1st Militia Company' marching there that morning. As well as the bad weather, Thomson was delayed by natural springs which damaged the earthworks.[51] Mulcaster recorded that work started on 27 February. Jones stated that the work did not start until 26 March 1810, which, like the date for the start at Montachique, is wrong.[52] The weather was affecting the whole area and Ross, stationed at Mafra, commented that breaches in the defences were more likely to be made by the weather than the French![53]

Work at Ericeira and Carvoeira had commenced immediately after Wellington's visit. Rice Jones' journal recorded him visiting Ericeira with Fletcher to select accommodation on 15 February 1810 and moving there three days later. He reconnoitred the roads in the area before starting work on the redoubts on 19 February, 'picked out the redoubts [95–97] near the three mills above Carvoeira in readiness for the two companies of the Militia of Figueira [da Foz] to begin tomorrow.' On 28 February, Captain Chapman visited and places were selected for destroying the road from Picanceira to Mafra and also on the road to Marvão, 'the principal roads are to be prepared by means of mines; all the others are to be broken up immediately.'[54] Rice Jones noted that local peasant labour was being used for the redoubts and volunteer miners from the British line regiments at Lisbon for breaking up the roads. In mid-March, additional workmen were obtained from the local *ordenanças*. On 24 March 1810, a Portuguese engineer officer, *Major* Francisco António Raposo arrived 'to take over part of the works', although Rice Jones does not explain which works.

There were at least eight Portuguese engineer officers identified as working for Fletcher on the Lines. Portuguese returns show the same officers present in February, March and April 1810, although most did not start until the end of February. This coincides with the increase in the construction work on the Lines. The eight officers were:

Segundo Tenente Henrique Luiz Aschoff
Capitão Francisco Villela Barboza
Capitão Luiz Máximo Jorge de Bellegarde
Major Manoel Joaquim Brandão [de Souza]
Capitão Joaquim Norberto Xavier de Brito
Major Lourenço Homem da Cunha d'Eça
Major Bernardo José Pereira dos Santos Franco
Major Francisco António Raposo[55]

---

50   Thompson, *Mulcaster*, p.89.
51   Thompson, *Mulcaster*, p.92.
52   Jones, *Sieges*, Vol.3, p.18.
53   REM: 4501-86, Ross to Dalrymple, 25 April 1810.
54   Shore, *Engineer Officer*, pp.51–52.
55   AHM: PT-AHM-DIV-1-14-096-070-M0020.

Another Portuguese engineer officer, *Major* José Francisco António Dias was also recorded as employed at Abrantes, working with the Royal Engineer, Captain Peter Patton. Other officers from the Portuguese engineers would work on the Lines at later dates. The number was much greater than that documented in English language sources.

On 26 April 1810, Rice Jones was ordered to hand over his work to fellow Royal Engineer Captain John Thomas Jones, who had just arrived in Portugal. Clearly the construction work was still underway. The formal handover was on 7 May 1810 and John Jones worked here until he was given the overall command of the construction on the Lines at the beginning of July 1810. Mulcaster commented on 19 June 1810, that John Jones and Lieutenant John Hulme RE were laying out four more redoubts.[56]

The first guns arrived at Torres Vedras on 11 March 1810; two 12-pounders, with one 12-pounder and five 6-pounders the next day. More arrived in the following days.

On 14 March, Mulcaster recorded his first visit to Enxara dos Cavaleiros to mark out the two redoubts that Fletcher had recommended (Forts 28 and 29). On 19 March, he moved his quarters there and started 'on the eastern redoubt' (Fort 29) the next day. He had requested 120 *ordenança* workmen.[57] On 18 March 1810, Mulcaster recorded in his diary 'Bonaparte has announced his intention to the senate of again visiting the Peninsula and is even said to have arrived at Vitoria,' a timely reminder to all that time to complete the defences could be limited. These two forts were the only ones in the centre of the defences, and well back from what would become the first line. As well as the main Torres Vedras road they would also cover the roads from Dois Portos and Sobral.

Mulcaster started the work at Montachique on 28 March 1810. His first impression was that the ground was very rocky, which would make building the forts much more difficult. On 31 March, he 'marked out four or five redoubts.' A Portuguese engineer officer arrived on this day to assist, *Segundo Tenente* Henrique Luiz Aschoff, a 25-year-old, who had been commissioned in 1809.[58] On 1 April 1810, the first two redoubts were traced out. The working relationship with Aschoff did not start well. On 2 April, Mulcaster noted 'Mr Aschoff begins his operations by sending the wrong letters to the different *Sargento Mores* [for workmen]. The next day he found 'Mr Aschoff digging up the parapets instead of the ditches of the lower work.'[59] A second engineer officer, Lieutenant Samuel Trench RE joined having just arrived in the country on 28 March 1810. Three more redoubts were traced out on 3 April and the 'remaining five' on 6 April 1810 (nine in total).

On 9 April 1810, Fletcher and Mulcaster marked out the redoubts at Freixial (Forts 49–51) between Montachique and Bucelas. Mulcaster

---

56 Thompson, *Mulcaster*, p.106. It was probably only three; 88, 90 and 91. The other four (89, 92, 93 and 94) were finished.

57 Thompson, *Mulcaster*, pp.87–89.

58 Sousa Lobo, *Defesa*, p.327, says Aschoff spoke English and he was working on the city defences and at São Julião, not on the Lines of Torres Vedras.

59 Thompson, *Mulcaster*, p.91.

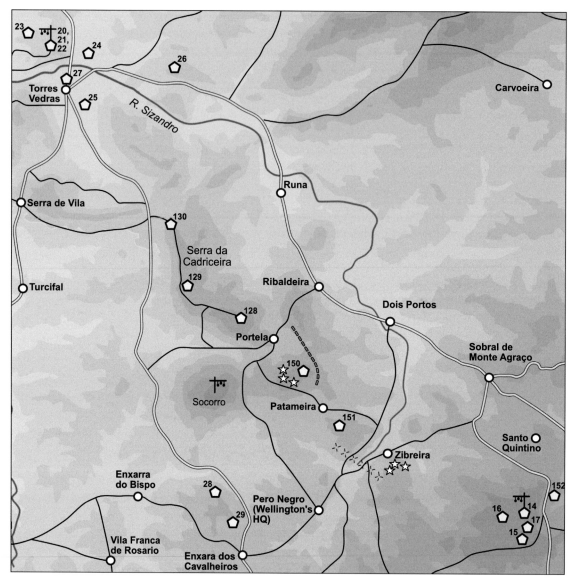

Forts 28 & 29.

continued to be involved in most forts that were under construction at this time. On 13 and 19 April, he reported visiting Venda do Pinheiro with Ross (between Malveira and Montachique). The construction must have been well advanced as he noted that nine guns had arrived.[60] Ross was responsible for the construction of these works. In April 1810, Ross moaned to Sir Hew Dalrymple that he now had his 'hands full having commenced twenty-three redoubts, from Serra de Xipro [Chipre] at the left of the pass of Mafra to Cabeça de Montachique'. A month later, that number had increased to 27.[61]

---

60   Thompson, *Mulcaster*, p.92.
61   REM: 4501-86, Ross to Dalrymple, 25 April 1810 & 25 May 1810.

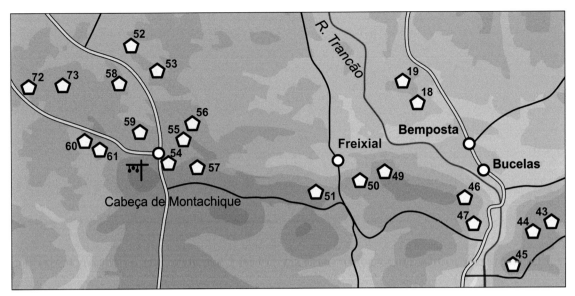

Bucelas, Freixial and
Montachique.

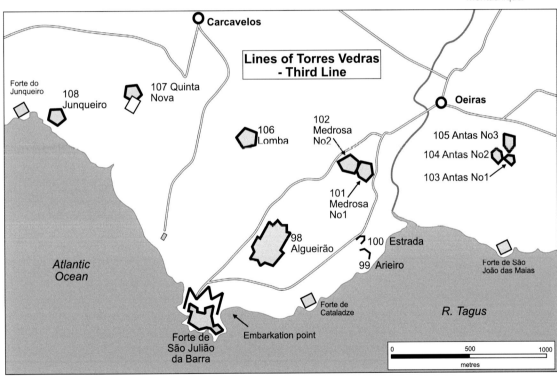

Early defences at São Julião.

Additional defences were also started at São Julião. Captain John Squire RE, who had arrived on 28 March 1810 was given responsibility for completing Forts 99–108. Squire complained that the works 'are in a forward state [and] my services might easily be spared … it is not very agreeable to direct the completion of works which have been begun by others.' His view of the progress was not accurate and was because he wanted to follow his own bizarre idea of being sent to survey Cartagena with the view of making it a second Cadiz.[62] He commented in the same letter that the 'working party consists of a regiment of Portuguese militia, half naked it is true, but a fine able bodied, willing, good humoured set of fellows.' Burgoyne commented in a letter dated 26 March 1810, that 'fort St Julian's is also improving under Wedekind's hands and works erecting on a small height in front of it.'[63] Six weeks later, Squire commented:

> Two officers with myself are employed in constructing works to cover the place of embarkation in the event of our being compelled to evacuate the country. Such a measure, I mean the securing our retreat is both prudent and necessary, and I believe that a more favourable spot could not have been selected, (bad as it is) than the little bay to the eastward of Fort St Julian. I think that long since, far greater execution should have been made for the defence of this position.[64]

So, clearly the works at São Julião were not in a 'forward state'. He was now saying the defences there were not sufficient. There was no more mention of an expedition to Cartagena. He also mentioned in the same letter that nearly 70 redoubts had been constructed.

Through May, Mulcaster's focus was on completing the works around Montachique but he was still frequently riding to Mafra, Torres Vedras, Ponte do Rol and Ericeira to check on progress. On 16 May, he was at São Pedro da Cadeira 'seeing the situation for the dams, without many of which they will never make much of the river.'[65]

It is not clear when work at Alhandra started. Mulcaster rode through Alhandra on 22 April, reporting 'means are taking to secure it by redoubts and an entrenchment.'[66] Initially, the work was just to prepare a ditch from the Tagus to the hills to the west. Wellington originally planned to place the bulk of his army in this area. Later these defences were significantly expanded.

As rumours about movement of the French near the border increased, the issue of workmen became a concern again. The problem appeared to be widespread rather than associated with a particular area. Fletcher wrote to Forjaz on 3 April 1810:

> I have the honour to acquaint your Excellency, that I have this morning received a letter from the military governor of this place, mentioning that the ecclesiastics of Ericeira, have refused to furnish their proportion of aid towards the works now carrying on in that neighbourhood. The ecclesiastics of the convent of this place [Mafra] have also acted in the same manner and have openly complained of their being required to contribute to the fortifications … All the officers of Justice of this district are also reported to have declined giving their share of assistance …

---

62   BL: ADD63106, Squire to Bunbury, 7 April 1810.
63   BL: ADD41962, ff.197-202, Pasley papers.
64   BL: ADD63106, Squire to Bunbury, 27 May 1810.
65   Thompson, *Mulcaster*, p.98.
66   Thompson, *Mulcaster*, p.94.

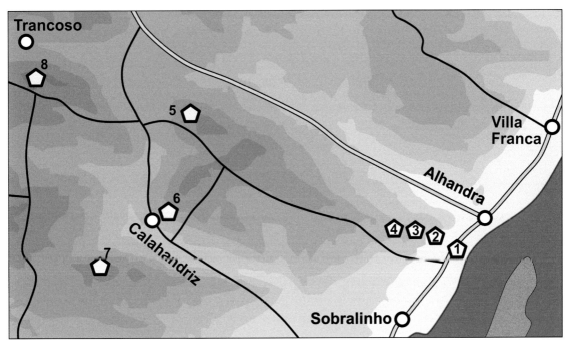

Initial defences at Alhandra.

It falls very heavily on the poor, that those who are wealthy should be allowed to refuse their aid … in which they are more immediately interested.[67]

Mulcaster also complained loudly about the 'shameful deficiency' when he found only 250 workmen at Montachique on 24 April 1810.[68] Even much later, when the arrival of the French was imminent, there were still serious problems with obtaining manpower. John Jones wrote two letters to Forjaz on 5 and 10 September 1810, reporting that his complaints about the lack of workmen at Alhandra were being ignored by the local officials.[69] Similar issues with manpower on the city defences have been discussed above.

There is very limited correspondence between Fletcher, Wellington and the engineer officers through April, May and June 1810. Wellington had issued his orders and there was little for him to add. Fletcher was riding round the various sites, so orders were being given verbally. We have to track progress by snippets from other correspondence.

67   AHM: PT-AHM-DIV-1-14-020-06, images M0006-7.
68   Thompson, *Mulcaster*, p.95.
69   AHM: PT-AHM-DIV-1-14-020-03, images M0003-0010.

Table of when work commenced, up to the end of June 1810

Area	Month started
São Julião (São Julião & Fort 98)	Nov 1809
Torres Vedras (Forts 20-27)	Nov 1809
Sobral (Forts 14-17)	Nov 1809
Castanheira	Jan 1810
St Pedro da Cadeira phase 1 (Forts 30-32)	Jan 1810
Mafra	Feb 1810
Serra de Chipre	Feb 1810
Murgeira	Feb 1810
Ponte do Rol	Feb 1810
Ericeira & Carvoeira	Feb 1810
Vialonga	Feb 1810
Ribamar, Marvao, Picanceira (Forts 88-94)	Feb 1810
Bucelas	Feb 1810
Arruda	March 1810
Enxara dos Cavaleiros (Forts 28-29)	March 1810
Montachique	March 1810
São Julião phase 2 (Forts 99-108)	April 1810
Freixial (Forts 49-51)	April 1810
Mafra to Montachique	April 1810

When Edmund Mulcaster visited the Ribamar area on 16 June, he noted that four redoubts were complete.[70] These were 89, 92, 93 and 94. By the end of the month, Fletcher reported that the remaining three, 88, 90 and 91, had also been completed, although this does not appear to be accurate.[71] As late as 1 August 1810, the reports stated that they would be 'finished shortly', although the guns had been installed in mid-July.[72]

On 8 June 1810, Fletcher wrote to Wellington with an update of the works completed to date. Following a discussion, an updated report was issued on 25 June 1810. Fletcher was preparing to hand over responsibility to one of his subordinates whilst he joined Wellington and the army on the Portuguese frontier. The report as printed in the *Supplementary Despatches* was in three parts, the first detailing the 108 forts that had been completed, followed by a 'General Abstract' of these 108 works. This was followed by further tables showing an additional 16 works (as summarised in the addendum table below). This is wrong as the defences included in this addendum were not started until July 1810 or later. The three reports have been incorrectly placed together.

---

70 Thompson, *Mulcaster*, p.105.
71 These are shown as a late addition in Fletcher's report of 28 June, Wellington, *Supplementary Despatches*, Vol.6, p.544.
72 REM: 5501-59-18, Jones to Fletcher, Lisbon, 18 July 1810; Jones to Fletcher, Lisbon, 1 August 1810.

Fletchers Report to Wellington, 25 June 1810, Summary[73]

(Fort numbers in brackets)	Works	Troops	Number and Nature of guns				
			How	24pdr	12pdr	9pdr	6pdr
First Line							
From Alhandra to Calhandriz valley (1-6)	6				13		7
To shut the road through Calhandriz valley (7-8)	2	400			6		
From Calhandriz to rear of Sobral (9-13)	5	1,220			8	7	
Heights of Sobral de Monte Agraço (14-17)	4	2,600	3		18	11	9
Serra de Ajuda (18-19)	2	500			4	3	
Torres Vedras (20-27)	8	3,800	3		15	18	6
Enxara dos Cavaleiros (28-29)	2	550			3	4	
From Ponte do Rol to São Pedro da Cadeira (30-32)	3	970			6	5	
Total First Line	**32**	**10,040**	**6**		**73**	**48**	**31**
Second Line							
From Tagus to Caza de Portella [Casa da Portela] (33-42)	10	2,460			29	18	
Pass of Bucelas (43-47)	5				10	4	
Redoubt to cover retreat from Bucelas (48)		200			2		
Pass of Freixial (49-51)	3	460			6	2	
Pass of Montachique (52-57)	10	2,160			12	12	
Covering road from Mafra to Montachique (62-73)	12	3,070			25	16	
Pass of Mafra (74-87)	14	3,650			30	13	
Between Mafra and Sea – north (88-94)	7	1,770			20		
Between Mafra and sea – south (95-97)	3	880			7		
Total Second Line	**65**	**14,600**			**141**	**65**	
Position of Fort St Julian's (98-108)	**11**	**3,850**		**20**	**48**	**9**	**6**
General Total	**108**	**28,490**	**6**	**20**	**262**	**122**	**37**

Fletcher added an addendum to the table above, showing the latest works but this was later than June, probably October 1810.

73 Wellington, *Supplementary Despatches*, Vol.6, pp.545–546. Note: The inference was that all these forts were completed, the forts in the addendum being describing as 'works lately completed'.

[Addendum to Report; author's summary – Date not known]

Description	Works	Troops	Number and Nature of guns				
			How	24pdr	12pdr	9pdr	6pdr
First Line							
Redoubts lately constructed around Alhandra (114-120)	7	1,330			16	9	
Redoubts lately constructed on heights of Calhandriz (121-124)	4	1,200			9	4	
Redoubts lately constructed between São Pedro da Cadeira and the Sea (111-113) Ordered 18 July	3	520			11[74]		
Position at St Julian's (109-110) 109 started 18 July 1810	2	330			12		
Total for Addendum	16	3,380			48	13	
Total for Table plus Addendum	124	31,870	6	20	310	135	37

There are some slight differences between these tables and those shown in Jones' *Sieges*.[75] Apart from the obvious, that Jones' tables show the final count of forts, there are some minor differences in the armament in the forts. It may be that the number of guns in the forts were altered after Fletcher's report of 25 June 1810.

The map below shows the 97 works on the first and second Lines that were completed by June 1810. Forts 98–108 were on the third Line at São Julião. The defences along the Tagus and the Atlantic coast were still weak. Wellington expected a French advance down the right bank of the Tagus and intended to place the bulk of his troops there. He believed that if an attack was made to the west, he would have enough warning to move troops to block it.

Work was continuing, even on the 'finished' forts. Mulcaster noted on 23 June, that he laid out the last of the traverses at Torres Vedras and the following morning 'roused the men up early to finish the glacis.'[76] Five weeks later, Jones commented that the works at Sobral 'cannot be considered as finished.'[77]

In Fletcher's letter of 24 June 1810, he stated that he intended to set off to join Wellington on the Portuguese border in the next few days, taking with him most of the senior and experienced engineer officers who had been working on the Lines.[78] Overall control would be given to Captain John Jones who had only been in the country since April 1810.

There was still a lot of work to do.

---

74   Calibre of guns not specified.
75   Jones, *Sieges*, Vol.3, pp.94–100.
76   Thompson, *Mulcaster*, p.107.
77   REM: 5501-59-18, Jones to Fletcher, 1 August 1810.
78   Captains Chapman, Goldfinch, Mulcaster, Ross and Squire; Lieutenants Rice Jones and Thomson.

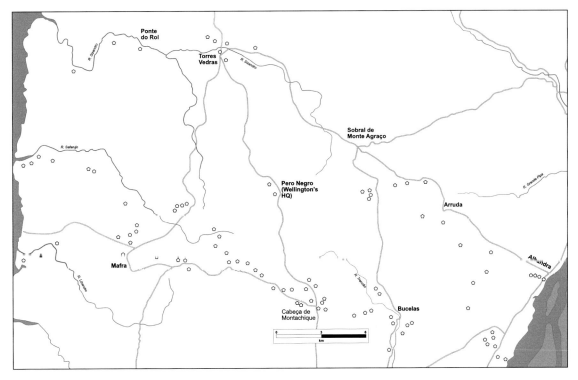

Forts completed by June 1810.

Arming the Lines

John Jones' book on the Lines said the guns used 'were all Portuguese iron ordnance, on carriages of a most primitive construction, with such low trucks as to be perfectly immoveable over broken ground and consequently not to be immediately rendered useful to an enemy.'[79]

The carriage construction was very important as Wellington did not want the French to capture possibly hundreds of guns which could be used to attack the second and third Lines. Jones also said all the guns were provided from the Portuguese Arsenal in Lisbon under *Tenente General* José António da Rosa and mounted by Portuguese gunners 'and the local carts succeeded in transporting 12-pounders into situations where wheels had never gone before.'[80] This was not all correct; the guns were not exclusively Portuguese. As early as February 1810, Wellington had written to Beresford:

> Have you given the orders for the artillery to be collected for the occupation of our works in the hills? I have written to Fletcher to desire him to see that Rosa and Fisher [Royal Artillery commander] settle definitely which posts shall be filled with our ordnance, and what by yours [Portuguese]; and to have the guns sent to the posts forthwith. I believe that we ought to take St Julian for ours [i.e. British guns], as they are upon travelling carriages, which it might be very inconvenient to lose.[81]

79   Jones, *Sieges*, Vol.3, p.17.
80   Jones, *Sieges*, Vol.3, p.85.
81   Gurwood, *Dispatches*, Wellington to Beresford, 23 February 1810.

It would appear that Wellington was suggesting using British 24-pounders on the third line. These guns were in Lisbon to make up a siege train and he was not willing to risk these guns in more exposed locations. Two weeks later, Wellington wrote to Berkeley:

> Having found, upon referring to the returns of the ordnance and the ordnance carriages in possession of the Portuguese government, that there are not a sufficient number of guns, with carriages, to arm the different works in front of Lisbon, which are now constructing and which it is intended to construct, to the northward of Lisbon, even with the addition of the heavy ordnance on travelling carriages embarked in the store ships in the Tagus. I shall be much obliged to you if you will place at my disposition the ordnance, the carriages and the stores belonging to the Russian ships of war [blockaded by the Royal Navy] in the Tagus. If you should consent to adopt this proposition, I shall request you further to make them over to Col. Fisher, the Commanding Officer of the British Artillery at Lisbon.[82]

This would potentially have made available about fifty 24-pounders, two-hundred 18-pounders and fifty 12-pounders. The problem with mixing guns of different nationalities was they had slightly different bores leading to issues with power, accuracy, and possible blockages.

Burgoyne also commented in March 1810 that the 'heavy [siege] train, [a] great part of which has been already landed and some mounted on these new works.'[83] In June 1810, Fletcher informed Wellington that Berkeley had reported that 24- or 18-pounder cannon would be delivered to St Julian's in the next few days. He also noted that the 12-pounders would take another three weeks for completion of carriages. He added that 'Lieutenant Colonel Fisher would relieve the heavy guns first.' It is likely that the British 24-pounders were installed at São Julião and then replaced when the Russian heavy guns became available.[84] Later, after the Lines were occupied, Wellington ordered any British or Portuguese 12-pounders to be handed over to Berkeley. These were probably to be used in the forts that Berkeley's seamen were occupying on the Tagus.[85]

The most extreme option came when Liverpool wrote on 2 October 1810 saying that, if necessary, Wellington had permission to remove all the lower deck guns from Berkeley's fleet in the Tagus, complete with the sailors and marines to man them. 'Such an arrangement may provide you … with a battery of 100 or 150, 32-pounders.'[86] One has to assume that this would have been discussed with the Admiralty before the offer was made, but possibly not with Berkeley. Using these larger guns would only have fitted with Wellington's plan by keeping these big guns for the embarkation point; they

---

82 Gurwood, *Dispatches*, Wellington to Berkeley, 6 March 1810. The sailors had returned to Russia but the Royal Navy would not allow the ships to leave.

83 BL: ADD 41962, Pasley Papers, ff.197-200, Burgoyne to Pasley, 26 March 1810.

84 Wellington, *Supplementary Despatches*, Vol.6, p.537.

85 Gurwood, *Dispatches*, 1st Edition, Wellington to Berkeley, 16 October 1810.

86 Wellington, *Supplementary Despatches*, Vol.6, p.604.

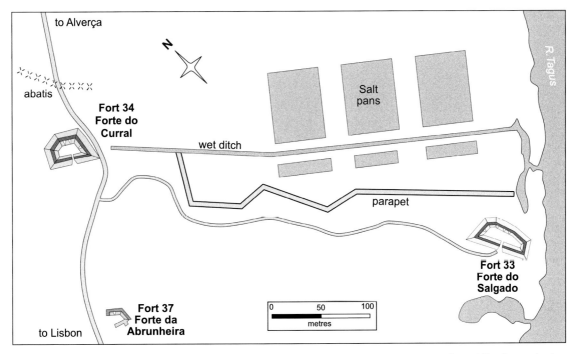

Second Line: forts on banks of Tagus.

could not have been used elsewhere. The smaller 9 or 18-pounders would probably have been of more interest. There is no evidence that this option was ever seriously considered.

What the Engineers and Others Thought of the Lines at this Time

One of the most surprising aspects of the construction of the Lines, is the lack of confidence shown by Allied officers about their usefulness. Lieutenant Colonel Alexander Gordon, one of Wellington's senior ADC's, having just ridden round the works with Wellington in February 1810, commented:

> Having seen all these places as well as the works already constructed, I can speak confidently with respect to their strength, but it is quite impossible with our force to hinder the enemy from turning them, the roads are so numerous in every direction that it would require a far greater force than ours to guard them … I am convinced when it comes to the push, we will abandon this country without fighting.[87]

Five months later, in July 1810, Fletcher wrote to Robert Morse, the Inspector General of Fortifications (the most senior Royal Engineer) providing information on the Lines.[88] This letter is unusual in a number of ways. First,

---

87   Rory Muir, *At Wellington's Right Hand* (London: Sutton Publishing, 2003), p.84.
88   TNA: WO55/958, Lisbon, 4 July 1810. The abstract of forts and guns was the same as had been sent to Wellington on 25 June 1810. Wellington, *Supplementary Despatches*, Vol.6, pp.545–546.

it appears that little information had previously been sent home on the works the engineers had been working on for eight months. Secondly, Fletcher expressed concern about how secure the lines would be when attacked: 'The length of the Lines … is so great that but a small proportion can be occupied by troops, and as the ground is in many places practicable for artillery … I do not feel … we are by any means secure.'

Picton, whilst waiting near the Spanish border entertained similar views:

> About 25,000 men are collected … to take advantage of an imprudent movement of the enemy or to continue our retreat towards the positions between the Tagus and Torres Vedras where we calculate to make a successful stand, at least for some time, so as to carry our reputation unimpaired aboard the transports which are in readiness to carry us off.[89]

If senior commanders, the senior engineer, and even Wellington's confidant still had grave reservations about the plan, it is understandable that the government was also concerned.

Other engineer officers were also expressing concern, although there is a question if these concerns were real or just showing the frustration they felt, being stuck in the rear whist the army was daily expected to be resisting the French invasion. The engineer officers believed that a breach at any point would render the whole defensive line (be it the first or the second) indefensible. Burgoyne commented:

> … what can be the real utility of defending a little corner of this country when the enemy come in sufficient force to render the event certain I cannot conceive and that Lord Wellington expects them in such force is pretty plain from his demanding the quantity of tonnage required to carry off the [army] … but this is not the worst, his Lordship has got the idea that the ground on some part of that shore is very favourable for defending [a] long [time] and then embarking in [the] face of the enemy; now I understand that no-one but himself can perceive this and at any rate it is an operation that in however favourable [a] situation a general would willingly avoid if he could.[90]

In another letter a few weeks later, he was even more critical:

> I think it a most barbarous infamous policy … we call on the people to make the greatest efforts to oppose the enemy in concert with us, while all our preparatory measures are to ensure a retreat for ourselves. Who of them will not take the earliest opportunity to negotiate their peace when they perceive, which is public enough, our intention? … If the thing is practicable, we should do it manfully and not give the slightest hint that we will desert the cause; if it is not so, why should we indulge them with false hopes and endeavour to make them commit themselves with their martial forces who only want the excuse to work them to the quick. Poor Portuguese! I should really pity them, but that I feel assured that

---

89   Robert Havard, *Wellington's Welsh General* (London: Aurum, 1993), p.128.
90   BL: ADD 41962, ff.197-200, Burgoyne to Pasley, 26 March 1810.

they will not commit themselves by any very serious acts of hostility and I doubt but if it comes to a hasty retreat we shall have more British shot by the arms we have put in the hands of the Portuguese than Frenchmen.[91]

Engineer officers should have been more qualified to comment, as they knew what was being built whilst most army officers did not. Squire was one of a number who clearly did not fully understanding Wellington's intentions, writing:

> … we find all our strength applied to fortifying a line, which surely neither ought nor can be defended, if the enemy possess a force very superior to ourselves, and they I would imagine will never invade Portugal without an army against which it is impossible even for our combined force to contend in the field … I understand that it is intended to collect the main body of the army on the heights of Alhandra and there to offer battle to the enemy, while the redoubts garrisoned by Portuguese troops shall defend the other parts of the position. This I confess appears to me a most extraordinary arrangement. While we are anxiously expecting the glories of a fight at Alhandra; will not the enemy penetrate by way of Mafra; or between Mafra and the sea, march direct upon St Julian and perhaps cut off two thirds of the army from its shipping? All this appears to me so very obvious that I feel persuaded that this extraordinary line will never be defended; and that our own redoubts and entrenchments with about 300 pieces of artillery will only serve to swell out a French Bulletin, and to expose us to the ridicule of both our friends and enemies.[92]

Another engineer, George Ross wrote home:

> I am still here toiling with the poor Portuguese to make a colony of redoubts. Still far from the scene where expectations dwells … If my unfortunate little redoubts ever come in play, or those of my neighbours, we shall in all probability reach England through France. I am no great judge of these high and weighty subjects: but if they should ever be named as a sin we have to answer for, I hope the military world will be kind enough to consider that we make them but do not invent them. If the twenty-seven redoubts in my neighbourhood were upon wheels and could travel quick as thought, they might by a fortunate application of them prevent a French column penetrating with impunity … But will it be of any use should he prefer manoeuvring to get between you and your ships. Our army cannot be strong on the whole line; where it is weak the redoubts surely will never stop a French column.[93]

Squire was writing privately to Henry Bunbury, Military Undersecretary to the Secretary of State for War and Ross was writing to Sir Hew Dalrymple. It is difficult to believe that these opinions were not being circulated at home at the highest levels. This was the sort of comment that would be reaching the government and making them nervous.

They were not helping Wellington.

---

91   BL: ADD 41962, ff.201-2, Burgoyne to Pasley, 4 April 1810.
92   BL: ADD63106, Squire to Bunbury, 27 May 1810.
93   REM: 4501-86, Ross to Dalrymple, 25 May 1810.

7

Construction of the Lines, July to October 1810

On 6 July 1810, Fletcher wrote to Captain John Jones, formally handing over responsibility for the completion of the defences.[1] From the tone of the letter Fletcher clearly believed that the work was nearing completion:

> As you find the works completed, and as you think the officers can be spared, I request you will employ them in making accurate surveys of the different positions … You will, I imagine, soon find it practicable to part with a proportion of the men of the line now employed in the department, and they will then be sent to Lisbon; but I think some of the men should be kept to destroy bridges and roads at the last moment … I conceive you will shortly have it in your power to dispense with the services of the Figueras and Torres Vedras regiments of militia, and I request you will report when you can do so. I beg you will also let me know when you think the services of the Portuguese Engineers are no longer required.

Fletcher's letter also mentioned the installation of the remaining artillery, the fitting of artillery platforms and the boarding out of the magazines, to make them more water resistant. Whilst a number of the senior engineer officers had joined the army, Jones still had 16 officers 'under his orders', including three Portuguese:[2]

Royal Engineers – Captains Holloway, Williams and Dickenson; Lieutenants Stanway, Thomson, Forster, Trench, Piper, Tapp, Reid and Hulme.
King's German Legion Engineers – Captain Wedekind and Lieutenant Meinecke.
Portuguese Engineers – *Majors* Manoel Joaquim Brandão de Souza, Lourenço Homem da Cunha d'Eça, *Capitão* Joaquim Norberto Xavier de Brito

---

1   Jones, *Sieges*, Vol.3, pp.223–224. Many of the letters between Fletcher and Jones are printed in Jones, *Sieges,* pp.223–253. The originals are held in the Royal Engineers Museum at Chatham and show that the printed versions are not always complete. Where this is important, it will be pointed out.
2   Jones, *Sieges*, Vol.3, pp.19.

Certainly, two and possibly all of the Portuguese engineers were senior to Jones, so the issue of seniority still needed to be managed; they were certainly not 'under his orders'. Another officer, *Major* José Manuel de Carvalho was working at Oeiras in July 1810, although it is not clear when he started. Captain Charles Holloway who was working on the defences at Peniche was senior to Jones, so also, was not under his orders. Captain Sebastian Dickenson was junior but was working away from the Lines at Setúbal to the south of the Tagus.

The number of Portuguese engineers mentioned, appears too low. Whilst there is no definitive list of the Portuguese engineers who worked on the Lines of Torres Vedras, there are several mentioned in letters as well as the details in Bamford's, Sousa Lobo's and Ayres' works.[3] It would make sense for more to be involved.

At the start of August, Jones reported the locations of the engineers:

Captain Holloway	– Peniche
Captain Wedekind	– Sick
Captain Dickinson	– Setúbal
Lieutenant Meineke	– Oeiras
Lieutenant Stanway	– Via Longa[4]
Lieutenant Forster	– Alhandra
Lieutenant Trench	– Sobral
Lieutenant Piper	– Alhandra
Lieutenant Tapp	– survey of position / Lisbon duty
Lieutenant Reid	– São Pedro da Cadeira [& Ponte do Rol]
Lieutenant Hulme	– Mafra and Ericeira district.[5]

Captain Williams,[6] who had been at Sobral and Lieutenant Thomson,[7] who had been at Ponte do Rol had left to join the army. Jones made no mention of the Portuguese engineers. All three were working in the Bucelas, Ajuda, Montachique area.[8] Is this because he did not consider they were under his command, being senior officers? At the time that Fletcher departed to join the army on the frontier, he suggested that Jones could dispense with some of the Portuguese engineers, militia soldiers and tradesmen from British regiments.[9]

3   Thompson, 'The Portuguese Engineers in the Peninsular War', pp.53–55. Lobo, *Defesa*, pp.317-330. Christovam Ayres de Magalhães Sepúlveda. *História Organica e politica do Exercito Portuguez* (Lisbon: 1910), Vol.5, p.339.

4   Stanway was omitted from the published version, but he is mentioned in the original. This may be an error, or because Stanway was withdrawn about this time to prepare detailed plans of the defences.

5   REM: 5501-59-18, Jones to Fletcher, 9 August 1810; Jones, *Sieges*, Vol.3, p.240. The printed and original letters are quite different.

6   REM: 5501-59-18, Fletcher to Jones, 24 July 1810. Williams was still on the Lines on 18 August 1810 and in early September was building defences on the river Zêzere at Punhete.

7   REM: 5501-59-18, Jones to Fletcher, 12 July 1810.

8   See Thompson, 'The Portuguese Engineers in the Peninsular War', pp.54.

9   REM: 5501-59-18, 6 July 1810.

When Fletcher reached the army, there was a change in plans. In early July, the expectation was that Ciudad Rodrigo would soon fall and the invasion could be imminent. The engineers were called up to the army on the basis that there would be no time for further work on the Lines. Ciudad Rodrigo surrendered on 10 July 1810, whilst Fletcher was travelling up to headquarters. The French now had two choices, either to besiege Almeida or to bypass the town and invade Portugal. The garrison under Brigadier William Cox, was about 4,500 strong and could have been blockaded. Almeida was invested on 24 July and the trenches opened on 15 August 1810. The French did not appear to be in a hurry, and Wellington was given more time to strengthen the defences.

Soon after arriving at headquarters, Fletcher wrote to Jones, ordering another redoubt to be constructed at São Julião. This had previously been considered and the increased threat of imminent invasion made defence of the embarkation point a priority. Fort 109 was north-east of Oeiras and would significantly improve the strength of the embarkation defences. It was a substantial fort, 'being of a description not to be carried by assault' and proposed for 4–500 men and 'not less than' six 12-pounders.[10] Jones received the letter on 18 July, replied that evening, and set off the following morning to commence the work.

As well as the engineering challenges, Jones was quickly involved in local politics. He reported receiving a letter from Charles Stuart, the British Ambassador to Portugal, who had received a complaint from the Marchioness of Abrantes about the damage being caused to her salt pans on the banks of the Tagus. The engineers wanted to flood them to render the area impassable. Having revisited the area, Jones was able to report that, at least temporarily, an alternative solution had been found.[11]

Quickly following on from the order to add to the defences at São Julião, came further instructions that:

> … the position at Alhandra should be strengthened as far as possible whether by scarping or works and I have therefore to request that you will examine that ground and that you will cause redoubts to be commenced at such parts as may afford good flanking points and as may appear to be at the same time favourable for the construction of enclosed works … Should you find parts of the height that are favourable for scarping, you will employ a body of workmen upon them, to render those places impracticable.

And:

> … that two or three good redoubts should be established between the work at São Pedro da Cadeira and the sea [Forts 111–113]. I think you will find one good situation at a hill about half way between [fort] no 32 and the sea, one near the sea, and a third at a point at which there was to have been a dam made. They

---

10   Jones, *Sieges*, Vol.3, p.224. Final size was for 500 men, seven 12-pounders and one howitzer.
11   REM: 5501-59-18, Jones to Fletcher, Lisbon, 12 & 18 July 1810. Neither in Jones, *Sieges*.

should not I conceive be for less than 200 men and three or four pieces of artillery each.[12]

These instructions were to strengthen both ends of the first line, so it can be surmised that Wellington was now considering the possibility of defending the first line. Jones wrote, this 'change was contemplated, probably in consequence of the invaders engaging in the siege of Almeida.'[13] These orders are far too early for that. It was only a week since Ciudad Rodrigo had surrendered and there had been no French movement since. The Allied forward positions held by the Light Division were still in front of Almeida. It would be another week before this screen was pushed back and another month before the trenches were opened in front of Almeida. Wellington could not have known that he would have nearly three months more to improve the defences, but a decision had been made enhance the first line with a view to making it defensible. The more time Wellington was given, the stronger it would be.

Table of when work started between July and October 1810[14]

Area	Month started
São Julião phase 3 (Fort 109)	July 1810
São Pedro da Cadeira phase 2 (Forts 111-113)	July 1810
Additional defences at Alhandra (Forts 118-9)	July 1810
Scarping hills to west of Alhandra	July 1810
São Julião. Trench between Forts 106 & 107.	September 1810
São Julião. Defensive line (Fort 110)	September 1810
Calhandriz (Forts 121-124)	September 1810
Portela, Quintela (Forts 125-126)	September 1810
Scarping of Serra de Serves	September 1810

On 20 July 1810, Jones reported back on his survey for the new fort (109) at São Julião. He wrote that the ground was extremely rocky and the plateau on top of the hill was too small for the size required and proposed two levels to hold the main body and the reserve troops. Two days later, having had more time to examine the ground, he was able to report that in most places the layer of rock was not very thick, and the fort could be built of the size proposed. Jones also suggested that a parapet could be prepared on the left side to 'provide a secure space for lodging a body of men. It may be added at any time.'[15] The diagram in Jones' *Sieges* also shows that a substantial layer of *trous-de-loup* (pits with spikes in bottom) were installed in front of the fort.[16]

In one of his letters, Jones expressed concern about not getting prompt responses. There clearly was some issue as Jones' letters of 18 July were

---

12   REM: 5501-59-18, Fletcher to Jones, Alverça da Beira, 18 July 1810. Also, Jones, *Sieges*, Vol.3, pp.224–225.

13   Jones, *Sieges*, Vol.3, pp.19–20.

14   Jones, Sieges, Vol.3, pp.224–228.

15   REM: 5501-59-18, Jones to Fletcher, Lisbon, 20 & 22 July 1810. Fletcher agreed to the proposal on 26 July 1810.

16   Jones, *Sieges*, fig.11, at end of Vol.3.

not received by Fletcher until 27 July 1810. This will not have helped with decision making. The delay dropped to 5–6 days, but this still seems long at such a critical time.[17]

Having started Fort 109, Jones turned to the other orders. On 25 July, he wrote to Fletcher making his proposals for Alhandra:

> … the position has been carefully examined and such parts of it have been marked for scarping as appear eligible, and various flanks and redoubts have been traced out in situations favourable for sweeping the face of the hill. A body of peasantry has been demanded and will commence these operations tomorrow and I feel I may venture to assure you that within six weeks or two months labour, the whole of the front of the position shall be made as strong as can be reasonably be desired.

However, he was unsure that scarping could make the left flank secure and recommended placing 'two good redoubts on the summit of the hills which overlook the valley and the ground rising from it … I find that in the first instance about fourteen guns and five other small works will be required.'[18]

Jones argued that these redoubts would also cover the retreat of troops from any defences on the plain and would make it very difficult for an enemy to hold any positions they captured. Approval was given a few days later and they became Forts 118 and 119. Fletcher prioritised this construction, detailed above, strengthening the plain at Alhandra.[19]

In the same letter, Jones reported that he was going to São Pedro da Cadeira the next day and hoped to start three forts (111–113) on 27 July 1810. Jones now raised a practical question. This was the height of summer and there was no accessible water supply near where many forts were to be built. He asked if it would be 'expedient' to provide water casks for the workmen as 'it is not possible to exist for six hours under fatigue in summer without some liquid'. On 28 July 1810, Jones confirmed that the three forts had been commenced. The one nearest the sea (113) was smaller than ordered and held only two guns and 'by taking advantage of the perpendicularity [sic] of the cliffs, fifty men will now be sufficient'.[20]

On the border, the French aggressively pushed the allied advance guard away from Almeida on 24 July 1810. Craufurd's Light Division about 4,000 strong was attacked by Soult with 24,000 men and forced into a disorganised retreat. There was no evidence yet that a siege of Almeida was planned. Wellington was concerned that the French might not wait to complete the siege and bypass the fortress. As a precaution, he started moving his army further west, he did not want to get caught, like Craufurd had been on 24 July. Writing to Hill, Wellington said 'as soon as they shall have got together their force, they will make a dash at us, and endeavour to make our retreat

---

17 S.G.P. Ward, *Wellington's Headquarters* (Oxford: Oxford University Press, 1957), p.124. About 70 miles (110km) per day for couriers was inferred.

18 Jones, *Sieges*, Vol.3, pp.238–239. There are two letters of this date in the original papers. The printed version is only part of what looks like a draft letter. Both letters contain different information. REM: 5501-59-18, Jones to Fletcher, 25 July 1810.

19 Jones, *Sieges*, Vol.3, p.227.

20 REM: 5501-59-18, Jones to Fletcher, St Pedro da Cadeira, 28 July 1810.

as difficult as possible.'[21] He was wrong, but it was better to be prepared. The French were waiting for a siege train, which did not arrive for another three weeks.

On 29 July 1810, Fletcher wrote to Jones reporting that 'we seemed to have commenced our march towards your part of Portugal'. Fletcher asked for the new works to be made defensible against musketry as a minimum. No mention was made of the other works, so Fletcher must have been confident that they were complete and armed. Jones received the letter on 1 August and acknowledged its receipt, and also of a separate private letter which must have told Jones to keep secret the fact that the withdrawal had started.[22]

Jones continued with a report on progress. All the defences at São Julião were in a 'tolerably finished state' except 107, Quinta Nova, where they were having some problems getting sufficient depth in the ditch due to rocky ground. He also reported that the new fort, 109, would be complete in about 10 days. The three new forts near Picanceira and Marvão (88, 90 & 91) were also nearly complete. At São Pedro da Cadeira, work was progressing slower than expected due to a lack of workmen: 'The *Capitão Mores* say all their Ordenenzas of a middle age are taken from them for the militia and that none are left but boys and old men. I made application last week to the Secretary at War to issue orders to enforce the attendance of as many men as possible.'[23]

Jones had also asked Forjaz, the Secretary of War, to move the Figuera da Foz Militia regiment from Mafra to Alhandra where there was a greater need of workmen.[24] At Sobral, Jones reported that 'the works there cannot be considered as finished' although he did also say 'as a field work it is certainly complete enough for any purpose [that] may exist'. The weather continued to hinder progress:

> The rains last week did much damage to the works in the Mafra District, and we have had constant parties employed to repair them. The Ponte do Rol river [Sizandro] swelled very much and the water carried away every pile which had been driven for the foundation of the dam. The [hollow?] outwork at St Julian's is like a well, and the water can only be got out by bailing.

The same day, Jones wrote to Captain Wedekind at São Julião asking him to make completion of the new fort the priority 'Without any exception the workmen under your orders are soly [sic] to be employed in making the works in the [vicinity?] of Oeyras defensible'. He asked for a temporary magazine to be built and for the ditch to be completed and palisaded.[25]

Whilst orders for additional work continued to flow down from headquarters, there was also a stream of letters asking for the release of resources. Requests to release the only other engineer captain (Williams)

21   Gurwood, *Dispatches*, Wellington to Hill, Alverça, 27 July 1810.

22   Jones, *Sieges*, Vol.3, pp.226–227; REM: 5501-59-18, Jones to Fletcher, Lisbon 1 August 1810. The private letter is not present.

23   REM: 5501-59-18, Jones to Fletcher, Lisbon, 1 August 1810. See also AHM: PT-AHM-DIV-114-169-020.

24   AHM: PT-AHM-DIV-1-14-169-020.

25   REM: 5501-59-18, Jones to Wedekind, Lisbon, 1 August 1810.

were continuous through July and August. Letters from headquarters almost alternated between recognising he was needed on the Lines and asking for him to be released to join Major General Leith's division. The only other two engineer captains were working with no support on defences at Setúbal and Peniche.[26] Similarly, there were several requests to release the Figueira da Foz Militia regiment even though it made up a significant proportion of the available workforce. It is really difficult to see how the several engineer officers with the army were more useful there than finishing the construction of the defences around Lisbon. Jones was also being continually reminded that he was supposed to be allocating engineer resources to prepare detailed plans of the Lines, when he did not have enough to control the building work. Fletcher commented on 3 August that he wanted to give a copy to Wellington as he 'has frequently asked me for it.'[27] Following Jones reporting on 8 August, that 'after next week, many of the works now in progress will be completely finished', Fletcher ordered two officers to be taken off the building work to prepare plans.[28]

Some of the work being requested appeared unnecessary at this time. On 9 August, Fletcher asked Jones to look at Fort 50 near Freixal as 'it was much plunged in to from ground close to it.' He went on to say the fort was stronger than it needed to be and should 'have been little more than an emplacement for guns.' If enemy troops were on higher ground near this fort, the position was lost and spending time reworking it was not worthwhile.[29] Four weeks later Jones reported that he was working on the redoubt but 'with very little advantage or effect', a polite way of saying it was a waste of time.[30]

Early in August Jones was still spreading his limited resources amongst the many tasks. In a letter of 3 August, he reported:

> No's 90 and 91 are already in such a good state of defence, that I yesterday took all the workmen from them (except 50 men each to finish) and sent them to St Pedro [da Cadeira] which will … [be in] a fair state of defence by Wednesday evening next. The other [redoubt] will not be so soon ready as we have met with much stone in excavating the ditch … I have no doubt whatever that it will be ready in time … I have deemed it right to [direct?] Captain Williams … at Sobral and confine his exertions solely to defence; such as clearing the ditches, filling up the openings through the counterscarp etc. By this arrangement I have been able to draw off 100 men from Sobral for Alhandra.[31]

---

26   Captains Holloway and Dickenson.

27   REM: 5501-59-18, Fletcher to Jones, Celorico, 3 August 1810. Part of the letter is printed in Jones' *Sieges*, but not this section.

28   REM: 5501-59-18, Fletcher to Jones, Celorico, 18 August 1810 & Jones to Fletcher, Lisbon, 20 August 1810.

29   REM: 5501-59-18, Fletcher to Jones, Celorico, 3 August 1810. Part of the letter is printed in Jones' *Sieges*, but not this section.

30   Jones, *Sieges*, Vol.3, p.247.

31   REM: 5501-59-18, Jones to Fletcher, Via Longa, 3 August 1810. Only part of the letter is printed in Jones, *Sieges*, p.329.

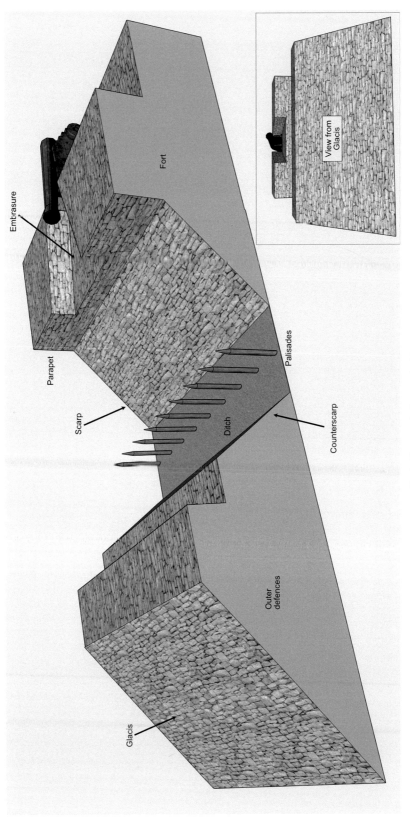

Typical layout of a fort on the Lines.

View from Glacis

Embrasure

Parapet

Scarp

Palisades

Ditch

Counterscarp

Fort

Outer defences

Glacis

i

The Lines of Torres Vedras © Chris Collingwood (www.collingwoodhistoricart.com)

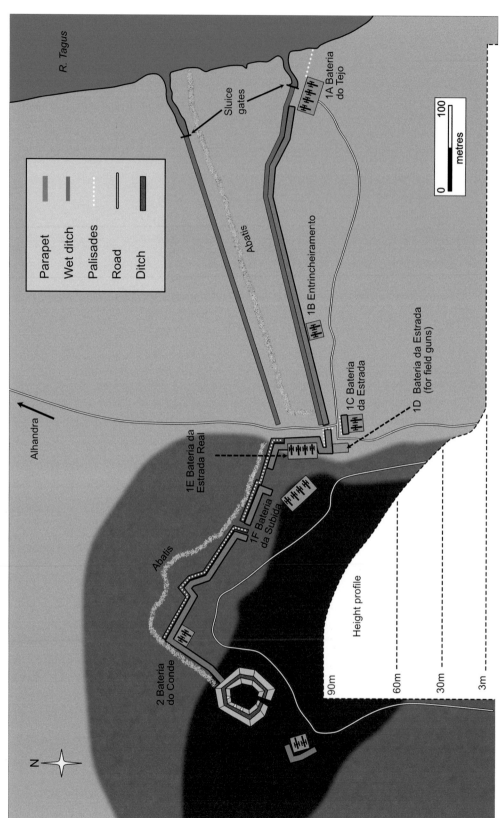

Defences and heights at Alhandra.

Church in Sobral town square.

Mount Socorro from Fort São Vicente, Torres Vedras.

Ciera Indicator Telegraph

= Repeat number

1

2

3

0 Start & Stop

4

5

6

To send code 123, the signal would be: 0 1 2 3 0

To send code 355, the signal would be: 0 3 5 = 0

Portuguese (Ciera) indicator telegraph with arm positions.

Photo from Fort 40 looking north towards Alhandra.

Summit of Serra de Serves from Fort 40.

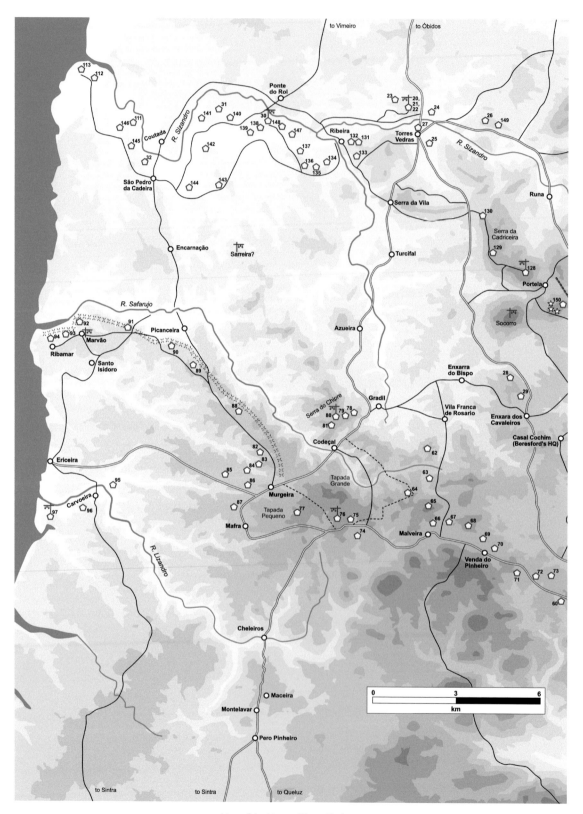

Map of the Lines of Torres Vedras.

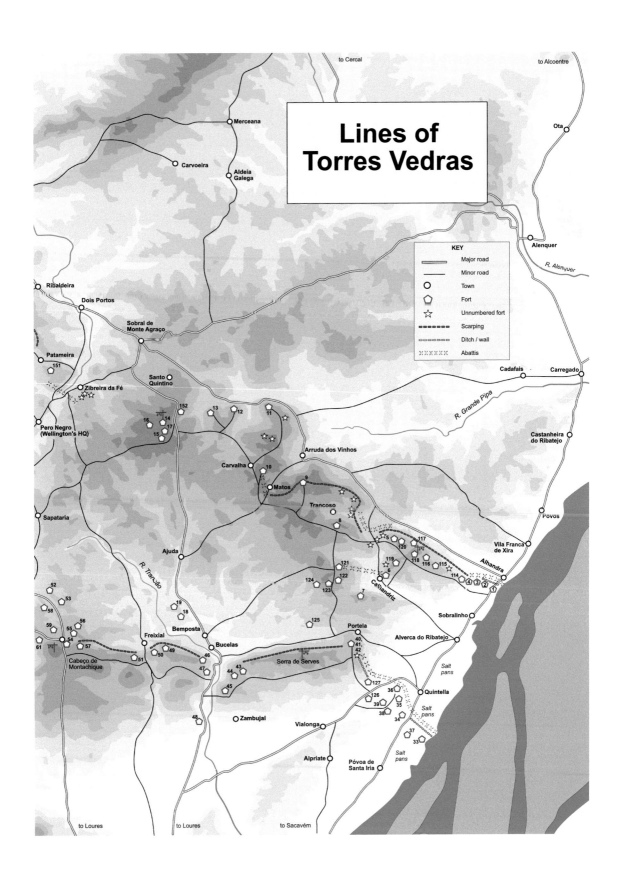

Lines of
Torres Vedras

KEY

	Major road
	Minor road
◯	Town
⬠	Fort
☆	Unnumbered fort
▪▪▪▪▪	Scarping
▫▫▫▫▫	Ditch / wall
✕✕✕✕	Abattis

to Cercal

to Alcoentre

Ota

Alenquer

R. Alenquer

Merceana

Carvoeira

Aldeia
Galega

Ribaldeira

Dois Portos

Sobral de
Monte Agraço

Cadafais

Carregado

Patameira

151

Santo
Quintino

152

13

12

11

R. Grande Pipa

Zibreira da Fé

Castanheira
do Ribatejo

Pero Negro
(Wellington's HQ)

16

14

17

15

Carvalha

10

Arruda dos Vinhos

Matos

9

Sapataria

Trancoso

8

Povos

Ajuda

R. Trancão

5

117

120

Vila Franca
de Xira

121

119

118

116

115

6

Alhandra

124

122

114

4

3

2

123

7

1

52

53

Calhandriz

58

Sobralinho

59

56

55

125

Portela

Alverca do Ribatejo

54

57

Bemposta

Freixial

19

18

Bucelas

40,
41,
42

61

51

50

49

46

Cabeço de
Montachique

Serra de Serves

Salt
pans

47

43

44

Quintella

45

127

36

Zambujai

48

126

39

35

Salt
pans

38

34

Vialonga

37

33

Alpriate

Póvoa de
Santa Iria

Salt
pans

to Loures

to Loures

to Sacavém

ix

Fort São Vicente, Torres Vedras.

Stone facing of Fort 40.

View north from Fort 18 covering main road from Sobral to Lisbon.

Gun embrasure at Fort 18, Ajuda Grande.

View from Fort 28, Pequena da Enxara, looking towards Mount Socorro. Main road from Torres Vedras to Montachique goes left to right in front of Mount Socorro.

Embarkation point at Fort São Julião da Barra.

Fort 27 Castelo de Torres Vedras.

Fort São Julião da Barra.

Fort 27, Castelo de Torres Vedras and town from Fort 20, São Vicente.

Pero Negro, Wellington's headquarters.

Casal Cochim, Beresford's headquarters.

Richard Fletcher RE. (Royal Engineers Museum)

John Thomas Jones RE. (Royal Engineers Museum)

View of Alhandra from heights near Fort 2, Bateria de Conde.

Fort 95, tunnel and steps up to main fort.

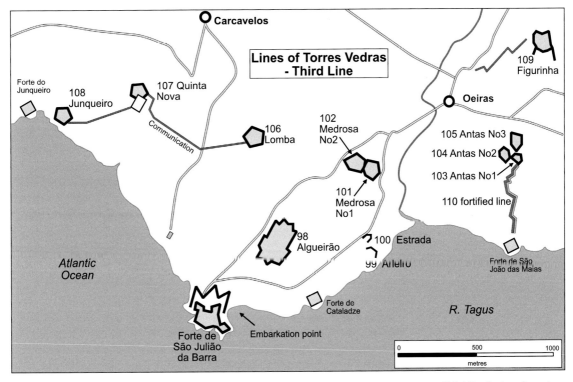

Third Line final configuration.

He noted in the letter that in the last 48 hours he had ridden about 110 kilometres visiting the various works around the Lines.[32] The following day, he intended to return to Alhandra 'and mark out the new works.' These were probably 114–117 and 120. Jones' expectation on 8 August 1810, was that by the middle of August most of the work would be completed.

There was clearly still concern about the embarkation point. On 14 August, Fletcher asked if:

> … it would if practicable … to connect the redoubts on the left [106 & 107] by a common trench in which bodies of troops might be placed in security from cannonade, who could support the intervals and communicate with facility with any particular point that might be pressed … and further, if the same sort of course could be introduced to advantage between the southern of the three mill redoubts (on the right) [103] and the Tagus.[33]

Although not explicitly mentioned, Fletcher and Jones would have been aware that two weeks had passed and there had been no further retreat by the allied army. More time was available for more defences. It was not until a letter of 19 August that Jones was told that the siege of Almeida had started.[34]

---

32 São Julião, Lisbon, Mafra, Ericeira, St Pedro da Cadeira, Torres Vedras, Sobral, Alhandra and Via Longa.

33 Jones, *Sieges*, Vol.3, p.228.

34 REM: 5501-59-18, Fletcher to Jones, Celorico,19 August 1810.

The letter also reported that the army was moving forward, east of Celorico, so there was even more time to improve the defences.

Jones made another detailed examination of the defences around São Julião. He confirmed that a communication between Forts 106 and 107 was feasible and he had 'always considered it a desirable thing to connect the redoubts.'[35] He was less positive about construction between Fort 103 and the Tagus, arguing 'the ground apparently naturally rocky and unfavourable for working. Any cover or other defence erected there would consequently be a work of considerable time and labour to execute.' He proposed instead forming a new work that 'might easily be thrown up in the stone quarry a little more in the rear by taking advantage of the excavations already found and that such a work would answer every purpose of defence and security to the right of the position.'[36]

Fletcher responded on 27 August, 'I thought that some sort of line there would have a much better command of the ground … than a work situated at the stone quarry in the rear … I wish to abide entirely by what you think best on the spot.' Confusingly, Jones' reply on 3 September 1810, reported marking 'out a line to the right of the mill redoubts at Oeyras (*agreeably with your letter of the 27th ult*) and which I hope in ten days' time to render an obstacle to an enemy attempting to penetrate that flank.' The words in brackets above, were not in the original letter, only in the printed version. Jones' inference is that he was following directions from Fletcher's letter of 27 August, which he was not. Fletcher left the choice to Jones. Looking at Jones' estimate of the time to complete the line, it is likely that when Jones looked again, he decided that constructing the line was not as difficult as he first thought.[37] This position, number 110, is the only defensive line numbered in the Lines of Torres Vedras, probably because it was originally intended to be a fort.[38]

Captain Wedekind reported progress at São Julião on 11 September:

With the means I have at present (600 men and tools for only 600 men) I calculate to have the fleche near the seaside in some state of defence … by the end of next week or the 21st of this month … The soil where the fleche is, is as bad as possible that of the lines is more favourable; the ditches are opened at a distance of 170 yards, 6 feet deep and 4 feet high parapet. There are about 200 yards of ditch to be opened.

No 109 red[oubt] is palisaded and I shall leave there tomorrow only 100 men to improve the glacis and counterscarp on the west side. The masons are about laying the three last platforms of stone which will be done tomorrow or next day. The guns are mounted and the magazine complete.

---

35   REM: 5501-59-18, Jones to Fletcher, Lisbon, 20 August 1810.

36   REM: 5501-59-18, Jones to Fletcher, Lisbon, 22 August 1810. Jones had previously said the quarry redoubt was his preference; see letter of 20 August 1810.

37   REM: 5501-59-18, Jones to Fletcher, Lisbon, 3 September 1810. Jones, *Sieges*, Vol.3, p.246.

38   REM: 5501-59-18, Fletcher to Jones, Celorico, 31 August 1810. The numbers were in part of the letter not printed in Jones, *Sieges*, Vol.3, p.230.

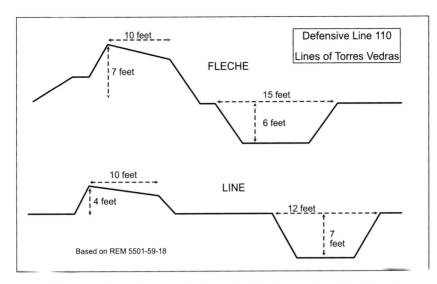

Profiles of defence 110, fleche and line.

To begin the lines of communication on the left of the position, I could employ very well 500 more men, but for every additional hundred of men I must thank you to supply me at least with fifty spades or shovels. The soil admitting in most places to be opened with *Enxadas* [hoes].

I would propose to begin the opening of these lines between 106 and 107 there being about 800 yards distance between these two redoubts and quite open ground. I shall have the lines marked and traced out by Monday next to begin in case you can send men and spades or shovels. I hope I can spare also by that time 200 men of the Militia for the communications.[39]

Wedekind's report clarified that the salient points on the line were being constructed in a more substantial manner than the connecting parapet. His attached diagram (below) shows this clearly. Wedekind also differentiated between the eastern line 110, which comprised of a trench and a parapet and the western lines between Forts 106 & 107 which was a covered way (parapet only).

In carrying out the survey on 20 August, Jones realised that there was a hill 6–700 yards in front of the new fort (109) which overlooked it enough 'to admit of it being attacked with a probability of success.' He recommended using powder to blast the hill to reduce its height by 3–5 metres, which would make it unusable. He estimated it would take 100 men, 14 days to blast the hill top.[40]

Finally, the amount of work to be completed was reducing and there were more civilians available for the remaining tasks. The issue of dismissing the Figuera da Foz Militia was raised again by Fletcher. Jones had written to Forjaz on 1 August 1810, asking for them to be moved from Mafra to Alhandra. Following the latest enquiry, he updated Fletcher:

---

39   REM: 5501-59-18, Wedekind to [assumed Jones], 11 September 1810.
40   REM: 5501-59-18, Jones to Fletcher, Lisbon, 17 & 22 August 1810.

I am no longer desirous of retaining them, having failed in my best endeavours to move them from Mafra, in which district we now procure peasantry sufficient for the work … on the 4th [August], Don Miguel [Forjaz] replied, that the regiment having been stationed at Mafra by order of Marshal Beresford, it was necessary to have the Marshal's order for their removal. I wrote to Marshal Beresford's head-quarters that same day to request their removal to Alhandra but my letter has never been honoured with any notice. Immediately on receipt of your letter yesterday, I wrote to the commanding officer of the regiment, to say, that his men are no longer required … I conceive however, that some further order to the colonel will be necessary for their removal.[41]

Jones' letter crossed with one from Fletcher saying 'I am directed by the commander of the forces to desire you will acquaint the officer commanding the Figueras Regiment of Militia that the further services of that corps on the works will be dispensed with.'[42] Although this militia regiment was being sent away, the lack of workmen was still a problem in some areas. Lieutenant William Forster RE, who was responsible for the work at Alhandra reported:

I am sorry to say there are very great deficiencies in the number of my workmen, I have included a statement of the actual number sent by the different *Capitãos Mores*, and also the number demanded by me, in my first requisition. Their inattention and neglect is carried to such a height, that I think nothing but the most vigorous measures will produce a change in their conduct. The following are the most culpable and those I would particularly recommend for chastisement.
Capitão Mor of Alenquer
Capitão Mor of Coruche
Capitão Mor of Merceana and Aldea Gallegos [Aldeia Galega da Merceana]
Sarjento Mor of Alverca
Sarjento Mor of Povos and Castanheira

He continued: 'If when you report the *Capitãos Mores*, you were to include the *Juiz de Fora* of this town, it would be of service to him.'[43] Jones was more positive reporting to Fletcher on 20 August 'If we go on with the same means for a month longer, we shall not have a man employed on our present works'. Unfortunately, that did not happen. On 10 September, perhaps triggered by another letter of complaint of the same date from Forster,[44] he complained to Fletcher that despite complaining to Forjaz, he had not been able to get more than 1,300 workmen when, in his opinion the district should be able to supply 5,000. This was delaying the work to complete the defences at Alhandra and

41   REM: 5501-59-18, Jones to Fletcher, Lisbon, 18 August 1810. Letter printed in Jones, *Sieges*, Vol.3, pp.241–242 with wording changes. The printed version says 'I wrote to Marshal Beresford that same day to request their removal to Alhandra *but have not yet had any reply*'.
42   REM: 5501-59-18, Fletcher to Jones, Celorico, 19 August 1810.
43   REM: 5501-59-18, Forster to Jones, 20 August 1810.
44   REM: 5501-59-18, Forster to Jones, 10 September 1810.

also starting the additional defences to the left of the town.[45] Two days later, Jones was clearly getting very frustrated about the manpower issue:

Do press Lord Wellington to write severely to Don Miguel Forjaz to see that we are supplied with men. Don Miguel always refers me to an imbecile [General] Don Antonio Xavier de Noronha [Governor of Estremadura province] and that imbecile refers me to a [still greater?], Don Laurenco Homen, a man absolutely under my orders. They seem to think that what we are doing is not regarded as anything at Headquarters. They give me abundance of civil words but not the slightest assistance. Every week our parties decrease and if something is not done, we shall soon dwindle down to nothing.[46]

The issue of the supply of workmen would not go away.

Having been told on 19 August that the French had started the siege of Almeida and the allied army had moved forward, Jones believed there was time for further improvements in the defences. A new proposal was made:

Alhandra however does not altogether satisfy me as a position, I should fear an enemy with a very superior force would penetrate by the hills on the left and get possession of the [serra?] in the rear of it. A movement which would not only turn all our defences but might perhaps lead to the capture of the whole force on the Alhandra position, which would then find itself surrounded and its retreat cut off. Above A dos Matos [near Calhandriz] on riding over the ground it appeared to me that we ought to form there a position for 1,500 men which should effectively prevent such an enterprise … I cannot avoid thinking that five thousand men at Alhandra and say two thousand more strongly entrenched to the left of it would thoroughly connect the country from the Tagus to the Ajuda valley … [and] ought to resist almost any numbers.[47]

Fletcher, immediately responded:

The redoubt near Trancoso [Fort 8] was thrown up under a hope that it might prevent an enemy from turning the position of Alhandra with artillery; infantry would, I believe, undoubtedly, do it. If, on a minute examination of the ground, you think that 1,500 men might be so intrenched as to prevent the last-mentioned species of force from penetrating, the object is, I conceive, highly important … I shall be truly obliged by your ideas at large on this matter.[48]

Jones quickly submitted his proposals and on 2 September 1810, he was informed that Wellington thought 'it is desirable to strengthen the ground on the immediate left of the valley, and he would have you begin without

---

45   REM: 5501-59-18, Jones to Fletcher, Lisbon, 10 September 1810. Fletcher passed the complaint to Wellington on 15 September 1810, AHM: PT-AHM-DIV-1-14-010-30-m0002. No letter from Wellington to Forjaz can be found.

46   REM: 5501-59-18, Jones to Fetcher, Lisbon, 12 September 1810.

47   REM: 5501-59-18, Jones to Fletcher, Lisbon, 20 August 1810. This part of the letter is not printed in Jones, *Sieges*, Vol.3, pp.242–243.

48   REM: 5501-59-18, Fletcher to Jones, 24 August 1810. Jones, *Sieges*, Vol.3, p.229.

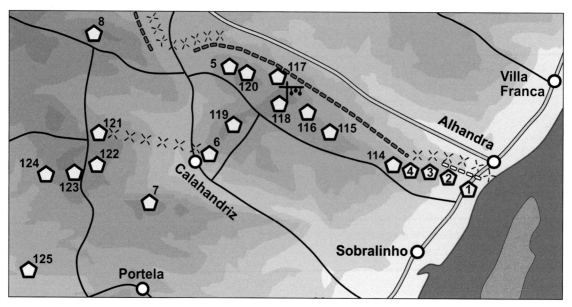

Final configuration of Alhandra Defences.

loss of time.'[49] Fletcher, recognising that time could be short asked him to 'progressively strengthen the ground in whatever way you think best.'[50] After a further detailed examination, Jones reported:

> … it has appeared possible by scarping etc to confine the advance of troops over that ground to the space occupied by the narrow ridge formed at the head of the valley. The ridge is of the hardest rock and a very gentle slope towards the left cannot be cut through with any effect. We have therefore commenced upon the construction of two redoubts to oppose the passage of it. In order to prevent an enemy profiting by the cover that the ravine affords to him we have begun upon a small advance a redoubt looking into it, but as this work is very much plunged into from high ground at a short distance both in front and rear, to prevent an enemy gaining and keeping possession of it, it will be necessary to construct the third redoubt on the right [four in total].[51]

These positions would become Forts 121–124.

The surrender of Almeida on 27 August 1810 triggered another bout of concern about an imminent retreat. Fletcher discussed the situation with Wellington and another confidential letter was sent to Jones. Wellington did not want news that a retreat was starting to get out to the population. Unlike the previous letter of 29 July 1810, this was more about detail rather than completion of fortifications. Jones was instructed to start felling trees to make abatis, to put the powder and ammunition in the magazines and to ensure that the mines for roads and bridges identified for destruction were all in place. The scale of abatis was extensive. It was not just on the banks of the Tagus. Fletcher commented 'there are many parts of the line between

49   REM: 5501-123, Jones to Fletcher 29 September 1810.
50   Jones, *Sieges*, Vol.3, p.232.
51   REM: 5501-59-18, Jones to Fletcher, Lisbon, 10 September 1810.

Morugueira [Murgeira] (in the pass of Mafra and Ribamar) in which trees may be felled to advantage.' From Murgeira to the coast at Ribamar was about 10 kilometres. Lieutenant William Reid reported starting this work on 6 September 1810 and Jones made visits over the next few days advising on the placement of the defences.

One task which Wellington continued to put off until the last moment was the destruction of the embankments on the river Tagus around Alhandra to clear the field of fire. The defences required the forts to be able to fire on the river, and gunboats on the river to fire on the land. The flooding without these walls would be extensive and would be a major inconvenience to the population in the future.[52] The issue of the salt pans was reconsidered. Although, following complaints, the salt pans had not been flooded and instead additional ditches had been cut between them, it was now accepted that flooding the salt pans as well would be a much more effective barrier. Fletcher had asked the question and Jones replied, 'I would like to proceed again with the original cut as it is in every way better.'[53] The decision was only being put off; when the French approached, the salt pans would be flooded. The owner, the Marchioness of Abrantes, wanted it delayed as long as possible. There was a need to balance the risk to the defences against the profits of the owner.

Two days later, Fletcher raised the subject of drinking water. He had not replied to Jones' previous query about supplying water casks for the troops. The provision of water buckets for the use of the artillery had been included from the start, but water for the garrison troops had not. Fletcher commented 'it would certainly be desirable, and I am sure there will be no objection to the expense of the purchase if the Commissariat cannot supply.'[54] Jones replied, saying he was working to collect casks for 10,000 gallons of water. Fletcher replied:

> Lord Wellington has consented that the water-casks should be supplied and will order the Commissary General to furnish or pay for them. I assume for two hundred hogsheads or vessels that would contain equal to that quantity; that is allowing that there are about one hundred works that may require them, and that on an average they may contain 250 men, two hogsheads or one hundred and twenty-six gallons will give rather more than two quarts per man [2.25 litres]. This will be in all 12,600 gallons, somewhat more than you mentioned. You will of course divide them as you see fit.[55]

Two quarts per man is about half the modern recommended daily intake for an adult. More would be required if it was hot or physical work was being undertaken. A hogshead, containing about 285 litres, would have weighed over 300 kilogrammes. This was about the capacity of an ox cart. Two hundred

52   Jones, *Sieges*, Fletcher to Jones, 31 August 1810, Vol.3, p.231.
53   REM: 5501-59-18, Fletcher to Jones, 1 September 1810. Jones, *Sieges*, Vol.3, p.247.
54   REM: 5501-59-18, Fletcher to Jones, Celorico, 1 September 1810.
55   REM: 5501-59-18, Fletcher to Jones, Gouveia, 11 September 1810. This part of the letter is not printed in Jones, *Sieges*.

ox carts would be required to provide the initial stock and there would need to be a minimum of 200 carts per day to replenish the water when the forts were occupied. This supply would not be sufficient if all the forts were fully manned, although realistically, not all forts would be manned all the time. Whilst the first line was occupied, the forts in the second line would have fewer troops in them, and when not directly threatened would be able to send troops out for water. Once the hot weather had finished the demand for water would reduce. However, the water supply would run out very quickly if a fort was under threat from the French. It is likely that the commissary did not provide all the casks approved by Wellington as Jones was confident that he could commandeer the numbers needed at short notice from the local vineyards.[56]

Water matters were firmly on Fletcher's mind. On 6 September, he wrote: 'as we draw towards the rainy season, a complete system of drainage for our redoubts, would be as far as possible, very desirable … that the water should not remain in the ditches, as I should fear its effects on the scarps. Will you have the goodness to consider this matter.[57]

This seems very late to be 'starting' to think about drainage. The periods of rain already experienced since the works commenced 10 months earlier should have shown the engineers the importance of getting drainage right. Bearing in mind that in 1810 almost all the works were earthworks with no stone facing, heavy rain could and did cause serious problems. In reply to Fletcher's letter, Jones stated:

> … it absolutely necessary for this preservation during the winter. We have had a few showers lately, the effects of which have been generally to bring down the fascine work and deface the slopes and in some parts to bring down the scarp. Parties have been constantly employed repairing these damages. I will take the earliest opportunity of examining the superior slopes of the different works and give more plunge to any which may seem to require it.[58]

In later years. probably with some level of hindsight, Jones wrote 'to ensure an efficient system of drainage should always be a principal consideration with an officer commencing a work.' As an example, he noted that Forts 101 and 102 near São Julião had literally filled with water during the autumn of 1810.[59]

When the works were started in November 1809, there was a concern that a French invasion could come quickly and getting some forts in place was the priority, not perfecting the design. Through the spring and summer of 1810, as more time became available, the pressure was to quickly extend the defences. Construction was still being done against the clock. Several redoubts were being quickly thrown up as the allied army arrived and for

---

56 Jones, *Sieges*, Vol.3, p.250. There were two letters from Jones on this date. Jones has combined them and left some parts out. See also, Jones *Sieges*, Vol.3, p.233.
57 REM: 5501-59-18, Fletcher to Jones, 6 September 1810.
58 REM: 5501-59-18, Jones to Fletcher, Lisbon, 11 September 1810.
59 Jones, *Sieges*, Vol.3, p.78.

some months after. Although the construction had been going on for nearly a year, at any particular moment, the engineers believed they were working against the clock. It was too late to start making major changes. Having experienced the damage caused by the heavy rain through the winter of 1810, Jones recorded 'in 1811, most of the exterior slopes of the works of the lines were retained with dry stone walls.'[60]

In mid-September the constant flow of letters between Fletcher and Jones slowed considerably. Fletcher was moving with the army and was busy carrying out the orders of Wellington. There was little new work on the Lines, the focus was on finishing the current workload and carrying out the last-minute tasks of loading magazines, clearing fields of fire, creating abatis, and destroying roads and bridges. Jones reported on 22 September that the new forts around Calhandriz 'have been rendered as strong as they ought to be.' He continued:

> The difficulty of turning the position of Alhandra is now very great and I think if a redoubt for three hundred men was constructed somewhere about the centre of a line extending from the height of Calhandriz to the Serra de Serves. the attempt would be nearly desperate whilst we have an army in the field, but in that case, to secure the country with a few troops as far as the pass of Bucellas it would be advisable to scarp the Serra de Serves. I beg leave to recommend those two measures. I will be answerable to have the redoubt a finished work in ten days from its commencement, and I have little doubt that in fifteen or twenty days we could render the Serra de Serves utterly impassable for an organised body of troops.[61]

He received Wellington's approval to both proposals on the 30 September and Fort 125 was started immediately. The Battle of Buçaco had been fought on 27 September 1810, and Wellington was now retreating.[62] The army would be in the Lines in 10 days.

Jones' concern about the Alhandra position was understandable. As many commentators past and present have pointed out, if the Lines were breached in any place, the whole of the defences would be compromised. On the eastern end of the first line there were passes through the hills at Arruda (Matos pass to Ajuda), Calhandriz and at Dois Portos. Wellington intended to have troops stationed at these places. There were defences at Arruda (Forts 9 & 10). There were no forts at Dois Portos, a fact spotted by the French; we will come back to this. Behind the hills of the first line, were the hills that made up the second line. At the Tagus end, this was the Serra de Serves. The valley at Portela between the Alhandra heights and the Serra de Serves was a weakness. If the French took Alhandra and then marched by this route, they could enter the Bucelas gap and could race straight for Lisbon or encircle the defenders at Vialonga. Jones' recommendation to block the valley was sensible now that there was additional time to complete these works.

---

60   Jones, *Sieges*, Vol.3, p.78.
61   REM: 5501-59-18, Jones to Fletcher, Lisbon, 22 September 1810.
62   Jones, *Sieges*, Vol.3, pp.233–234. The letter was written from Coimbra.

Fletcher's letters of 30 September and 2 October were focussed on the final preparations: 'Every precaution should be taken at and near our works for their being immediately occupied and defended … I would therefore recommend your making every arrangement as to mining roads, felling abatis [sic], clearing away obstacles, dressing off slopes etc … I would not actually load the mines until the last extremity.' One final addition to the defences was ordered:

> As there might be a number of guns placed on the high point on the right of this valley [Via Longa] I think it might be desirable to throw up a redoubt on this spot, having six embrasures towards the low ground [Fort 126]. I think there should also be an emplacement for guns at the mill at the end of the wall on the left [Fort 127].[63]

These were the last to be ordered before the occupation of the Lines. Jones reported on 5 October that he had suspended work on scarping the Serra de Serves, which had just started the previous day, to start work on these two new redoubts. He also reported that he had started work on Fort 125 on 3 October.[64] The valley from Alverca to Vialonga was further strengthened by adding ditch and abatis between Fort 127 and Forts 40–42 on top of the Serra de Serves. There was also a small unnumbered battery at the opposite end of the wall from Fort 127, both of which were probably for field guns.

The initial construction phase was now drawing to a close. The allied army was approaching the Lines, and workmen were still rushing to complete the last forts. One of the instructions in Wellington's memorandum of 20 October 1809, was to 'fix upon spots on which signal posts can be erected upon these hills, to communicate from one part of the position to the other'.

That would not be easy.

---

63   Jones, *Sieges*, Vol.3, pp.234–235.
64   REM: 5501-59-18, Jones to Fletcher, Lisbon, 5 October 1810. There are several changes from the original in the letter printed in Jones, *Sieges*, Vol.3, pp.252.

8

Communications on the Lines

In planning the Lines of Torres Vedras, Wellington's expectation was that he would be attacked by a larger force and to defend the Lines, he would need rapid communications to enable him to move his army to counter any threat. His immediate priority in October 1809 was to get the main defences started at São Julião, Torres Vedras and Sobral. It was nearly five months before discussions started on the best method of communicating along the Lines.

Land based optical signalling was nothing new, examples could be traced back thousands of years. However, their messages had to be very simple. There was a renewed interest in the eighteenth century, but it was not until the French Revolution that the first sophisticated system was put in place. Frenchman Claude Chappe designed a large and complex telegraph with around 200 combinations, and which required permanent buildings. It was first introduced in 1794 and was a great success. At the peak of Napoleon's power, the Chappe telegraph system covered much of France, with branches into the Low Countries and Italy.

A transmission was made up of a sequence of numbers, each number referring to a word or phrase in a code book. The transmission numbers were cascaded serially up the line. The first telegraph put up the first number, which was then duplicated by the second station on the line. The second station then waited for the third station to put up the first number. When the second station had duplicated the first number, the first station would put up the next number and the second station would then duplicate it. This process was repeated to the last station. Transmission timings were amazing with this technology, for example the 475 miles from Toulon to Paris would take about 12 minutes.[1] The fastest method for the British to send a message from the Mediterranean to London would be by ship and would take 2–4 weeks, depending on the weather.

Other countries realising the potential, developed their own systems, but they were very expensive. The only telegraphs in Britain, constructed by the Royal Navy, ran from the Admiralty in London to the major naval ports.

---

1   G. Holtzmann & B. Pehrson, *The Early History of Data Networks* (California: IEEE, 1995), p.89. N.B.. 12 minutes for the first number to arrive, not the whole message.

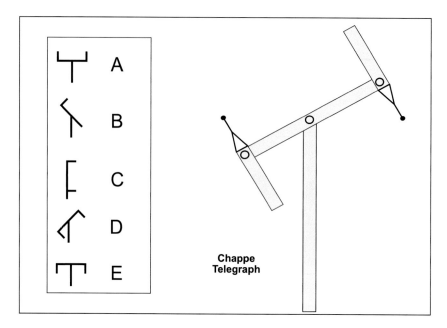

**Chappe
Telegraph**

French (Chappe) Telegraph.

There had been a system in place in Portugal for a number of years which communicated with Lisbon when ships were approaching the Tagus. Sea trade was the life blood of the Portuguese empire. In 1810, 60 years ahead of any similar development in Great Britain, the Portuguese military formed the *Corpo Telegrafico* and implemented a national telegraph system that connected Lisbon with Almeida, Abrantes and Elvas. The Portuguese telegraphs were designed by the civilian engineer Francisco António Ciera who developed three simple systems which were quick and cheap to produce, and all used the same code book.

Each instance could show a number between one and six and by combining with other instances could make a longer number. These numbers were then referenced to a word in the code book. Because only six numbers could be displayed, the numbers in the code book could only use the digits 1–6. It was however possible to represent all numbers by using multiple instances. These Portuguese telegraphs were not initially considered for use on the Lines.

The first mention of telegraphs for the Lines of Torres Vedras was on 1 April 1810 when Wellington noted that Fletcher had been talking to Rear Admiral George Berkeley, the commander of the British squadron based at Lisbon.[2] The Royal Navy had hundreds of years of experience of communicating at sea and it was logical to seek their advice. Berkeley's proposal was based on the current naval communication system. Like the Ciera systems, a sequence of balls and flags made up a number that could be referenced in a code book to give a word or phrase. Numbers beyond 30,000 were possible in a single instance. Berkeley had previously worked with coastal telegraphs when he was appointed in 1798 to command the Sussex Fencibles. In this role he had

---

2   Gurwood, *Dispatches*, Wellington to Berkeley, 1 April 1810.

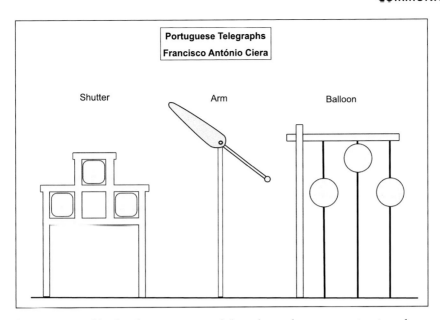

Portuguese Telegraphs

Francisco António Ciera

Shutter   Arm   Balloon

Portuguese (Ciera) telegraphs.

been responsible for the operation of the telegraphs communicating along 100 miles of coast and out to the patrolling ships.[3]

Messages were then made up of a string of numbers. The Royal Navy used a code book developed by Captain Home Popham and this was to be the basis of the land-based code book. At this time there were about 3,000 codes for words and phrases in the Popham code book with room for many more. Many naval terms would need to be removed and many land-based ones added. This telegraph was much more complex than the Ciera system, in terms of messages, cost, construction and the difficulty of operation.

Disappointingly, there is little exact detail on the number, construction or operation of the telegraph system on the Lines. The generally accepted number is 10, one of which was constructed after October 1810 (at Fort 128). There were possibly two other signal stations, excluding any telegraphs which were used to communicate with Lisbon.

There were up to five different telegraph systems operating in the area. The first was the new system developed by the Royal Navy for the Lines of Torres Vedras (labelled as the Lines Telegraph on the map below). The second was the Lisbon end of the national telegraph system using Portuguese telegraphs (labelled as the National Telegraph). Until the start of Wellington's retreat, the system would have been operating to Almeida and Elvas. By the time Wellington arrived in the Lines, it was all destroyed or removed, apart from the first telegraphs out of Lisbon which could still be used. This route went from Monsanto, near Lisbon to the Serra de Serves and then on to Monte Gordo, near Vila Franca de Xira. It is almost certain that there was a working telegraph on the Serra de Serves, as Jones specifically mentions it in a letter of 11 September 1810 after he had been asked by Fletcher to look at

---

3   De Toy, *Berkeley*, pp.214–215.

constructing defences round it.[4] What is not known, is if this was the original Portuguese telegraph or a new British one. One recent Portuguese article suggested a telegraph in Fort 40 (on the Serra de Serves).[5] If this telegraph is added to the generally accepted number of telegraphs (10), then the total would be 11, which is the number of telescopes purchased for use by the telegraph stations.

The third system was the telegraph from Lisbon to the royal palace at Mafra again using Portuguese telegraphs (Mafra Telegraph).[6] This would have allowed communication back to Lisbon. There is some uncertainty about whether this still existed after the Portuguese Royal family sailed to Brazil, but Jones specifically mentions it being used.[7]

The fourth system was one that is not mentioned by Jones. Berkeley also set up a communication line down the Tagus from his leading boats at Vila Franca and beyond back down to Lisbon (Navy Telegraph).[8] Berkeley would want to know what his sailors were doing independent of Wellington's communications. This system may have just been used internally within the Royal Navy, but it is more likely that it was also used to pass messages for the army.

Finally, Portuguese telegraphs were constructed to be located in the same places as the British telegraphs although as we will see they were never used.

There is another inconsistency. Two contemporary maps show another signal station at Sarreira, between Fort 30 (Grilo) and the forts on the Safarujo river near Marvão. This is not mentioned in any account but would have allowed communication between Fort 30 (Grilo) and the forts near Marvão, which could not see each other due to intervening hills. There is no contemporary account that this was used.

After the first mention on 1 April 1810, nothing else is heard until 24 April, when Wellington thanked Berkeley 'for the telegraph books.'[9] On 27 April 1810, Mulcaster noted in his diary: 'Received letter from Colonel to prepare signal posts.'[10] The following morning, work commenced on the Serra de Socorro preparing the ground for the first telegraph. Over the next few days, work also started preparing the ground at Montachique. On 5 May, Mulcaster noted that Fletcher and Lieutenant Davie from HMS *Barfleur* arrived at Socorro and the first telegraph was fitted. The mast at Montachique was erected the next day.[11] Silence descends again for three weeks until Rice

---

4   REM: 5501-59-18, Fletcher to Jones, Gouveia, 6 September 1810 and Jones to Fletcher, Lisbon, 11 September 1810.

5   José Paulo Ribeiro Berger, 'Os Exércitos em Confronto e a População da Capital sob a Proteção das Linhas de Defesa de Lisboa' in P.A Avillez (ed.), *Os Exército Português e as Comemorações dos 200 Anos da Guerra Peninsular* (Lisboa: Tribuna, 2008-11), Vol.3, p.209.

6   Originally also to Royal palaces at Ajuda, Salvaterra and Queluz. It is unlikely any of these were still operating. Luna et al, *Boletim*, p.77, says that the Prince had a telegraph from Belém to the terrace of the Mafra palace that went via Tapada (probably Fort 76, Sonível), Sabugo and Monsanto.

7   REM: 5501-59-18, Jones to Fletcher, 20 July 1810.

8   Robert Sutcliffe, *British Expeditionary Warfare and the Defeat of Napoleon* (Woodbridge, Boydell, 2016), pp.135–136; De Toy, *Berkeley*, p.505.

9   Gurwood, *Dispatches*, Wellington to Berkeley, 24 April 1810. It is not clear which telegraph books Wellington was referring to as three weeks later, he asked for copies of Popham's code book.

10   Thompson, *Mulcaster*, p.95.

11   Thompson, *Mulcaster*, pp.96–97.

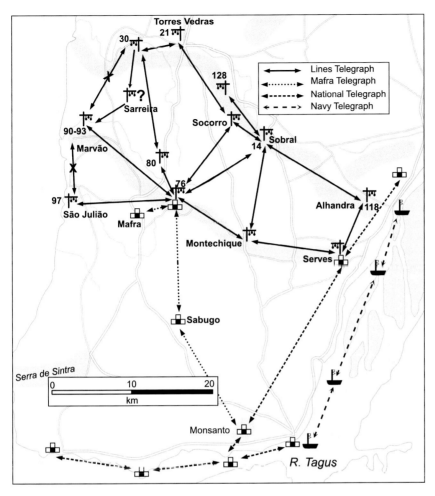

Telegraph networks around Lisbon.

Jones noted in his diary that he had purchased 11 telescopes for the signal stations.[12] There is no specific mention of constructing any of the other signal stations, but we know from passing comments that the one at Ponte do Rol (Fort 30, Grilo) was in place on 18 July and at Alhandra (Fort 118, Sinais) on 25 July 1810.[13]

There are a number of telegraph stations on the Lines that most writers agree existed. On the first line, there were five: Fort 118 (Sinais); Fort 14 (Alqueidão); Serra de Socorro; Fort 21 (São Vicente); and Fort 30 (Grilo). On the second line, it becomes less clear. All writers agree on: Serra de Montachique; Fort 76 (Sonível); Fort 80 (Forte da Quinta da Boa Viagem); and Fort 97 (São Julião). Not everyone includes one at the eastern (Tagus) end of the second line; the telegraph on the Serra de Serves. At the western end, there was a telegraph near Marvão. There are different views on its actual location and correspondence confirms that it was also moved in September 1810. Different sources place it in Fort 91 (Alagoa), Fort 92 (Picoto), or fort

---

12   Shore, *Engineer Officer*, p.54, 1 June 1810.

13   REM: 5501-59-18, Jones to Fletcher, Lisbon, 18 & 25 July 1810. The telegraph at Alhandra was in place before Fort 118 was built around it.

93 (Marvão), and one map shows it at the highest point above the town of Marvão.[14]

There are two criteria for visibility between telegraphs. First, were there any physical obstructions and second were they close enough. John Jones wrote that the maximum observable range of the British telegraph was about eight miles (13 kilometres).[15] The range of the Portuguese telegraph according to its designer, Francisco António Ciera was slightly longer at 15 kilometres.[16]

On 15 June 1810, Wellington who was at Celorico near the Portuguese border, wrote to Berkeley thanking him for the assistance he had given to Fletcher. He continued:

> There are however, two or three points in which I think you could [help] … One is to give us some of Popham's telegraph vocabularies. I am very desirous that the naval code of signals and cyphers should be cut out of these books, in order that no evil should result from their falling into bad hands. I should be very much obliged to you if you could [provide sailors] for each of these [signal] stations I cannot spare officers to go down and learn how to use a telegraph; and I am afraid of the mistakes and blunders, which will result from using them without instruction. Officers … who know something of signals, or sober signal men, one at each station, with one seaman at each, would be a sufficient establishment for the present.[17]

The navy will have been reluctant to supply their code books to the army. The code book was used by every ship in the Royal Navy and the loss of a code book would require the system to be changed across the navy. This had happened as recently as 1803 and led to the introduction of Popham's system. Wellington was clearly trying to address the naval concerns and mitigate the risk by asking for the naval signals be cut out. What was not considered was using the Portuguese telegraph code book which would have been more relevant to land-based operations in Portugal.

There is a further letter from Wellington to Berkeley on 24 June 1810 when in typical Wellington style he goes into great detail on his ideas for the design of the telegraph and the number of people to operate the telegraph stations:

> In respect to the yard, if the gentlemen of the navy will undertake to manage it for us, I have no objection to the yard being placed across the mast, or in any other way they please, but if we *unlearned* are to have anything to do with it, I should wish to have only one arm to the yard and I should think that if the yard was supported by means of two large sized blocks … there would be no difficulty in discovering the numbers intended. Number 2 would be under the block nearest

---

14   TNA: MR1-930-4.
15   Jones, *Sieges*, Vol.3, p.90.
16   AHM: PT-AHM-DIV-1-14-170-07, max distance two and a half Portuguese leagues, approx. 15 kilometres (nine miles).
17   Gurwood, *Dispatches*, Wellington to Berkeley, Celorico, 15 June 1810.

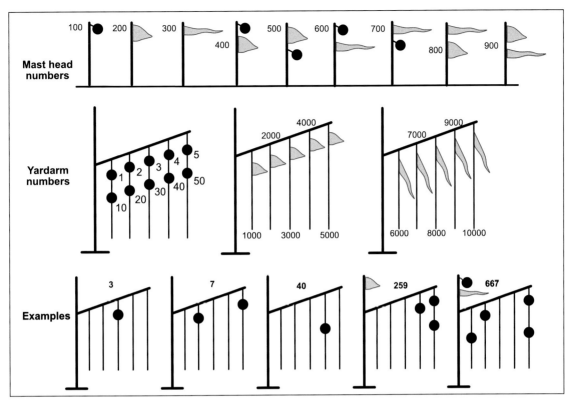

the mast; number 3 between the two blocks; number 4 under the most distant from the mast However upon all this you must be the best judge.

British Telegraph Codes, as described in Wellington's *Supplementary Despatches.*

Wellington continued:

> … the establishment at each station ought to consist of the person to be in charge of the signals, and one or two men to assist him … These officers and men should be paid and treated in every respect as parties from the fleet acting on shore. I write to Colonel Fletcher to request him to let you know what number of stations there are, and where they are and I request you will let him know how many officers or men you will send to each; he will arrange where they are to reside near the signal post and will desire the Commissary at Lisbon to provide for their rations.[18]

The issue of pay for the sailors would become a problem and this will be explained later.

It is surprising that several weeks after the work had commenced to construct the telegraphs, there was still discussion about the basic design of the telegraph. Was the solution being developed by trial and error? The masts had been put up, but at the end of June there was still no clarity on what apparatus was going to be hoisted to the top. Wellington had seen a

---

18   Gurwood, *Dispatches*, Wellington to Berkeley, Celorico, 24 June 1810.

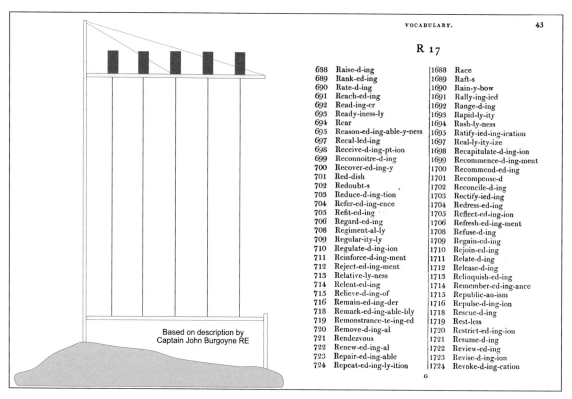

VOCABULARY. 43

R 17

688	Raise-d-ing	1688	Race	
689	Rank-ed-ing	1689	Raft-s	
690	Rate-d-ing	1690	Rain-y-bow	
691	Reach-ed-ing	1691	Rally-ing-ied	
692	Read-ing-er	1692	Range-d-ing	
693	Ready-iness-ly	1693	Rapid-ly-ity	
694	Rear	1694	Rash-ly-ness	
695	Reason-ed-ing-able-y-ness	1695	Ratify-ied-ing-ication	
697	Recal-led-ing	1697	Real-ly-ity-ize	
698	Receive-d-ing-pt-ion	1698	Recapitulate-d-ing-ion	
699	Reconnoitre-d-ing	1699	Recommence-d-ing-ment	
700	Recover-ed-ing-y	1700	Recommend-ed-ing	
701	Red-dish	1701	Recompense-d	
702	Redoubt-s	1702	Reconcile-d-ing	
703	Reduce-d-ing-tion	1703	Rectify-ied-ing	
704	Refer-ed-ing-ence	1704	Redress-ed-ing	
705	Refit-ed-ing	1705	Reflect-ed-ing-ion	
706	Regard-ed-ing	1706	Refresh-ed-ing-ment	
708	Regiment-al-ly	1708	Refuse-d-ing	
709	Regular-ity-ly	1709	Regain-ed-ing	
710	Regulate-d-ing-ion	1710	Rejoin-ed-ing	
711	Reinforce-d-ing-ment	1711	Relate-d-ing	
712	Reject-ed-ing-ment	1712	Release-d-ing	
713	Relative-ly-ness	1713	Relinquish-ed-ing	
714	Relent-ed-ing	1714	Remember-ed-ing-ance	
715	Relieve-d-ing-of	1715	Republic-an-ism	
716	Remain-ed-ing-der	1716	Repulse-d-ing-ion	
718	Remark-ed-ing-able-bly	1718	Rescue-d-ing	
719	Remonstrance-te-ing-ed	1719	Rest-less	
720	Remove-d-ing-al	1720	Restrict-ed-ing-ion	
721	Rendezvous	1721	Resume-d-ing	
722	Renew-ed-ing-al	1722	Review-ed-ing	
723	Repair-ed-ing-able	1723	Revise-d-ing-ion	
724	Repeat-ed-ing-ly-ition	1724	Revoke-d-ing-cation	

G

Based on description by
Captain John Burgoyne RE

Burgoyne's description of the British telegraph and Popham code book.

telegraph with a yard across the mast (i.e. on both sides of mast) in use at Almeida earlier in the year. He had asked for it to be replaced by a Portuguese 'arm' telegraph, although this was probably to standardise equipment and codes rather than a criticism of the effectiveness of the 'yard' telegraph. Also, the Portuguese telegraph was much simpler to construct when the previous telegraph was destroyed by enemy artillery fire.[19]

The Royal Engineer, John Burgoyne, described the design of a British telegraph used on the Lines. This is the only description of an actual mast that could be found: 'This telegraph consists of a mast with halyards and a long yard having five sets of halyards, each marked by a bit of wood fixed over them to make them more distinct at a distance. The whole code of signals are made by two flags … two pendants … and five balls.[20]

Burgoyne's description is similar to what Wellington proposed above, in that each ball position was marked to help the reader determine the position of the ball. The balls were visible from any angle but being able to see flags would be dependent on the wind direction (or lack of wind). Burgoyne's rough sketch shows the yard at an angle from the horizontal, as does one of the two sketches in *Wellington's Dispatches*.[21] It would make much more sense

19   AHM: PT-AHM-DIV-1-14-270-01_m0035 to m0038.

20   REM: 4201-68, Burgoyne Notebook, pp.36–37.

21   Wellington, *Supplementary Despatches*, Vol.6, pp.546–547. This is attached to a letter from Fletcher to Wellington dated 25 June 1810. The letter makes no mention of including details of the telegraph. Like the redoubts 'recently constructed' list on pp.545–546, the note on

for the yard to be horizontal to allow the receiving station to judge the height of the balls. As there were two vertical positions for the balls, a sloping yard would make identification harder.

Mulcaster noted in his diary on 6 July 1810 that he had been told he could not join the army on the frontier until he had 'safely housed the signal men.'[22] He was on his way north a few days' later, so Berkeley had clearly agreed to provide sailors and they had arrived on the Lines. About this time, command of the work on the Lines passed to John Jones when Fletcher rode north to join Wellington's army. Jones' first mention of telegraphs is on 18 July 1810, when he wrote to Fletcher reporting:

> … at every [signal] post I have visited, the sailors in charge say the distance between the stations is too great and that the masts are all too light for the yards – it blew rather hard on Sunday evening and two were [broken], that on Mount Socorro so badly that we were obliged to replace it. I shall … see Mr Leith the [Naval] lieutenant in charge of the signals and obtain his ideas as to a new construction and in the meantime, I have ordered stronger masts and yards to be prepared for each post. To render the Ponte do Rol signal visible we are now employed cutting away that angle of the pine wood which at present forms its background. The navy complain of the quality of the telescopes. If better can be [bought] in Lisbon I shall not hesitate in authorising the purchase of them. I write these observations previous to seeing Mr Leith. I hope to meet him tomorrow evening or the following morning.[23]

Jones also visited Rear Admiral Berkeley who told him that Leith had made no complaints about the masts, so 'whatever the officers at the different posts may think, Lieutenant Leith had not judged it necessary to say anything officially against them.'[24] Fletcher replied:

> I am sorry to hear so bad an account of the signal posts. We thought at the time of erecting them that from any one of them to the next nearest, the balls would be very visible, and this seemed to be the opinion of Mr Davie the officer who put them up. I … believe the principal fault lies in the telescopes and I feel confident that there will be no objection to you purchasing others of a better description, if you can find them.[25]

On 1 August 1810, Jones reported 'I witnessed the passing of intelligence in two minutes from Alhandra to Mafra by our chain of posts, so that now I have no fear of their answering when the weather is [?] clear'. A week later,

---

telegraphs could also be misplaced. The telegraph sketch Wellington had sent to Berkeley the previous day, does not match the design shown here and the yard is horizontal. Gurwood, *Dispatches*, Wellington to Berkeley, 24 June 1810. Note: This letter is only in the original edition of *Dispatches*.

22 Thompson, *Mulcaster*, p.110.
23 REM: 5501-59-18, Jones to Fletcher, Lisbon, 18 July 1810.
24 REM: 5501-59-18, Jones to Fletcher, Lisbon, 20 July 1810.
25 REM: 5501-59-18, Fletcher to Jones, 23 July 1810. The full letter is not printed in Jones, *Sieges*, Vol.3, p.226.

Jones confirmed 'Lieutenant Leith has the book of signals. The [signal] posts as far as I can judge answer very well.'[26]

As there is no contemporary commentary on how the telegraphs were operated on the Lines, we have to conjecture. Recent investigation by Portuguese historians proposed that the British telegraphs were used in a ring format where all messages were passed around all telegraph stations.[27] There are issues with this proposal particularly as some of the telegraph stations at the western (Atlantic) end of the ring could not see each other. Fort 30 (Grilo) to 91 (Alagoa) and also 91 to 97 (São Julião) were blocked by intervening hills. For this reason and others mentioned below, Jones' claim of a two-minute transmission time if the message was passed round all the telegraphs seems unlikely if not impossible.

As mentioned above, there is no conclusive evidence that the telegraph was mounted in Fort 91. There are conflicting accounts of it being sited in 91, 92 (Picoto), 93 (Marvão) or 94 (Ribamar). We know that Jones had received orders to move the telegraph from the 'Picanceira redoubt', either Fort 89 (Moxarro) or 90 (Penegache), to Marvão.[28] The order did not mention a redoubt when specifying Marvão. One contemporary map shows the Marvão telegraph in Marvão village, which is the highest point in the area, and this makes more sense than being in Forts 91–93.[29] Forts 89 and 90 could see Fort 30 on the first line, but none of those to the west (91–94) could. So, moving the telegraph to 'Marvão' would make a ring network even more unlikely and means that the move was for another reason. It is probable that the telegraph stations on the Atlantic coast served a different purpose. Their role may have been to watch for any French advance along the coastal paths and send warning. Fort 97 (São Julião), according to Mulcaster, was placed to watch the ford over the mouth of the Lizandro river.[30] If the role of the telegraph near Marvão was also to monitor the crossing points at the mouth of the Safarujo river, then the high point at Marvão or Forts 93 or 94 was the correct place. Also, it would explain why the telegraph was moved from Picanceira to 'Marvão', otherwise, if an enemy force approached the mouth of the Safarujo river, a messenger would need to travel some miles east to get to the nearest telegraph. For the same purpose, Fort 30 (Grilo) could also see the course of the Sizandro river from Torres Vedras all the way to the coast.

Another possible use of the coastal telegraphs at Marvão and Fort 97 was communication with offshore naval vessels. Part of Wellington's request for naval support was to have vessels off the coast to dissuade any advance along the coast by land or sea. A naval vessel would have no difficulty reading the signals and they were using the same code book. Berkeley had set up a system like this when he commanded the Sea Fencibles in Sussex in 1798.

---

26   REM: 5501-58-18, Jones to Fletcher, Lisbon, 1 & 8 August 1810.

27   Luna, et al, *Boletim*, p.118. Rui Sá Leal, one of the authors who has operated the replica telegraph told the present author that reading the signal with a tripod-mounted telescope was hard. If the telescope had to be moved or it was windy, it was even more difficult.

28   REM: 5501-59-18, 11 September 1810,

29   TNA: MR-1-930-4.

30   Thompson, *Mulcaster*, p.106.

A final benefit of positioning the Marvão telegraph in the village was because there would be a straight line to Fort 76 (Sonível) and on to the telegraph at Montachique. Having the telegraphs in a straight line was very important as we shall see.

There could be occasions when a message would need to go to all stations, such as a general warning of an attack, but in most cases a message could be directed to the nearest telegraph to the recipient, such as Wellington at Sobral or Hill at Alhandra. Wellington's General Order of 13 October 1810, stating that 'messages for Headquarters to be sent to the Sobral station' (Forte do Alqueidão) infers that messaging a specific location was possible.[31]

The biggest concern about messages going round all the signal stations, is the number of telegraph masts that would have to turn to reach the next point on the ring. The nature of the telegraphs required them to face each other with minimal offset, otherwise the signal could not be read. To go round all the telegraphs would require five or six telegraphs to turn. Turning a telegraph accurately would be a slow process and would need a telescope for each direction as the telescopes needed to be large, mounted on a sturdy tripod and accurately aligned. Continually swinging from one target to another would make reading signals even harder. Wind, disturbing the telescopes would be as problematic for reading signals as rain, fog or darkness.

The next problem with turning was that each message was made up of more than one number. Each telegraph that had to turn, would need to collect the whole message, turn and then retransmit the whole message. This would significantly slow down transmissions. Short signals would be vital.

The final problem with turning was the need to validate the message. On many systems, for example the Chappe system, the receiving station repeated each number to confirm they had received it correctly. Only then would the sending station transmit the next number element. It is not clear on the Lines if the receiving station repeated each number back to the sending station. The only mention found suggesting this happened is by Jean Jacques Pelet, Masséna's aide de camp, who observed that messages were repeated by the receiving station, but perhaps he is not the best judge.[32] There is not a clear instruction for repetition for the Popham codes, as used at sea. The Popham system generally did not repeat each message back to the sending ship. There were two responses to a message; 'message received' (affirmative flag) or 'message not understood' (affirmative and No.8 flags). According to the Popham telegraph book, the signal was kept up until it was repeated 'by ships in succession'.[33] The receiver could ask for the message to be repeated 'in cases of doubt'. There was a significant difference between the system used at sea and used on the Lines. On a ship, the whole message could be put up at once using different positions on the masts. This could not be done on land. If the message was not repeated, and the affirmative flag was used instead, the affirmative flag could be flown from the mast head and the mast would not

31   Gurwood, *Dispatches*, General Order, Rinho, near Sobral, 13 October 1810.
32   Howard, *Pelet*, p.233
33   Home Popham, *Telegraphic Signals or Marine Vocabulary* (London: Egerton, 1803), p.6.

need to be turned. It is unlikely that Wellington would have accepted this; the accuracy of the message was more important than the speed. This appears to be confirmed by a comment in the altered Popham Code books that the signal was not taken down until the next station repeats it.[34]

Without turning, there were three groups of telegraphs that could see each other in a straight line: on the first line, 118 (Sinais), 14 (Alqueidão) and Socorro; on the second line, Montachique, 76 (Sonível), and Marvão. Between the Lines, 30 (Grilo), 80 (Boa Viagem) and 76 were also in a straight line. On the first Line, Socorro would need to turn to communicate with Fort 21 at Torres Vedras. Similarly, 21 would need to rotate to communicate with Fort 30.

Jones does not mention a telegraph at the eastern end of the second line in his description of the telegraphs, which is surprising as it was an important position and there was a letter to him discussing a telegraph at that location. It is likely that that the remains of the Portuguese national telegraph system on the Serra de Serves would have been re-used. It was nearly in line with the other three telegraphs on the second line and could also see Fort 118 (Sinais) at the eastern end of the first line. A separate telegraph from Monsanto communicated with the telegraph on Serra de Serves (although there would need to be an intermediate telegraph station as Monsanto and Serves are about 20 kilometres apart). Sousa Lobo's recent work on the Lines supports the principle of a connection to Lisbon, although he suggests using different stations:

> The best equipped telegraph station, and communications 'node' to the rear, was the Serra do Socorro. From here it communicated to the south, with the 2nd Line, to the post installed on the Serra de Montachique; to the east was the post of Serra de Serves and to the west was Tapada de Mafra, at Fort 76 Sonível and Fort 92 Ribamar [92 is Picoto, 94 is Ribamar]. Montachique communicated with Castelo de S. Jorge, further south, through the signal posts of Serves and Monsanto.[35]

The distance from Socorro to Montachique is on the limit of visibility at 14 kilometres. It would be more reliable to send messages from Socorro to 76, or from 14 to Montachique, both distances being shorter. A third alternative comes from Jones who wrote that messages to Lisbon went from Fort 76, at Mafra to Monsanto via Sabugo.[36] This would have used the Portuguese telegraph system that was originally installed to allow communication between the palace at Mafra and Lisbon.

If it is assumed that the telegraphs at Fort 30, Marvão and 97 were primarily for communicating warning of an enemy advance along the coast, then a smaller ring transmission was possible using 118, 14, Socorro, 21, 30, 80, 76, Montachique, Serves and back to 118. The coastal telegraph's primary role was to send messages, not receive or relay them. Oman comments that a signal could be sent from the main station (probably Socorro) to either end

---

34   WP: 9/4/1/3&4, Popham code books in Wellington Archives.
35   Sousa Lobo, *Defesa*, p.235, author's translation.
36   REM: 5501-59-18, 20 July 1810.

of the first Line in four minutes. This again suggests that a ring system was not the only option.[37]

Although Socorro is seen as the primary telegraph station, it makes more sense for Fort 14 (Alqueidão) to have taken this role. It was where Wellington started every day, it was not much further from his headquarters at Pero Negro, and it was heavily defended. Socorro was undefended.

The complexity of the messages inferred by the Popham and Ciera code books were not representative of the messages that were actually sent. On the occasions where we know something about the codes used in allied telegraphs, a small set of codes were used to create messages that were relevant to the situation. The Ciera code book held by the Portuguese Marine Archives has many handwritten entries for people and places, after the main printed Portuguese vocabulary.[38] For example, Lord Wellington was 66343 and Torres Vedras was 66631. These additions will have avoided having to spell out words or phrases. At Almeida, earlier in 1810, there were codes that related to specific messages. For example, 'How many days provisions have you?' – code 9 – or, 'Can you hold out X days longer?' – code 13. The number of days would be given in the second number transmitted. In the Pyrenees in 1813, where a different mast and yard system were used, specific codes were given to units and actions.[39] For example, the message 'the 2nd Division to move to Cambo' could be created with four numbers, 504, 529, 510, 41; '2nd Division' – code 504 – 'to move to' – code 529 – 'Cambo' – code 510, a location, followed by the specific location, code 41, Cambo. Of more significance is that this 1813 telegraph system used the Popham code book. Original copies are held in the Wellington Archives and contain numerous entries for places on the Lines of Torres Vedras, places in Spain, Portugal and army units.[40] Places in the Pyrenees were added by hand after the Lines entries. This will almost certainly be the codes that were developed for initial use on the Lines of Torres Vedras. Jones inferred that this was the case; 'many sentences and short expressions peculiar to the land service being added.'[41] The Popham code books in the Wellington Archives are hand written and contain 'Lines' specific codes which are different from the standard Popham codes, e.g. 890 was 'Torres Vedras' as opposed to 'therefore'. This infers that the code book was partially rewritten whilst the physical telegraphs used the naval design.

The notes in Popham's code book help to determine how the system might have operated. The start of message code was a single flag at the top of the mast. This was left in place until it was copied all the way along the line, that is, to alert all the stations. Similarly, the 'start message' code in the Pyrenees in 1813 was number 500, a single flag. Something similar would have been used on the Lines. Each successive code was left in place until the next station had repeated the code. The description is clear, that the

37   Oman, *Peninsular War*, Vol.3, p.435. No source for the statement is provided.
38   Arquivo Central da Marinha (ACM): 1305-12.
39   WP: 9/4/1/7.
40   WP: 9/4/1/3&4.
41   Jones, *Sieges*, Vol.3, p.90.

message was cascaded down the line, one number at a time and the number was confirmed before the next number was sent. If the telegraphs were in straight line, then the message could be cascaded up the line one number at a time, which was the fastest method. If telegraphs had to be turned to pass on the message to the next signal station, the whole message would have to be collected before it could be passed on. This is almost certainly how the system would have operated on the Lines. It would also make sense if each telegraph station had the ability to direct a message to a particular location. This would save time and much unnecessary signalling if the destination of the message was known, and telegraphs were turned to use the most effective route to the destination.

However, solving the technical problems for the construction and messaging of the telegraphs was not the biggest problem Wellington faced in establishing his communication system.

Problems with the Sailors

At the beginning of September 1810, Wellington was faced with an unexpected problem. Berkeley had written to him asking for additional allowances for the sailors who were operating the telegraphs and threatening to withdraw them if they were not provided. Normally, officers received *bât* and forage money; the men, pay and allowances, both appropriate to the equivalent army ranks at the time.[42] Wellington replied that:

> The difficulty … [is not in] giving the officers and seamen additional rations …
> So much as in creating a precedent by the grant of this allowance … which may
> be very inconvenient to the service here after.[43]

Wellington said if the Admiral felt he had to withdraw the sailors, he would 'try to arrange to manage our signals without the assistance of these officers and men.' Berkeley had also written in July and August. Wellington in his letter of 2 September acknowledged that he had not replied to Berkeley's earlier letter because he 'felt considerable embarrassment upon the subject', probably because he could not agree to the extra allowances (even if he was sympathetic to the claim). Berkeley's September letter possibly was the first to contain the threat to remove the sailors.[44] This could not have come at a worse time as Wellington knew he would be retreating towards the Lines in the next few weeks. The discussion continued and Wellington wrote again to Berkeley:

> … there are several officers in this army [including] the Commissary General;
> and they all declare that they do not recollect one instance of the officers and
> seamen and marines having any additional allowance, either of provisions or pay,

---

42   TNA: ADM 1/4333, 23 January 1799. Thanks to Nicholas Blake for this info.
43   Gurwood, *Dispatches*, Wellington to Berkeley, Celorico, 2 September 1810.
44   De Toy, *Berkeley*, pp.502–503.

upon such service, [other than] *bât* and forage for the officers, or the allowance of Brigadier Generals for the Captains.[45]

Wellington continued saying he would write to the Secretary of State for a decision as he had no authority to alter the rates of pay or allowances.[46] It is inconceivable that the situation could be so serious that even after Wellington said he would seek guidance, Berkeley would remove his sailors at such a critical moment. Despite Wellington's assurances that he would seek advice, Berkeley ordered his sailors to leave on 12 September, as De Toy quotes Berkeley:

'... my desire of co-operating ... makes me very loathe to deprive you of a man of any description from the army ... but it appears really too great a hardship upon the sailor' ... [H]aving made his point, Berkeley did not keep the men from the signal posts too long. On the approach of the French and the allied army's occupation of the Lines, Berkeley sent the seamen back.[47]

It was about four weeks before Berkeley returned his sailors. He forced Wellington at short notice to arrange construction of an alternate telegraph system and train new operators as he was retreating towards Lisbon. This alternate system was still not ready two days before he arrived, was untested, and he was extremely worried about the situation. If as De Toy suggests, 'cooperation proved more important than a payment principle' then Berkeley should have left the sailors on the Lines whilst an answer was sought from London rather than forcing Wellington into a task that wasted a large amount of time and resources and put his whole defensive strategy at risk.

Following the threat from Berkeley, on 7 September 1810, Jones was asked to arrange for Portuguese militia to take charge of the signal stations vacated by the British sailors. Realising that there was no one who could operate the complex British telegraphs, Jones was ordered:

In consequence of the Admiral having decided to withdraw the navy from the signal posts, Lord Wellington thinks we had better use the simple sort of Portuguese telegraph which we now employ here. It is a mere upright with an arm, to one end of which is attached a light frame bound with black cloth, and to the other a piece of board about 15 to 18 inches square. I send you a sketch of the sort of thing with the dimensions, and I request you will have the goodness to get one made for each post as soon as possible, and have it carried to the spot where it can be put up in a few minutes. It is [secured by cords?] in the way of those of a tent. The length of each [joint?] is eight feet so that three give twenty-four feet in all. Perhaps it may not be necessary as you will be stationary to have them in joints, though if they were so, they would possess the advantage of being portable

---

45 Gurwood, *Dispatches*, Wellington to Berkeley, 9 September 1810.

46 It would appear that Wellington did not write until 19 October. Perhaps fighting the French was more important in the short term. Gurwood, *Dispatches*, Wellington to Liverpool, Pero Negro, 19 October 1810.

47 De Toy, *Berkeley*, pp.502–503.

in case it should become advisable to move them from one point to another. The men who work them are old seamen who have been examined for the purpose, I should think it would not be difficult to procure a number of these men at Lisbon … As we mean to use the books of Popham's code with these [telegraphs] … it would be desirable that the books now in the possession of Lieut. Leith should be turned over to you on his quitting the charge … The telegraph of which you have a sketch turns on the pivot which attaches it to the post and the different angles it makes marks the numbers.[48]

Fletcher's detailed description would suggest that Jones had not previously seen one of the Portuguese telegraphs. The original Ciera diagrams for the telegraph and the modern replica use a shaped arm, whist the specification above and the one used at Almeida talk about a black square. the black square being much easier to build and also having a larger surface area would be easier to read. Jones completely misrepresents the reason for the installation of the Portuguese telegraphs, saying they were 'placed at each post in readiness to be used in the event of any disaster occurring' to the British telegraphs.[49] They were constructed because of the removal of the Royal Navy signalmen and were not interchangeable with the British telegraphs.

Many seamen and *Corpo Telegrafico* soldiers were probably unemployed due to the Portuguese telegraph system being dismantled on the advance of the French. The telegraphs to Abrantes, Elvas and Almeida had been destroyed and there would have been many signallers without a job. Wellington said that 'old Portuguese seamen' had been operating the telegraphs on the Portuguese border earlier in 1810 and could also be used on the Lines. This would seem an excellent compromise as they would be familiar with the principles of naval signalling.

Jones replied immediately expressing his concerns:

The taking away the seamen from the signal posts will be a misfortune as they have just become thoroughly expert at passing the signals, and they now make the posts there answer admirably well. I think a N.C. Officer and two privates might be selected for each post whom we could instruct to pass the signals. I do not think we could ever teach Portuguese and even with soldiers I fear we shall never become very expert.[50]

This was quite insulting and would suggest that Jones did not know much about the Portuguese telegraphs. The Portuguese had a national telegraph system and a telegraph corps; the British had neither! On 18 September 1810, Jones reported that 'workmen are employed constructing the portable telegraphs ordered to be fixed up near the site of the present signal masts.' In the same letter he noted he had been promised Portuguese guards for the telegraphs.[51] By this date, Wellington had started his retreat from the border.

---

48   REM: 5501-59-18, Fletcher to Jones, Gouveia, 11 September 1810.
49   Jones, *Sieges*, Vol.3, p.26.
50   REM: 5501-59-18, Jones to Fletcher, Lisbon, 12 September 1810.
51   REM: 5501-59-18, Jones to Fletcher, 18 September 1810.

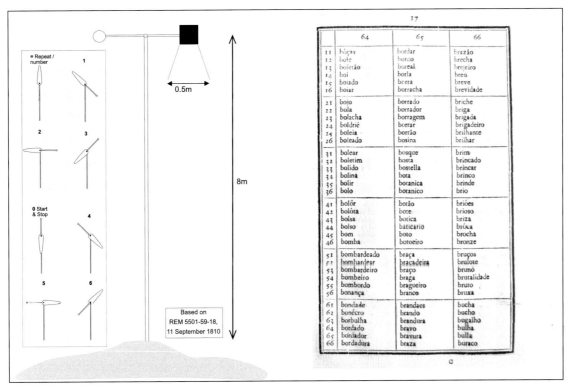

	64	65	66
11	bôças	bordar	brazão
12	bote	bordo	brecha
13	boletão	boreal	brejeiro
14	boi	borla	brea
15	boiado	borra	breve
16	boiar	borracha	brevidade
21	bojo	borrado	briche
22	bola	borrador	briga
23	bolacha	borragem	brigada
24	boldrié	borrar	brigadeiro
25	boleia	borrão	brilhante
26	boleado	bosina	brilhar
31	bolear	bosque	brim
32	boletim	bosta	brincado
33	bolido	bostella	brincar
34	bolina	bota	brinco
35	bolir	botanica	brinde
36	bolo	botanico	brio
41	bolôr	botão	briões
42	bolóta	bote	brioso
43	bolsa	botica	briza
44	bolso	baticario	brôca
45	bom	boto	brocha
46	bomba	botoeiro	bronze
51	bombardeado	braça	bruços
52	bombardear	braçadeira	brulote
53	bombardeiro	braço	brunó
54	bombeiro	braga	brutalidade
55	bombordo	bragueiro	bruto
56	bonança	branco	bruxa
61	bondade	brandaes	bucha
62	bonécro	brando	bucho
63	borbulha	brandura	bugalho
64	bordado	bravo	bulha
65	bordador	bravura	bulla
66	bordadura	braza	buraco

17

Portuguese arm telegraph.

There were two issues in quickly moving to the Ciera telegraph. First was visibility. There was no guarantee that the signals could be seen at the same distances. Some trials would be needed to confirm that messages could be read. If not, the size of the arm could be increased to improve visibility. One source said that the telegraph used at Abrantes on the national network was about 1 metre square rather than the ½ metre square suggested above.[52] This would of course require all the components to be more substantial. Secondly, you could not 'easily' use the Popham code book with the Portuguese telegraph. This does not appear to have been considered. Wellington should have understood this issue as he had used Portuguese telegraphs on the border in the summer of 1810. The Ciera code book could be used on both telegraph systems easier than the Popham code book could. The Popham codes on the Portuguese telegraph was the worst solution.

As an example, in the Popham code book, number 81 (attack) would be: =, 2, 1, 3 on the Portuguese telegraph (without start/stop codes). The number on the British telegraph mast could be shown in one instance; on the Portuguese telegraph, it would take six instances (including start/stop signals). As numbers got larger, the number of operations on the Portuguese telegraph increased. The number 1105 would still require one instance on the British telegraph and 14 on the Portuguese telegraph (including start/stop signals). Using the Portuguese telegraph code book rather than Popham's would have been quicker, requiring only five instances.

---

52   José Manuel Viera, Abrantes Militar 1810 Capitulo V, <https://coisasdeabrantes.blogspot.com/2017/06/>, accessed 3 November 2020.

119

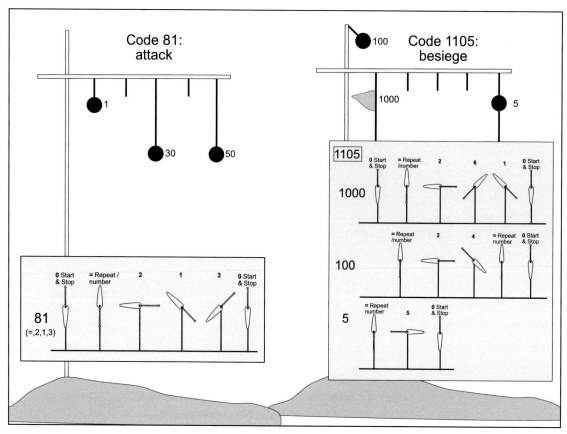

British and Portuguese telegraph number examples.

Wellington remained very concerned about the situation as he retreated to the Lines. His whole strategy for defending the Lines required fast signalling to be available as he planned to concentrate his army behind the Lines and quickly move them to counter any French attack.

As late as 5 October 1810, Jones was reporting 'the new telegraphs are not yet quite finished, but I expect tomorrow to have sufficient for the front line sent out.'[53] Clearly the sailors had not yet returned as this work continued. The first elements of the army arrived on 7 October and the bulk entered the Lines just two days later on 9 October 1810. Although it is not documented, it appears that Wellington and Berkeley reached some arrangement about the use of sailors on the telegraphs, perhaps common-sense prevailing in agreeing to their use pending a decision from London on extra allowances. Wellington, when writing to Liverpool asking for directions on 19 October, commented that the sailors had been removed but were returned after the army arrived in the Lines.[54] A General Order dated 13 October 1810, stated that: 'When any officer [wants to send] a message to the Commander of the Forces, it is only necessary to send it to the nearest telegraph and to request the *officer of the Navy* [author's italics] at that telegraph to communicate it

53 REM: 5501-59-18, Jones to Fletcher, Lisbon, 5 October 1810.
54 Gurwood, *Dispatches*, Wellington to Liverpool, Pero Negro, 19 October 1810.

to the Sobral station.' This statement also suggests that message could be directed to a particular location rather than being sent to all telegraphs.

Whilst the signalling on the Lines was a great success, the argument between Wellington and Berkeley was unnecessary and created great risk. Wellington did not get an answer on the request for extra allowances until December 1810. The amount agreed with Berkeley was 10s daily for lieutenants, 6s for midshipmen and 1s for sailors, a very generous allowance which was more than their normal daily pay.[55]

The success of the telegraphs on the Lines was summed up by one officer: '[The French] cannot give the least move but that we know it in the course of 15 minutes by telegraph, which we have in all directions. Whenever they think of moving, we know it directly.'[56]

When worked started on the fourth line of defences in December 1810 plans were made to extend the telegraph system south of the Tagus. In January 1811, 11 Portuguese telegraphs were ordered to be constructed for the south bank. The distance across the Tagus was short and communication across the river near Lisbon would not be a problem.

There is one final point that needs dealing with, the telegraph at Fort 128, Archeira. This telegraph was started after the allies arrived on the Lines in October 1810. There are two possible reasons for its construction. First to replace the telegraph on Mount Socorro just two kilometres south of 128, or second, to improve visibility to the front allowing faster communication of the French movements. Whilst Socorro was seen as the hub of the communication system as discussed above, its role appeared diminished when Wellington chose to base himself at Fort 14 (Alqueidão). Socorro's value would depend on whether Socorro or Alqueidão was being used to send messages south. If Alqueidão was being used, then Socorro became redundant. If Socorro was used as the hub, then the whole system was at risk as Socorro was not defended. The telegraph at 128 was protected by a substantial fort (500 men) and had the benefit of being able to see further into enemy territory. This new fort could see the telegraphs at Socorro, Alqueidão and Torres Vedras. Whilst the communication system was not used long enough to understand how it was originally intended to work, it is likely that the construction of Fort 128 and Wellington's decision to use Alqueidão as his base, reduced the value of Socorro, to a point where it could have been discarded and Fort 128 communicated directly with Forts 14 and 21.

Summary

The development and construction of the telegraphs on the Lines of Torres Vedras was a significant undertaking involving British and Portuguese engineers, and the Royal Navy. The perfecting of the solution took many months and could never be considered more than a partial solution. Bad

---

55   Sutcliffe, *Expeditionary Warfare*, pp.136–137. The citations do not show the allowances.

56   Andrew Bamford, *With Wellington Outposts, The Peninsular War Letters of John Vandeleur* (Barnsley: Frontline, 2015), p.39, Alcoentre, January 1811.

weather and darkness meant it could never be relied on. Generally, a rider was also sent with the same message to ensure it got through. When the telegraph was working it could save time; time that could be critical in getting troops to where they were needed. The only mention of their use is found in a letter from Wellington to Hill on 15 October 1810 when he advises Hill to 'Keep an officer at the signal post, and I will send you the orders by signal, as well as by message.'[57]

The Lines were only occupied for about six weeks. After that, the telegraphs would not be used again. In the same way that the Lines were not tested by the French, neither was the communication system's efficiency. However, in different circumstances, the telegraph system could have been vital in supporting the defence of the Lines.

---

57   Gurwood, *Dispatches*, Wellington to Hill, Ajuda, 15 October 1810.

9

The Campaign of 1810

Wellington's decision to build the Lines of Torres Vedras was based on his belief that there would be a powerful French Invasion of Portugal in 1810. What he was not sure about was when this would happen. The initial planning of the construction of the Lines was based on the worst-case scenario that the French would invade in Spring 1810, so quickly getting some basic defences in place was essential. The role of the army would be to delay the French advance, giving more time for the construction of defences. Wellington had discounted any possibility of defending the Portuguese frontier, it was too long and there were too many possible routes. In addition, moving between the various entry points was next to impossible due to the mountainous terrain and lack of good roads north to south. Wellington's army was not large enough to defend all the possible entry points, so decisions would have to be made on the most likely routes. If Wellington was wrong, then roads to Lisbon would be open to the invaders. One engineer officer commented: 'The Emperor is about to cross once more the Pyrenees, to restore tranquillity and happiness in the Peninsula. I suspect we shall be sent or driven home soon enough.'[1] This view was widespread. Ensign John Aitchison also remarked 'They say Bonaparte himself is to come into Spain with reinforcements.'[2]

The end of 1809 saw the Allied army moving from Badajoz back into Portugal, and in January 1810, Wellington moved his Headquarters to northern Portugal with Craufurd's light troops being pushed forward to the Spanish frontier. The two most likely invasion routes were from the north through Almeida, or from the south by Elvas. The most probable was from the north, as this would be the direct route from France where the reinforcements were coming from. The southern route would require crossing the Tagus. As previously mentioned, Napoleon delegated command to Masséna and this change in leadership lost any opportunity for a quick invasion. Masséna was not appointed until 17 April 1810 and was in no hurry to embark on this new challenge.[3] Of more significance was Napoleon's decision to not appoint a commander in chief in Spain. Napoleon could command obedience from his

1   REM: 4601-74, Mulcaster to Burgoyne, Torres Vedras, 2 January 1810.
2   W.F.K. Thompson, *An Ensign in the Peninsular War* (London: Michael Joseph, 1981), p.67.
3   Oman, *Peninsular War*, Vol.3, pp.199 & 212.

marshals; Masséna did not have that authority and one of the main reasons for his failure was the lack of co-ordination and co-operation from the other French forces. Masséna's subordinates included *Maréchal* Ney, *Maréchal* Soult and *Général de division* Junot. All headstrong, with opinions about their own capabilities and the weaknesses of their colleagues. Junot had led the French into Portugal in 1807 and believed that he should have had command of the new invasion.[4] He did not appear to share his knowledge from the previous campaign with his new commander.

Napoleon's planning for the third invasion started immediately after signing the peace treaty with Austria in July 1809. A proposal for Soult to invade in Autumn 1809 was rejected, with Napoleon preferring to wait for the reinforcements that were now available but would not arrive for some months. The original timescale involved an army of 100,000 troops including elements of the Imperial Guard concentrating in northern Spain in early 1810.[5] This force would not be ready until March 1810. The decision to delegate command meant further delays to the operation.

In February 1810, *Maréchal* Michel Ney advanced to Ciudad Rodrigo and summoned the town on the 13th. He had no siege equipment with him, but he hoped that the Spanish would surrender when threatened by a substantial force. The governor rejected the demand and Ney withdrew to Salamanca. Whilst this advance had little chance of success, it did worry Wellington who thought it could be the start of an early French advance on Portugal. There was certainly an increased urgency in the construction of the Lines. February saw the start of defensive work away from the three key sites of São Julião, Torres Vedras and Sobral. Through his intelligence network, Wellington was likely to have known about the concentration and advance of Ney before he received information about Ney's summons of Ciudad Rodrigo.

The campaign started without Masséna who did not arrive at Salamanca until 28 May 1810. Napoleon ordered Ciudad Rodrigo and Almeida to be taken before the invasion could start and there was no expectation that this would happen before the autumn of 1810. Would the French have hurried if they had known about the plan for defending Lisbon? Realistically, at this time, there was no evidence of a plan for extensive defences north of Lisbon. Up to the end of February 1810, there was some sporadic work to build defences on the city boundary and the three sites mentioned above. If Napoleon had sources of intelligence near Lisbon, he may have noticed an increase in the construction of defensive works in March 1810. There was almost certainly still not enough information to determine that substantial defensive lines were being built. The fact that Wellington was not near Lisbon could also have distracted their attention. Thiébault, the French general and historian, claimed he recommended that Masséna should have invaded as Junot did in 1807, with forced marches from the border to Lisbon, allowing nothing to slow the march.[6] He may have been right, but the way the campaign

---

4   Oman, *Peninsular War,* Vol.3, pp.197–198.
5   Oman, *Peninsular War,* Vol.3, p.209.
6   Arthur Butler, *The Memoirs of Baron Marbot* (Felling: Worley, 1994), Vol.2, p.308.

was organised meant this was never an option. It would have required the collection of vast stores of food and transport to feed the larger army.

Oman suggested a number of reasons why the Emperor was 'methodical' in his planning and concluded that he wanted to ensure the British were crushed and that there would not be a third failure following the evictions of Junot in 1808 and Soult in 1809.[7] Oman also alluded to the need for the French to collect supplies for the invasion, although a common criticism of Masséna's invasion was his failure to do that. Masséna must have been aware of the likely supply issues as it had been a problem for Junot in 1807, and Ney when he was operating in the border region in 1809–10. Kenton White's recent book shows that Masséna did collect substantial *depôts* before starting his invasion, but these would not last long.[8]

There was no significant French activity until the end of April 1810, when Ciudad Rodrigo was formerly invested. The scarcity of animals meant it had taken months to bring the siege train forward. Despite pleas from the governor, Andrés Pérez de Herrasti, for Wellington to lift the blockade, no action was taken. Wellington was not strong enough to attack this new French Army, as it was nearly 140,000 strong.[9] By the time Masséna had assigned garrisons and supporting forces, the invasion force would be about 65,000 and this was not enough. However, Napoleon believed this was sufficient to defeat 30,000 British. He continued to believe that the Portuguese army was worthless. Wellington's original plan was not to try to stop the French at the border and he stuck to this strategy. Whilst a victory over the French would temporarily delay an invasion, another invasion would follow. If Wellington lost the battle, Portugal would certainly be lost.

Following Herrasti's refusal to surrender, the French commenced a regular siege, opening their first trench on 15 June. Masséna remained in Salamanca with control of the siege delegated to Ney. The guns opened on 25 June 1810.

At the end of May, Burgoyne was ordered to repair the fort of La Concepción located between Almeida and Ciudad Rodrigo. Three days later, he was ordered to prepare mines to destroy the fort even as he completed the repairs. Wellington realised that he did not want the repaired fort falling into French hands, and also any troops left to defend it would be lost. Wellington knew he was going to retreat, whilst the French did not. Being seen to be repairing Fort Concepción meant the French did not know what his intentions were. Destroying it would have told the French he did not intend to defend the frontier. Wellington's planning for the invasion included surveying the routes for retreat and identifying choke points where the French could be delayed.

The siege of Ciudad Rodrigo dragged on until 10 July 1810, when Herrasti surrendered just before the French launched an assault through the breach. The French had lost 10 weeks before the fortress, in part due to the strong

---

7 Oman, *Peninsular War*, Vol.3, p.229.
8 White, *Key to Lisbon*, pp.79–80
9 Oman, *Peninsular War*, Vol.3, pp.200–206. By September 1810, there were 350,000 French troops in the Iberian Peninsula.

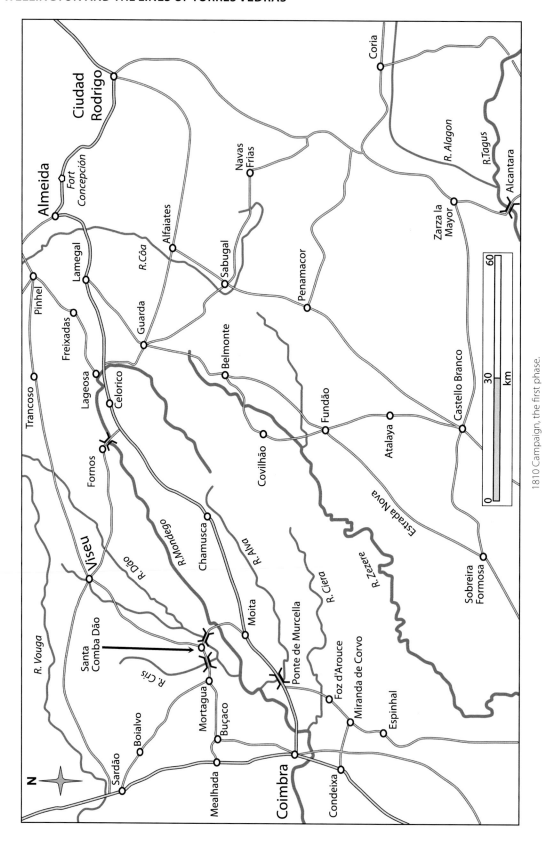

1810 Campaign, the first phase.

defence put up by the governor and his defending troops. They could have done no more.

The invasion was then further delayed as the French collected supplies. Both food and transport resources had been severely reduced during the siege and replenishment was needed before the attack on Almeida could begin. A strong reconnaissance by the French on 21 July 1810, had led to Fort Concepción being blown up. Craufurd's effective screening of the border area came to an abrupt end when the whole French VI Corps, 24,000 strong, advanced on 24 July 1810 and surprised the Light Division, catching them on the eastern side of the Côa river, in front of Almeida. Craufurd was forced to rapidly retreat across the river over the single small bridge, suffering over 300 casualties as a result. It could have been much worse for the overwhelmed allied defenders. Wellington, who had been suggesting to Craufurd that he should withdraw to the western bank of the Côa river, was not happy. The beginning of August saw a lull in operations as the French waited for new siege supplies.

Wellington, as on the Lines of Torres Vedras, ordered several telegraphs to be built in the border area to allow rapid communication. Telegraphs were constructed at several places including Almeida, Celorico da Beira and Guarda. Mulcaster noted that he had been ordered to 'construct a telegraph on the Lisbon principle.'[10]

Wellington was concerned about the delay in starting the siege of Almeida. Were the French planning to blockade Almeida and march directly on Portugal? Writing to Hill on 27 July, he said the French 'will make a dash at us' (Lisbon).[11] Two days later, Fletcher, who was now with the army, wrote to John Jones, who had been left in charge of completion of the Lines of Torres Vedras, informing him that the withdrawal had commenced, and the forts should be made ready for immediate occupation. Because many of the forts were not complete, Fletcher specified a minimum of blocking the entrances, preparing the magazines and making the parapets ready for muskets. Wellington continued to delay creating the abatis as this would require the destruction many thousand cork and olive trees.[12] It was over two weeks before Wellington's concerns about an immediate advance were proved false, when the French started the siege. However, most of the forts that would be ready when the French arrived in early October had been started and many were complete. Even if the French had made 'a dash' after taking Ciudad Rodrigo, the defences at Lisbon would already be formidable.

The French opened the trenches in front of Almeida on 15 August 1810 and the batteries were ready on 25 August 1810. Then disaster struck when a French shell lit a trail of gunpowder which led to the main magazine, resulting in an explosion that destroyed a large portion of the town and left the governor with no option but to surrender on 27 August 1810. Wellington's hope that Almeida could hold out until the autumn had been ruined. Fletcher

---

10   Thompson, *Mulcaster*, 8 August 1810.

11   Gurwood, *Dispatches*, Wellington to Hill, Alverca, 27 July 1810.

12   Jones, *Sieges*, Vol.3, pp.226–227 also REM: 5501-59-18, Fletcher to Jones, Celorico, 27 July 1810.

immediately informed Jones in Lisbon and on 31 August 1810, Wellington gave permission for the trees to be felled to construct the abatis.

The French now faced the same problem as on their advance to Ciudad Rodrigo, the scarcity of food, ammunition and particularly transport for their supplies. Also, Masséna needed to reorganise his forces before the French army, 65,000 strong, began their advance on 15 September 1810. The French surprised Wellington by staying north of the Mondego on roads that were much worse than those on the southern bank. Having stripped Viseu,[13] the French then advanced towards Coimbra which led them to the ridge of Buçaco (Bussaco) where, on 27 September 1810, Wellington repulsed several attempts to dislodge him inflicting 4,000 casualties for the loss of 1,000.

The next day, the French turned Wellington's position and he continued his retreat towards Coimbra. When the leading French units reached the city, they embarked on a disorganised orgy of looting that destroyed much of the food which Masséna needed for his advancing army. This delay of a few days gave Wellington's troops an opportunity to retreat in a more leisurely fashion, which was very useful as the roads were crowded with refugees fleeing from the conflict. Two routes were used for the retreat. Hill with Hamilton, Fane and Le Cor retired to Lisbon by Espinhal, Tomar and Santarém avoiding Coimbra. The bulk of the army moved to Coimbra, all except the rear guard passing through the city on 30 September. They then followed the route through Condeixa to Leiria. South of Leiria, Picton diverted to the Caldas da Rainha to Torres Vedras road with the remainder taking the route through Rio Maior and Alenquer.

The French did not leave Coimbra until 4 October, the delay consigning the invaders to many days of marching in torrential rain, but they did not know that yet. On the 7 October the bulk of the French army were at Leiria and the following morning set-off south in the rain.

As Wellington withdrew in front of the advancing French army, another element in his defensive plan was initiated. Using the traditional Portuguese principle of calling the population to arms, the countryside over which the French advanced was abandoned, with the people fleeing and all foodstuffs (supposedly) being destroyed. In Wellington's memorandum to Fletcher ordering the building the Lines, he stated: 'They [the allied army] should stand in every position which the country could afford, such a length of time as would enable the people of the country to evacuate the towns and villages, carrying with them or destroying all articles of provisions and carriages, not necessary for the allied army.[14]

Wellington repeated the same message in his proclamation to the Portuguese civilians when the invasion was imminent.[15] The speed of Wellington's retreat after the Battle of Buçaco appeared to catch the authorities and the population by surprise and, unfortunately, the population of Coimbra were given little warning to leave their homes and destroy anything useful

---

13   Donald Horward (ed.), *The French Campaign in Portugal. An Account by Jean Jaques Pelet* (Minneapolis: University of Minnesota, 1973), pp.164–165.

14   REM: 5501-91-1.

15   Gurwood, *Dispatches*, Proclamation to the people of Portugal, 4 August 1810.

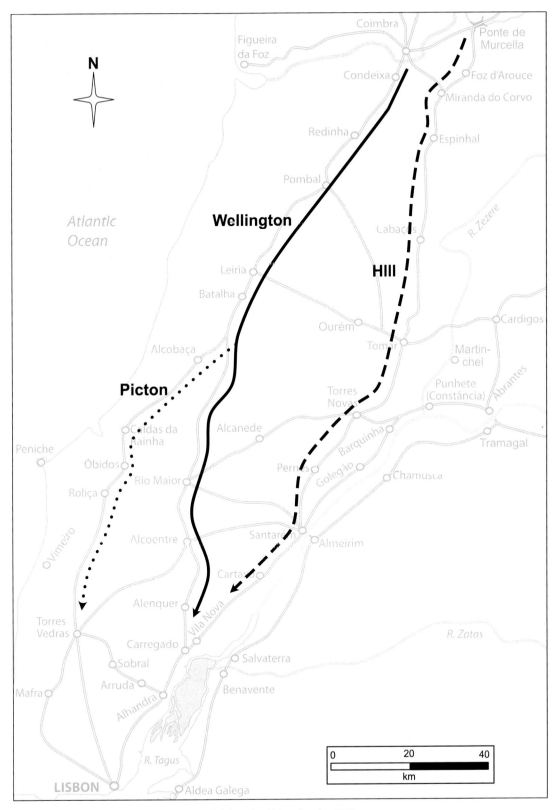

Withdrawal to Lisbon October 1810.

to the enemy. The advancing French managed to collect some supplies, but much was destroyed at the last second by the retreating allied army or damaged by the looting French troops. However, what was collected was not enough. The French advanced into a wasteland where there was insufficient food for the invading troops or their animals. When the French eventually came up to the Lines, they would find themselves with a formidable obstacle in front, and limited resources to stay or even retreat.

It was the responsibility of the Portuguese government to order the population to abandon their homes. They had done this, but there was a marked reluctance to enforce it. Wellington had been pressed to abandon the agreed strategy of retiring from the frontier when the moment arrived and was being pushed, almost threatened by the Regency, to stand and offer battle to halt the invasion. Wellington's response was similarly strong:

> I beg you will inform the Regency and above all, Principal Souza, that … I will not suffer them … to interfere with [my arrangements for the army] … I know best where to station my troops and where to make a stand against the enemy … I recommend to them to look to the measures for which they are responsible … to provide for the tranquillity of Lisbon and for the food for the army and of the people.[16]

When Wellington announced after the Battle of Buçaco that he was withdrawing, there was a desperate scramble by the citizens of Coimbra to leave. Although they had been told several weeks previously that it might be necessary, when reality arrived many had only a day to collect what they could carry and escape from the French.

Wellington was still confident in the strategy he had chosen for the defence of Portugal and remained positive in reporting progress to his government. Writing to his brother Henry, he said:

> … we shall make our retreat … without much difficulty, or any loss. My opinion is, that the French are in a scrape. They are not a sufficient army for their purpose, particularly since their late loss, and that the Portuguese army have behaved so well; and they will find their retreat from this country a most difficult and dangerous operation.[17]

To Colonel Henry Torrens, Military Secretary at the Horse Guards, he wrote: 'we make our retreat with great ease', although he did comment that there had been a few stragglers amongst the less experienced regiments.[18] He was similarly positive when writing to Lord Liverpool: 'With few exceptions, the troops have continued to conduct themselves with great regularity, and they have suffered no fatigue … the enemy suffer great distress. The

---

16   Gurwood, *Dispatches*, Wellington to Stuart, 6 October 1810.
17   Gurwood, *Dispatches,* Wellington to H. Wellesley, 3 October 1810.
18   Gurwood, *Dispatches*, Wellington to Torrens, 4 October 1810.

THE CAMPAIGN OF 1810

inhabitants of the country have fled … carrying with them every thing [sic] … which could be deemed useful to the enemy.'[19]

Locally he was more critical, and clearly straggling and stealing were a problem. In a General Order dated, 3 October 1810:

> There are more stragglers from these three [British] regiments [in Leith's Division] than from all the others of the British army taken together, which must be occasioned either by the neglect of the officers or by the soldiers being unable to keep up with the march … The Commander of the Forces requests that Major General Leith will communicate these orders to the Portuguese troops … particularly the Lusitanian Legion … Major General Picton is requested not to allow the troops of his division to enter any town unless necessarily obliged to pass through it.[20]

Three soldiers were hung at Leiria for theft to make an example and stop the bad behaviour.[21] In later letters he complained about the amount of food that was left by the population and the failure of the Portuguese government to communicate and enforce the evacuation policy. Whoever was at fault, it was the civilians who suffered the most. As one soldier commented: 'The road was so crowded with the flying inhabitants that the troops could scarcely move on. It was a most distressing and lamentable sight, to see a whole people leaving their houses and homes to the fury and rapacity of the cruel invaders.'[22]

He went on to recount the drunken pillaging and robbery being carried out by the retreating allied soldiers. It was not just the invaders who were preying on the inhabitants. Whilst Wellington might have been 'officially' positive about the organisation of the retreat there were clearly issues apart from the short notice to the population. Military supplies had to be abandoned or destroyed as the French advanced. So, blaming the population for not removing their possessions appears unfair. There were clearly many issues of bad behaviour by the troops and there were occasions where the rear guard was not handled well. Considering how long the allies had to prepare, the whole operation felt hurried. Had the French marched straight through Coimbra and continued the pursuit it probably would have been much worse for both the allied army and the civilians.

The arguments over blame and responsibility for the withdrawal and the evacuation of the civilians continued for many weeks after the retreat.[23] The problem Wellington faced was that many Portuguese, and in fact many British officers, believed that Wellington intended to pass straight through Lisbon and embark. The continuous retreat after Buçaco, abandoning one Portuguese town after another, reinforced that belief. Jones reported from

19   Gurwood, *Dispatches*, Wellington to Liverpool, 5 October 1810.
20   Gurwood, *Dispatches*, General Order, dated, Leiria, 3 October 1810.
21   Oman, *Peninsular War*, Vol.3, pp.408–409.
22   Steve Brown (ed.), *The Autobiography, or Narrative of a Soldier. The Peninsular War Memoirs of William Brown of the 45th Foot* (Solihull: Helion, 2017), pp.53–54.
23   See for example Gurwood, *Dispatches*, Wellington to Stuart, 1 November 1810.

Lisbon with some concern that 'No-one will believe that the army will halt till it reached St Julian's, and all authority and order is beginning to be lost.'[24] Second Lieutenant George Simmons also wrote that he was 'meeting numbers of poor people, making their way to Lisbon in the most wretched plight, telling us the British army were in full retreat before the French.'[25] Since most people in the government and all the population were not aware of Wellington's plan or the existence of the Lines, it was not a surprising conclusion to be made by the Portuguese.

As Wellington approached Lisbon, he wrote to Colonel Warren Peacocke, the military governor, asking for all recovered convalescents in Lisbon to be moved to Montachique. He also asked for most of the Royal Artillery in the city to be moved to the same place. He wanted these troops ready to move when the army reached the Lines.[26]

The majority of the allied troops arrived at the Lines on 9 October 1810 with the rear guard entering the next day. Picton's division, travelling by themselves had arrived at Torres Vedras on 7 October. Guides were present to take the various units to their allocated positions. Some of the forts were already occupied by militia and their magazines were full. Engineer officers were assigned to each district to support the local commanders and with responsibility to continue construction work and repairs.

Two days later the leading French troops arrived and got their first sight of the Lines of Torres Vedras. Oman summed up the significance of this moment: 'The high-water mark of the French conquest in Europe was reached on the knoll by Sobral [in October 1810].'[27]

---

24   Jones, *Sieges*, Vol.3, p.253.

25   W. Verner (ed.), *Major George Simmons. A British Rifleman* (London: Greenhill, 1986), pp.110–111.

26   Gurwood, *Dispatches,* Wellington to Peacocke, Alcobaça, 5 October 1810.

27   Oman, *Peninsular War*, Vol.3, p.436.

10

The Lines – October to November 1810

The allied forces concentrated in the Lines now gave Wellington a numerical advantage over the invading French army. British troops with their regiments were about 35,000 strong. The Portuguese units had about 25,000, many of whom had fought at Buçaco, making a total of about 60,000 in the Anglo-Portuguese army. There were also two divisions of Spanish troops with another 8,000 men. To defend the forts on the Lines, Wellington had about 8,000 Portuguese militia and 3,000 artillerymen with possibly a further 10,000 *ordenanças*, although that number is not clear. The French army spread out over many miles in front of the Lines was probably no stronger than 50,000. Wellington continued with his strategy of defeating the enemy through attrition, not battle.

As previously described, Wellington's original intention was to defend the position of the second line using the forward strong points of Torres Vedras and Sobral to slow down the French advance. Due to the additional time to prepare the defences, Wellington was now confident that he could hold the invaders at the first line. He still believed the most likely attack route was down the northern bank of the Tagus river. The weak point in the defences was the gap between Sobral and Runa where there were no forts and there was access to minor roads to Montachique, Bucelas and Mafra. Wellington placed the bulk of his forces near the Tagus and at Sobral. On 10 October 1810, the troops were located as follows:[1]

Unit	Location
1st Division	Sobral
2nd Division	Alhandra
3rd Division	Torres Vedras
4th Division	Dois Portos
5th Division	Enxara dos Cavaleiros

---

[1]	James Wyld, *Memoir annexed to an Atlas containing Plans of the Principal Battles, Sieges and Affairs in which the British Troops were Engaged During the War in the Spanish Peninsula and the South of France* (London: Wyld, 1841), p.39 fn. Also Gurwood, *Dispatches*, Distribution of Allied Army, 10 October 1810.

Unit	Location
6th Division	Ribaldeira
Light Division	Arruda
Campbell's Portuguese Brigade	Torres Vedras
Coleman's Portuguese Brigade	Torres Vedras
Pack's Portuguese Brigade	Towards Alenquer in front of Sobral
Hamilton's Portuguese infantry	Vila Franca
Le Cor's Portuguese infantry	Alverca
De Grey's cavalry Brigade	Ramalhal in front of Torres Vedras
14th Light Dragoons	Towards Abrigada north of Sobral
Stapleton Cotton with 3 regiments of cavalry	Santo António do Tojal near Loures (modern Santo Antão do Tojal)
Fane's cavalry	Loures and Vila Franca
Headquarters	Santo Quintino, near Sobral

Pack, De Grey and the 14th Light Dragoons were still some way north of the Lines acting as a covering force.

The deployments on 9 and 10 October were done in atrocious weather which made movement by road difficult and movement off-road nearly impossible. This will also have slowed down the advance of the main French forces, which meant that when the Lines were encountered it was by cavalry, and they had to wait for the infantry to arrive before any further action could be taken.

On 6 October 1810, Wellington wrote to Fletcher confirming his intention to split the Lines into six districts and appointing engineer officers (regulating officers) and commissaries to each district.[2] They were:

District	Location	Regulating Officer	Supporting Engineer
First Line			
1	Sea to Torres Vedras	Captain Mulcaster	Lieutenant Thomson
2	Sobral to Calhandriz	Captain Goldfinch	Lieutenant Forster
3	Calhandriz to Alhandra	Captain Squire	Lieutenant Piper
Second Line			
4	Tagus to Bucelas	Captain Burgoyne	Lieutenant Stanway
5	Bucelas to Mafra	Captain Dickinson	Lieutenant French
6	Mafra to the Sea	Captain Ross	Lieutenant Hulme

Letters were also sent to each regulating officer detailing the forts they were responsible for and the numbers of soldiers available to occupy them.[3] Most accounts of the two main Lines, refer to seven districts. This structure was not put in place until after the French retreated. On 20 March 1811 the original six districts were still being used. By May 1812, the change to seven districts had been made but the exact date of the change is unknown.[4]

---

2 Gurwood, *Dispatches,* Memorandum to Lieut.-Col. Fletcher, Royal Engineers and the Commissary General, Rio Maior, 6 October 1810. Also letter to Regulating Officer(s), dated, Rio Maior, 6 October 1810.

3 The original of the letter sent to Burgoyne is in the Royal Engineers Museum; REM: 5501-108-8.

4 REM: 5501-59-1, was still referring to district 3, Alhandra on 20 March 1811. In Jones' *Sieges,* Vol.3, pp.94–100, the tables showing 7 districts in dated May 1812, as is the original in REM: 5501-59-18.

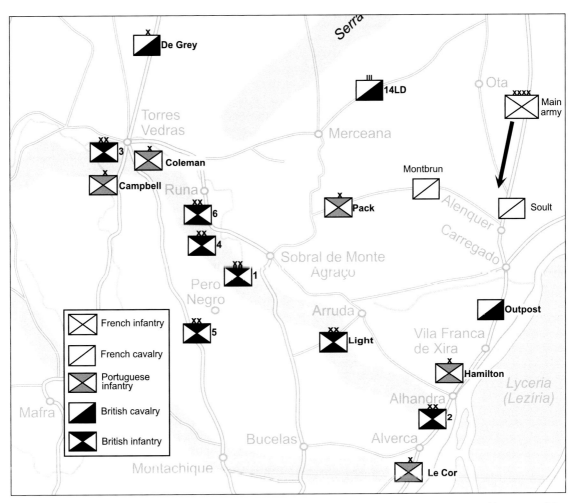

Positions of forces around the Lines, 10 October 1810.

Wellington's instructions, allocated militia, artillery crews and tents to each district, the 'troops to be assembled at headquarters forthwith'.

District	Militia	British artillerymen	Portuguese artillerymen	Ordenança artillerymen	Tents for men
1	2,470	70	140	250	2,500
2	1,300	40	140	300	2,000
3	400	60		60	5,000
4	1,100		80	500	5,000
5	2,400	50	120	480	10,000
6	700	40	230	350	10,000
Total	8,370	260	710	1,940	34,500

The tents were ordered for the use of both the soldiers in the forts and the army although why the majority were ordered for the centre and western end of the second line is puzzling. That was not where they were needed which was the centre and east between the lines.

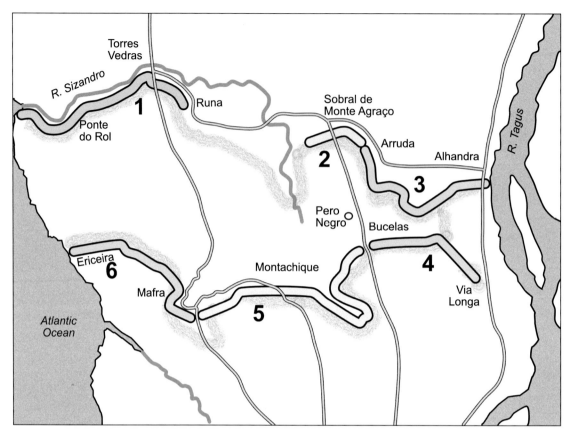

Districts on Lines of Torres Vedras – October 1810.

It is also puzzling why Portuguese engineer officers were not assigned as several had worked on the construction of the Lines. Possible reasons were: ease of command and communication through all officers appointed belonging to the same corps; no issues of seniority as all were under the direct command of Fletcher; or possibly that the Portuguese engineers were employed elsewhere improving other defences.

In Wellington's memorandum and the letter to the regulating officers, Wellington referred to appointing an 'officer commanding' assumed to be a more senior line officer. The regulating officer would issue instructions 'till an officer to command the troops within it [the district] shall be appointed'. This message was reinforced in a later letter to Beresford:

> Regulating officers are appointed to the several fortified districts as follows: and I shall be obliged to you if you will direct the officers commanding the militia and the ordenança and regular artillery, to report themselves, and to apply to these officers for orders.[5]

This structure would raise the typical seniority issues as the senior engineer officers were captains and all the officers commanding regular, militia and

---

5   Gurwood, *Dispatches,* Wellington to Beresford, Alemquer, 7 October 1810.

ordenança would probably be senior unless there were superior officers in command of each district. The actual command structure becomes less clear as there is only one clear case where a superior officer was appointed to command a district. On 6 October 1810, Wellington appointed Major General John Sontag to command the troops in district one at Torres Vedras, a command he retained until after the French withdrawal in March 1811. It appears that the Portuguese *Tenente General* José Miranda, commander of the militia in Northern Estremadura, was appointed to command district six. This information comes from a letter of Royal Engineer, Captain George Ross, who wrote that he had declined the position as regulating officer having met Miranda:

> He has been here but two days, but it could require only two hours to convince me that no motive ought to induce me to take any responsibility under a person so totally different from what I conceive a general ought to be. He is also surrounded by about 30 Portuguese, whose first appearance does not presuppose one in favour of their military qualities, and a few hours conversation convinces me that though they might be very well as Portuguese Marquesses and Counts they have little to recommend them as brother sticks or props to the superannuated hero of Roussillon. I have not yet learnt what is thought of my refusal.[6]

As Ross was still in district six in February 1811, it can be deduced what his superiors thought of his refusal. There is no other mention of Miranda having a command role on the Lines although his militia regiments were present, and he would have remained in overall command of them.[7] This does leave the question of who were the superior officers in each district? The only place where this was relevant was on the first line. When the first line was occupied there would be few troops on the second line. The regulating (engineer) officers on the second line could retain overall command of the construction and maintenance of the defences without the need for a superior officer being present. On the first line it would then make sense for the superior divisional officer to command both the regular troops and the second line troops placed in the defences. This is probably what happened, with Lieutenant General Hill commanding around Alhandra and Brigadier General Craufurd around Arruda. But, this was not what Wellington's correspondence said. As late as 8 October 1810, Wellington gave Hill full details on the forts and the troops around Alhandra and then commented 'Captain Squire, of the Engineers, has been appointed as the regulating officer of this district, in order to assist whoever may be appointed to command the troops in it.'[8]

Wellington's letter appointing Sontag to command at Torres Vedras gives an insight to his thinking at the time. Although written only one day later than his instructions of 5 October, Wellington had already ordered more troops to Torres Vedras. He told Sontag that he was sending a British battalion, the 2/58th, which was on garrison duty in Lisbon (probably because its strength

---

6   REM: 4501-86, Ross to Dalrymple, Mafra, 19 October 1810.
7   Oman, *Peninsular War*, Vol.3, p.431. Soriano, *História*, Vol.3, pp.223–225.
8   Gurwood, *Dispatches,* Wellington to Hill, Arruda, 8 October 1810.

had dropped to about 300). Two battalions of Portuguese militia, 1,700 strong had also been ordered up. He continued: 'I shall add another British regiment, a Portuguese regiment of the line and another regiment of militia, if I should find that the enemy manifests any intention of moving in that direction.'[9]

No other part of the Lines was allocated regular troops and Sontag was being given three battalions, including two British; why? There are a number of possibilities. First, Torres Vedras was away from where the bulk of the allied army would be positioned. If it was attacked, it would have to hold out longer than any other part of the line. It would be even more dangerous if Picton's 3rd Division, which was assigned to the district, was moved to support an attack to the east. Second, the main forts at Torres Vedras were north of the river Sizandro and consequently more exposed. If there was flooding in the river valley, the forts could be cut off from any support. Again, the defenders might have to hold out for some time. Third, Wellington was concerned that the first attack might come at this point in the defences. Writing to Picton on 8 October, he said 'I think the attack will be on our left, by Torres Vedras.'[10] He also said this to Lieutenant General Sir Brent Spencer, commander of the 1st Division, the same afternoon.[11] Wellington was clearly worried because the French had not yet arrived in front of Alhandra. He wrote that he had no information that the French had arrived at Rio Maior. If they were not there, then they could be on the Caldas to Torres Vedras road. They had not taken this route, the French were just advancing much slower than Wellington expected. Picton had arrived in Torres Vedras late on 7 October 1810. With him was engineer John Burgoyne, who recorded in his journal on the following day: 'As General Sontag had not arrived, nor Mulcaster [Regulating Officer], nor the militia, etc, appointed to this district, I assisted General Picton in making temporary arrangements with the Portuguese troops of the line.'[12]

Burgoyne had clearly seen the orders given to given to Sontag as he recorded details from them in his journal. Burgoyne noted that Mulcaster arrived during the day but said nothing of the expected troops. That evening, Burgoyne received his orders, sent on the 5 October, appointing him to be regulating officer in district four. He set off the next morning for his new headquarters at Bucelas and recorded when he arrived that the *ordenança* artillerymen were present but, most of the regular artillerymen and all the militia were missing. Having spent 10 October allocating the *ordenança* artillery amongst the redoubts, he was ordered the next day to immediately send 200 of his artillerymen to Alhandra. It would appear that Lieutenant General Hill, on the first line, on the most probable route of attack was also short of the troops assigned to his district. All of this would suggest that the arrangements were not as smooth as many accounts suggest. It does raise the question, when the speed of the retreat was fully understood, why Wellington

---

9   Gurwood, *Dispatches,* Wellington to Sontag, Rio Maior, 6 October 1810.
10   Gurwood, *Dispatches,* Wellington to Picton, Arruda, 3 ½ pm, 8 October 1810.
11   Gurwood, *Dispatches,* Wellington to Spencer, Arruda, 3 ½ pm, 8 October 1810.
12   REM: 4201-68, journal entry dated 8 October 1810.

did not start sending out orders for moving troops and appointing officers on the Lines until 5 October 1810, one week after he commenced his retreat from Buçaco and two days before the first units of his army arrived? This could have been done several days earlier and avoided the scramble that appears to have occurred. Another example of late orders is Wellington's request to John Jones, the engineer in charge of completing the defences, on 5 October, to appoint guides to lead the retreating troops to their allocated positions. Each district would need an officer and four others, with detailed knowledge of the locality and at least three of them needed to be mounted. So, 30 knowledgeable locals with 18 horses need to be found and equipped, in 48 hours.[13] Jones will have had nothing else to do at that critical point!

Wellington's correspondence went very quiet on 9 and 10 October, suggesting that he was busy moving round the new defensive positions and finalising arrangements.

According to Soriano, there were 15 militia regiments present in the Lines. He records their numbers and locations slightly differently from Wellington's memorandum of 5 October, but Soriano was positioning actual regiments rather than numbers of troops. They were:

Portuguese Militia Regiments present on the Lines of Torres Vedras, October 1810[14]

Regiment	Location and Commander	Strength
	Torres Vedras	
Lisboa Oriental	*Coronel* Marcellino José Manso	485
Lisboa Occidental		659
Setúbal	*Coronel* Visconde de Villa Nova de Souto de El-Rei	472
Alcacer do Sal	*Coronel* João Infante de Lacerda	615
		2,231
	Sobral	
Atiradores Nacionaes de Lisboa oriental	*Major* Leonardo Sabino Salvalici	355
Atiradores Nacionaes de Lisboa occidental		406
		761
	Póvoa and Alhandra under command of *Coronel* Carlos Frederico Lecor	
Santarém	*Coronel* José Clímaco de Azevedo Moncada	488
Idanha	*Tenente Coronel* Fernando Tudella de Castilho	573
Castello Branco	*Tenente Coronel* Luiz da Cunha Castro e Menezes	529
Covilhã	*Tenente Coronel* Francisco Eduardo da Silva Fragoso	457
Feira	*Tenente Coronel* Francisco Correia de Mello	569
		2,616
	Bucelas	
Termo de Lisboa occidental	*Tenente Coronel* Manuel Monteiro de Carvalho	662
Thomar	*Tenente Coronel* Jorge de Mesquita	538

13   Jones, *Sieges*, Vol.3, pp.235–236.

14   Soriano, *História*, Vol.3, pp.223–225. Total strength was 9,163, present was 8,206. These numbers are very close to Oman, *Peninsular War*, Vol.3, p.431. Oman does not give a reference, but it is likely to be Soriano. René Chartrand, *Fuentes de Oñoro, Wellington's Liberation of Portugal* (Oxford: Osprey, 2002), p.27, had different militia numbers. No source is given.

Regiment	Location and Commander	Strength
Torres Vedras	*Coronel* Lazaro Cardoso Amado	707
		1,907
	Mafra	
Vizeu	*Coronel* João de Azevedo e Souza Mello e Vasconcellos	**691**
Total	(there were another 1,000 reported as sick)	**8,206**

Soriano's details of the Portuguese artillery numbers are different from Jones'.[15]

Artillerymen present in the Districts.					
		Jones		Soriano	
District	Brit	Port	Ord	Port	Ord
1	70	140	250	164	271
2	40	140	300	163	331
3	60		60	284	182
4		80	500	242	964
5	50	120	480		
6	40	230	350	251	350[16]
Totals	260	710	1,940	1,104	2,098
Portuguese			2,650		3,202

Jones' figures for district three, Alhandra, which are the same as in Wellington's memorandum, must be wrong. Initially, this was the most critical part of the line and the number of artillerymen is very low. Jones had written that there were 3,200 Portuguese artillerymen present which matches Soriano.[17] There is substantial detail on the numbers, commanders and locations of all the Portuguese troops in Soriano's work.[18]

Through the awful weather from 8 to 15 October the allied troops huddled in any cover they could find. The tents that had been ordered had not arrived. Some were fortunate to find cover in the villages, but many were stuck in the open. The Portuguese occupying the forts were allowed to find cover away from the redoubts as long as they stayed close to them.

Whilst the marching was finished for a few weeks, the work was not. Many soldiers were immediately put to work to strengthen the defences that they now occupied. Around Arruda, the Light Division was ordered to dig defensive positions on the heights, to improve and repair the redoubts and to strengthen the defences in the Matos pass (behind Arruda).[19] The engineer John Squire reported that an abatis was added to the defences on the banks of the Tagus.[20] John Burgoyne noted that Hill was at Alhandra

---

15   Jones, *Sieges*, Vol.3, pp.86 and 125–127. Soriano, *História*, Vol.3, pp.225–226.
16   This figure is missing. Soriano says the total was 3,202 and 350 matches the figure given by Jones.
17   Jones, *Sieges*, Vol.3, p.86.
18   Soriano, *História*, Vol.3, pp.225–230.
19   R. Burnham, *Wellington's Light Division in the Peninsular War. The Formation, Campaigns and Battles of Wellington's Fighting Force: 1810* (Barnsley: Pen & Sword, 2020), pp.321–323.
20   BL: ADD63106, Squire to Bunbury, 10 October 1810.

'which is strengthening very much.'[21] One soldier noted that 'Those off duty were employed throwing up batteries and breast works or breaking up roads … we remained thus for five weeks'. This soldier was based on the front line near Zibreira (da Fé) and the batteries would have been for field guns, not part of the main defences.[22]

Some of the officers who had doubted the effectiveness of the defences were now more positive. Gordon, Wellington's ADC, commented on 5 October, 'I think we shall give him a sound drubbing' and a few days later 'our army is in high spirits and no-one fears the result of the approaching termination of the campaign.'[23] Quite a change from his opinion in February. But there were still doubts at the highest levels. Hill commented on 13 October 'it [the defensive position in front of Lisbon] is strong but rather too extensive for our numbers.'[24] The retreating allied army had a few days to settle into the defensive positions and when the French approached, they were ready. Wellington's trap was sprung.

The Royal Navy's Preparation for the Defence of Lisbon

Wellington's good working relationship with Berkeley continued to provide huge benefits. The Royal Navy's primary and essential role of keeping the shipping lanes open and escorting convoys continued to be successful. In addition to this, Berkeley had the unenviable task of trying to keep control of the civilian crews on the 250 strong fleet of troopships and transports. This was the fleet that would bring Wellington's army home if he was forced to embark. The crews were bored and caused trouble both on and offshore. Being civilians, there was little Berkeley could do to control them.[25]

For the defences around Lisbon, the Royal Navy did much more than provide a few sailors to operate the telegraphs on the Lines. As early as March 1809, Craddock had considered the use of gunboats on the Tagus, so the idea was not new. In June 1810, Wellington wrote to Berkeley:

> I would also request you to consider of the assistance which you will have it in your power to give us in the way of armed vessels. The right of our position will be at Alhandra, where the Tagus begins to open, where you could give us great assistance and security. I should [also] think that a gun boat or two, stationed on the coast between Mafra and Maceira [5km south of Mafra], would be of service, in case the enemy should attempt to push a column along the beach.[26]

There was no mention of patrolling the river Tagus or the Atlantic coast in Wellington's original Memorandum of 20 October 1809, but such a necessity

21   REM: 4201-68, journal entry for 16 October 11810.
22   Christopher Hibbert (ed.), *A Soldier of the 71st* (London: Leo Cooper, 1975), p.54.
23   Muir, *Right Hand*, pp.118–119.
24   Sidney, Edwin, *The Life of Lord Hill GCB, Late Commander of the* Forces (London: John Murray, 1845), p.147.
25   De Toy, *Berkeley*, pp.498–500.
26   Gurwood, *Dispatches*, Wellington to Berkeley, Celorico, 15 June 1810.

must have been anticipated. Berkeley was likely to have raised it even if Wellington did not. One of Wellington's concerns was a French advance south of the river Tagus, which would require any attempted crossing to be resisted. It was reasonable to assume that the large Royal Navy presence would oppose such an attack. Wellington was probably more interested in what Berkeley could do to strengthen the right flank of the Lines away from the estuary and up the river. The answer was, a lot, but this is not reflected in many accounts.

Oman and Fortescue say very little about naval support. Both mention two battalions of marines guarding St Julian's and the surrounding area. Oman does however report that gunboats 'infested the Tagus estuary'.[27] Similarly, Jones says very little about the role of the Royal Navy. He mentioned briefly that there were some marines to help defend Lisbon, that marines were used on left bank at Almada (the fourth line), and there is one mention of gunboats on the Tagus near Fort 33, but that is it. More recently, books by Grehan and White noted that marines and sailors were supporting Major General Fane on crossing the Tagus and defending the 'island' of Lezíria (Lyceria).[28]

There appeared to be a recognition in England that the war was coming to a crisis point and that the whole of the military resources in Portugal needed to be put at the disposal of Wellington. As mentioned earlier, Liverpool had written on 2 October 1810, giving Wellington permission to remove all the lower deck guns from Berkeley's fleet in the Tagus, complete with the sailors and marines to man them. Even more surprisingly, Wellington was given permission to abandon them if necessary.[29]

Berkeley enthusiastically provided resources to support Wellington's activities, sometimes too enthusiastically. There were occasions when he risked the anger of the Admiralty by taking actions that they would not approve of. In the early days of October 1810 as Wellington retreated, Berkeley was very busy organising armed vessels for use on the river. This was a substantial undertaking.

The largest was HMS *Audacious* (74) which was sent 'up the river as far as possible to provide support for the boats and batteries.' It is not explicit how far up *Audacious* went but based on the fact that the smaller HMS *Vestal* was anchored off Póvoa, it is unlikely that *Audacious* went any higher. HMS *Vestal* was an old 28-gun frigate which had been converted into a 16-gun troopship earlier in 1810.[30] Berkeley had fitted out *Vestal* as a hospital ship with two similarly fitted flat boats in attendance.[31] *Vestal* was also part of a chain of ships passing telegraph messages along the river.

On 7 October 1810, Berkeley reported to Wellington that he had fitted two 18-pounder cannon on one of the transport ships and had 'a flotilla

27 Oman, *Peninsular War*, Vol.3, pp.431, 434, 436. Fortescue, *British Army*, Vol.7, 543.
28 Grehan, *The Lines of Torres Vedras,* pp.139, 151. White, *Key to Lisbon,* p.198. The Portuguese word for this low-lying, flood-prone land in the river is *Mouchão*.
29 Wellington, *Supplementary Despatches*, Vol.6, p.604.
30 Cy Harrison, *Three Decks – Warships in the Age of Sail*, <https://threedecks.org/index.php?display_type=show_ship&id=6691>, accessed 7 July 2020.
31 De Toy, *Berkeley*, p.505.

of flat boats ready to act on the river'. The transport was probably around 300 tons, about the size of a frigate. Berkeley was happy to risk a transport in the narrow confines of the river at Alhandra but would have been less happy risking one of his frigates. Wellington asked Berkeley to move them to Alhandra and informed him that the riverbank had been levelled to provide a clear field of fire for the boats.[32] It is likely that this transport ship was the forward element of the telegraph ship chain.

A flat boat was a shallow draft vessel ideal for use in coastal waters or rivers. They were primarily designed to transport troops but could also carry a small gun in the bow. The Royal Navy had two designs, one was 12 metres long and would carry about 50 tightly packed men plus a naval officer, gunner and 20 oarsmen. The smaller design was 10 metres long and carried 16 oarsmen. They only need 60 centimetres of water, which allowed them to get close to the banks of the river.[33] There are no details of which types were in use on the Tagus. With no troops on board, they could have carried a larger gun. An 18-pounder cannon might have been possible; an 18 or 24-pounder carronade would have been easily carried. Both De Toy and Sutcliffe mention mortar/howitzer vessels which were likely to be flat boats fitted with a mortar or carronade.[34]

The correspondence regularly refers to 'gunboats'. The Royal Navy did have specific designs for gunboats which were broadly the same shape, but larger than the flatboats. A typical version was about 15 metres long, weighing 40 tons, with an 18-pounder cannon mounted in the bow and an 18-pounder carronade on a swivel mount in the stern. The gunboat also had mast and sails. It is not clear if any of these vessels were present. There is one letter where a gunboat mounting a 24-pounder is mentioned. This must have been a substantial boat is it was noted that it could not go above Salvaterra.[35] It is more likely that most would have been ships' boats from the fleet with a bow mounted cannon. The number of boats carrying guns is not known but could have been more than 100.[36] One contemporary letter from an infantry officer suggested there were 2–300 boats with guns.[37]

On 7 October 1810, Berkeley reported to Wellington that the defences at Cascais and at the fort of Santo António de Cascais still contained cannon. Wellington replied, saying that he thought these guns had been previously removed, and would be grateful if Berkeley arranged to have them removed and taken to São Julião. These guns could have fired on the loaded transports as they left the embarkation point.[38]

Berkeley recognised there might be a need for naval help onshore, he had about 450 marines with him and had requested further marines to be sent

32   De Toy, *Berkeley*, p.505. Gurwood, *Dispatches*, Wellington to Berkeley, 8 October 1810.
33   Hugh Boscawen, *The Origins of the Flat-Bottomed Landing Craft 1751–1758* (London. National Army Museum, 1985), p.24.
34   De Toy, *Berkeley*, p.505; Sutcliffe, *Expeditionary Warfare*, p.134.
35   Gurwood, *Dispatches*, Wellington to Berkeley, 3 November 1810.
36   De Toy, *Berkeley*, p.506, mentions 'several gunboat divisions, some of over 20 boats.'
37   Bamford, *With Wellington Outposts*, p.26.
38   Gurwood, *Dispatches*, Wellington to Berkeley, 8 October 1810. De Toy, *Berkeley*, pp.504, 505 fn.

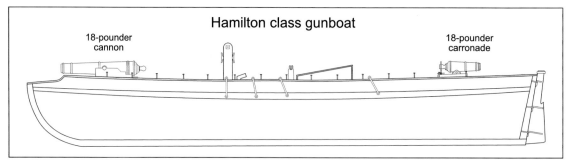

Hamilton class gunboat

18-pounder cannon

18-pounder carronade

British Gunboat.

from the UK, eventually making a disposable force of about 2,000 men.[39] These troops took over responsibility for the embarkation point at São Julião, some of the forts on the river and some guard duty in Lisbon, releasing troops back to Wellington's army.

The Royal Navy was now ready for the arrival of the French.

From the French Arrival up to 14 November 1810

The French advance guard first approached the Lines on the morning of 11 October 1810. The bulk of the French army was a day's march north, exhausted after three days marching in the rain. The weather was still very poor so there will have been limited visibility of the formidable obstacle they were approaching.

Montbrun's cavalry which had spent the night around Alenquer pushed south on the main road towards Vila Franca de Xira and on the minor road towards Sobral. At Vila Franca, *Général de brigade* Pierre Soult's cavalry brigade found the advanced position of the British on the banks of the Tagus, two kilometres in front of the first line at Alhandra. He quickly ejected them but when he came in sight of Alhandra realised he was going no further. Similarly, when Montbrun approached Sobral, he realised it was occupied and his flanking forces had reported allied defensive positions to the east at Arruda, and to the west at Zibreira and beyond. As he had no information on the strength of the allied troops in the area, he took no direct action, reporting the findings of his patrols back to Masséna. Wellington was in a similar position; he knew that French troops were approaching but did not have enough information to determine where an attack would come. He was hopeful that the first attack would not be to the west around Torres Vedras but at either Alhandra or Sobral. He accordingly issued two sets of instructions to his commanders on how they would need to react.

Oman's description of Wellington's analysis on 11 October is wrong; it was Arruda that would be 'tough' not Alhandra, as Oman suggested. Wellington, writing to Craufurd, believed the French were marching on Alhandra, but: 'They can make no impression upon the right … and they must therefore endeavour to turn Hill's position … by its left … This is a tough job also,

---

39   Oman, *Peninsular War*, Vol.3, p.434. De Toy, *Berkeley*, p.504.

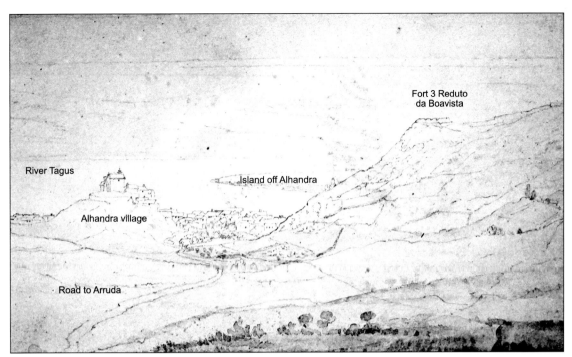

Fort 3 Reduto
da Boavista

River Tagus

Island off Alhandra

Alhandra village

Road to Arruda

Pencil sketch of Alhandra.
(REM: 5501-29-13)

defended as the entrances of the valleys are by redoubts and the villages by abatis etc.' Wellington thought that the French would try and fail against Hill at Alhandra and then move west to Craufurd's positions position at Arruda and the Matos valley.[40]

Wellington had expressly pointed out to Craufurd that the pass of Matos behind Arruda was critical. The loss of this pass would allow the French to turn the defences at Alhandra and from there could move inland towards Bucelas. The French of course did not know this but having seen that the route was well defended they would look further west, to where the bulk of Wellington's army would be waiting.

On 12 October, the first French advance was towards Alhandra by Taupin's infantry brigade, however there was no contact. Later in the day Junot's VIII Corps arrived at Sobral and after a skirmish ejected the allied advance guard from the town. The defenders only retreated to a height a few hundred yards away, still well in front of the main positions on the heights south of Sobral. A soldier of the 71st recounted that they were chased from Windmill Hill through the town and up to Gallows Hill, where they halted and dug themselves in. You can still stand on Gallows Hill (Alto da Forca) today and see the vista of the defences to the south and the town of Sobral to the north.[41]

Around Alhandra, the French continued to explore the defences and *Général de brigade* Sainte-Croix was killed near Vila Franca by a shot from

40   Oman, *Peninsular War*, Vol.3, p.438. Gurwood, *Dispatches*, Wellington to Craufurd, 11 October 1810.

41   Hibbert, *Soldier of the 71st*, pp.50–51.

KEY

Major road	
Minor road	
Town	○
Fort	⬠
Unnumbered fort	
Scarping	
Ditch / wall	
Abattis	

Cadafaes

R. Grande Pipa

Vila Franca

Alhandra

117

114

115

116

118

120

5

119

6

Calahandriz

1

Arruda

Trancoso

8

121

122

9

123

Matos

124

11

10

Carvalha

12

13

152

Ajuda

14

17

15

16

19

Santo Quintino

Sobral de Monte Agraço

R. Trancão

Dois Portos

Zibreira

km

0   3

Alhandra to Sobral.

one of the gunboats that had arrived that day.[42] He was probably the first of many French to suffer from the attentions of these vessels. It is said that the naval party under Berkeley's nephew landed, recovered Sainte-Croix's body and buried him with full military honours. Pelet stated the French recovered the body.[43]

On 16 October, Burgoyne recorded that there were 14 gunboats in the Tagus and a transport brig 'manned with some 18-pounders' was moored off Alhandra. He also noted that the French has installed a battery of four guns on the riverbank at Vila Franca to keep the gunboats away.[44] This was probably in response to the death of Sainte-Croix. Another report of 22 October mentioned 22 gunboats and a 'luggar with a long 18-pounder.'[45]

With clear evidence that the French were concentrating around Sobral, Wellington called in his divisions. Hill and Craufurd remained in their positions near the Tagus to resist any attempt to break through on the riverbank. It was still possible that the French could launch simultaneous attacks on Sobral and Alhandra. Most of Wellington's troops were within half a day's march of each other so reinforcements could be moved quickly to any threatened spot.

On the morning of 13 October, Wellington had four divisions in the six-kilometre gap between the heights of Sobral and Portela do Bispo. There were no defences on the heights around Portela, as Oman (and many others) claimed, they had not been built yet. Forts 128–130, 150 and 151 were not started until after the skirmishes in October 1810. There was a 12 kilometre gap at this time between Forts 16 at Sobral and 26 near Torres Vedras. From east to west the divisions were: 1st Division (Spencer), 3rd Division (Picton), 4th Division (Cole) and 6th Division (Major General Alexander Campbell).[46] Pack's Portuguese brigade held the forts on the summit at Sobral. In reserve was the 5th Division (Leith) behind Zibreira and the two Portuguese brigades of Coleman and Archibald Campbell behind Ribaldeira.

In addition to the infantry, Wellington ordered forward a substantial force of artillery, in total nine brigades of foot artillery with one foot and one horse artillery brigade in reserve. Nearly 70 guns were facing the French across this relatively narrow defile. Wellington also ordered earthworks to be built for the artillery.[47] He could afford to concentrate almost all his field artillery in the central location as the positions to the east and west were supported by the heavy guns in the redoubts.

Wellington had also made provision for additional support from the 2nd Division. On 13 October he had ordered one of Hill's brigades back to Bucelas, leaving the other two brigades and Lecor's militia at Alhandra. Wellington justified the move by explaining that this brigade would be in

---

42   Gurwood, *Dispatches*, Wellington to Stuart, 12 October 1810.
43   De Toy, *Berkeley*, pp.506–507. Horward, *Pelet*, pp.220–221.
44   REM: 4201-68, Burgoyne journal, entries for 16 & 21 October 1810.
45   De Toy, *Berkeley*, p.509.
46   Oman, *Peninsular War*, Vol.3, p.441 fn. Oman seemed to be having an 'off day' when he wrote this chapter. He had the divisions in the wrong order in the main text but correct in the footnote.
47   Gurwood, *Dispatches*, Memorandum for Colonel Murray, Quarter Master General, 13 October 1810.

a better position to react if the French penetrated the Matos or Calhandriz valleys.[48]

The French at Sobral could see the force that was waiting for them to attack was much stronger. Masséna had chosen to examine the positions around Alhandra this day, and it is likely that Junot had no authority to launch a major attack. In the afternoon the French were concerned about their right flank, which was threatened by the allied troops blocking the road near Dois Portos. Junot decided to push them back and launched some light troops against Cole's division. For the next few hours, a lively skirmish ensued with both sides feeding in more troops. On the allied side, the 7th Fusiliers and the Brunswick Oels (light infantry) were reinforced by Hervey's brigade of the 11th and 23rd Portuguese Regiments. Wellington, watching the skirmish from Alqueidão fort told Cole: 'If you can maintain your ground without engaging in a serious affair, I wish you to do it … if you should be obliged to retire from Dois Portos, go to Ribaldeira and blow up the bridge which is mined.'[49]

There was one bridge to the west and one to the south of Dois Portos and both bridges were destroyed around this time. Wellington could see that the French were not very strong, and he did not see any benefit in getting involved in major skirmishing over ground he had no intention of holding. The French, having pushed Cole's advance guard back, maintained their position. Wellington reported that Colonel Hervey had been wounded in the engagement and the two Portuguese regiments 'again distinguished themselves upon this occasion.'[50] Casualties were about 150 on each side, showing that the skirmish became quite serious.

Another skirmish occurred to the east at Alhandra where a battalion sized force probed the allied position. The attempt was quickly abandoned when the scale of the defences was recognised. It is probable that Masséna was present to watch how the allies reacted as he did exactly this the following day.[51] Pelet who had been sent by Masséna to complete a reconnaissance at Sobral whilst he was at Alhandra reported: 'The mountain on which we find the principal work of the enemy rises before Sobral as that of Bussaco above Moura.'[52]

This was a choice of words designed to discourage his commander from trying an attack. Oman's comment that 'it was astonishing he [Masséna] had made no attempt earlier to judge with his own eye of the strength of Wellington's line of defence' is flawed.[53] The first infantry contact between the opposing forces was on 12 October. Masséna visited Alhandra on 13 October and Sobral on the 14 October. On each of these visits a small attack was made

---

48   Gurwood, *Dispatches*, Wellington to Hill, Ajuda, 15 October 1810. The order to move one of Hill's brigades to Bucelas on the 13 October is not in the Dispatches. This order must have been later in the day as his letter to Hill of 8:00am does not mention moving troops to Bucelas.

49   White, *Key to Lisbon*, p.188. Da Silva (ed.), *A Vida Quotidiana nas Linhas de Torres Vedras* (Torres Vedras: CMTV, 2010), p.168.

50   Gurwood, *Dispatches*, Wellington to Liverpool, 13 October 1810.

51   Horward, *Pelet*, p.226.

52   Horward, *Pelet*, p.230 fn. Masséna will have read this report before going to Sobral on 14 October.

53   Oman, *Peninsular War*, Vol.3, p.442.

to see how the defenders responded. Masséna had also sent out his trusted lieutenants to look at the surrounding area over these two days. As the scale of the defences was unexpected, Masséna was collecting information to determine the next step for his army.

Overnight on 13/14 October the French had moved four cannon behind barricades on the outskirts of Sobral without attracting the attention of the allied advance guard 200 metres away at Monte da Forca. The French artillery commander reported great difficulty moving his guns forward due to the bad weather, the state of the roads and the lack of forage for his animals, the first corps guns not arriving until 13 October. Masséna arrived at Sobral about noon on 14 October and watched the assault that followed. Pelet wrote that the attack was proposed to Masséna after he had arrived at Sobral rather than one that had been pre-planned.

Like the attack the day before at Alhandra, this was just to irritate the defenders and see how they reacted. The attack was undertaken by the fourth battalion of the 19e Ligne with support from the regimental grenadier companies and the hidden artillery. The choice of an inexperienced battalion suggests more about 'blooding' a raw unit than a serious attempt to push back the allies. The initial advance of the French dislodged the allied advance guard from their trenches on Monte da Forca. The success was short-lived as the defenders were quickly reinforced and then pushed the French back into the town returning to their original positions.

It is unlikely that Masséna learnt anything from the attacks that he witnessed. They were both small scale and were not pressed home. Neither needed the main defences on the Lines to open fire. Oman's claim that the French declined to renew the attack because of the 'redoubts visible along the Monte Agraço on the one hand and the Portello [Portela] heights on the other were of the most formidable description' is not correct.[54] As mentioned previously, the Portela redoubts had not yet been built. The reason why the French did not renew an attack was because they could see the fortifications on Monte Agraço and at least four red coated British divisions with nine batteries of artillery, behind fieldworks between Monte Agraço and Runa. Any major advance by Junot's corps of 12,000 could lead to a major defeat. They were outnumbered, outgunned and outflanked. One French officer who was present commented 'we lost 120 men to no purpose.'[55]

Did the French Know About the Lines?

Many accounts report Masséna's anger when he first saw the Lines and him saying the redoubts might be new, but the hills were not.[56] Were the defences a complete surprise to the French?

---

54 Oman, *Peninsular War*, Vol.3, p.443.
55 R. Brindle (ed.), *With Napoleon's Guns. The Military Memoirs of an Officer of the First Empire. Colonel Jean-Nicholas-Auguste Noël* (Barnsley: Frontline, 2016), p.104.
56 For example, White, *Key to Lisbon*, p.185.

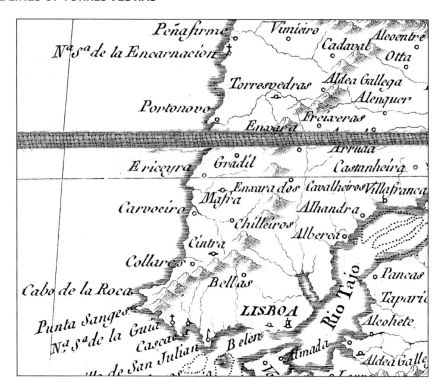

Lopez map showing the area north of Lisbon.

Pelet, tried to justify their lack of knowledge by blaming the Lopez maps which do not show hills north of Lisbon. In this he is correct, but there were a number of senior officers with the army that had been to that area recently. With Masséna were Junot, Loison and Thiébault (who started with them before being made Governor of Salamanca). Junot's chief engineer, Vincent, wrote reports and recommended fortifying the hills that Wellington used. Why had these not been brought to Masséna's attention? Pelet said at one point that Loison recalled hills in the area from his previous visit, why was Junot not questioned then?[57]

The first warning that the French received was not on 7 October 1810, as Pelet claimed but before the battle of Buçaco, at Viseu on 23 September where they were told: 'The English have an entrenched camp with redoubts and large ditches extending from Alhandra on the Tagus to Torres Vedras … at this moment it is occupied by some militia regiments.'[58]

Further confirmation came on 7 October, but the French felt confident that no fortifications could resist them. Conventional wisdom at this time was that fortified lines did not work; they could always be pierced by the attackers concentrating at one point whilst the defenders were spread across the whole defensive line. Wellington demonstrated this quite effectively in the Pyrenees at the end of 1813 by penetrating the French defensive positions

---

57   Horward, *Pelet*, p.222.
58   Horward, *Pelet*, p.222. Donald Horward, 'Masséna and Wellington on the Lines of Torres Vedras' in Alice Berleley (ed.), *New Lights on the Peninsular War* (Lisbon: British Historical Society of Portugal, 1991), p.124.

on the great river barriers. Pelet admitted that they had paid little attention as their maps showed wide flat terrain to the north of Lisbon. It is difficult to understand why Junot who had been in Lisbon several months did not have more concerns, particularly as it was his chief engineer, Vincent, who had written reports on the defence of Lisbon in 1807. It is understandable that the French did not take a defensive barrier too seriously but blaming it on the lack of hills on Lopez' maps was not.

There is no justification for Masséna not knowing, unless you believe that Junot deliberately did not offer his commander the necessary information. There were also several experienced Portuguese officers including the traitors Marquess d'Alorna and Pamplona Corte-Real who who both owned land north of Lisbon. Having said all of this, if Masséna had taken the information he received on the Lisbon defences seriously, would it have changed any of his actions? Probably not; he would have had to advance anyway. The problem again, comes back to his invasion force not being big enough. There was nothing Masséna could do about that. Pelet also argued that: 'The cruel ravages carried out by the enemy reinforced our ignorance [of the existence of the Lines], for it seemed they would not have abused a country they wanted to save. One must never lose sight of this central idea, for otherwise we could be accused, with reason, of a lack of foresight, and even stupidity.'[59]

This argument does not work either. If Wellington was intending to evacuate, then you would have to assume that he was some sort of monster, if he would deliberately destroy the country without a care for the population because he personally had no further use for them. Portugal was still an ally in the fight against the French and callously destroying the nation would fracture this relationship and probably Britain's relationship with every other ally. Who would ever trust them again? Pelet misread the situation based on the uncaring French attitude to conquered countries, their people and their resources.

15 October to 14 November 1810

The skirmishes over the previous few days were all insignificant when you look at the size of the armies. There were 120,000 soldiers facing each other at very close quarters and there had been four minor clashes, none of them involving more than 2,000 men. Pelet's reports to Masséna were generally pessimistic. From the French positions in front of the Lines, Pelet could see much of the defences in the Second Line, he described seeing redoubts at Bucelas, Montachique and Mafra. He believed that the French were not strong enough to break through the two Lines and reach Lisbon, 'the attack of the enemy Lines would have cost us half of our actual army.'[60] Masséna having spent a few more days reviewing the defences was quickly coming to the same conclusion. Writing to Ney on 16 October, who was in reserve with

---

59   Horward, *Pelet*, p.222.
60   Horward, *Pelet*, p.234.

the VI Corps at Alenquer, he reported 'the enemy are dug in up to the teeth … I see great works bristling with canon.'[61] His army was similarly surprised by the situation. One soldier commented: 'This came as a terrible shock to us. We had thought ourselves to be victorious, to be near the end of a glorious campaign and about to move into winter quarters in the Portuguese capital.'[62]

The French morale must have plummeted when the expectation of a great victory and plunder in Lisbon was replaced by the prospect of living in the open, through the winter with poor supplies. The terrible weather of the previous few days and the difficulties that had already been experienced in obtaining food would be a taste of what was coming. Retreat must have looked attractive to the common soldier.

Masséna needed a new plan. What were his options? The idea of an assault was considered too risky; the idea of retreat politically unacceptable. With more troops, an attack might have worked. Communications back to Spain and France were already next to impossible, Masséna could not easily call for support from the other French forces in Spain. He was probably enough of a realist to know that the chance of him receiving substantial reinforcements was low; the other marshals and generals had their own local problems to deal with. He decided to send a messenger back to Paris to explain the situation and *Général de brigade* Foy was selected for this difficult role. In the meantime, the French VIII Corps around Sobral dug field defences to strengthen their forward positions; most of the army was already further to the rear.

The bulk of the II Corps was at Carregado with its leading elements near Vila Franca de Xira. The VI Corps was further back at Ota with the leading elements at Alenquer. Within days of the last skirmish on 14 October, the move to Santarém had started; the reserve cavalry and reserve artillery had been ordered there.[63] The French army was now spread over 50 kilometres, which was a risk. If Wellington had launched an assault from Sobral, Junot was likely to have been comprehensively defeated before any help could arrive. Fortunately, Wellington did not change his strategy even though many in his army questioned why he was not attacking the inferior French forces in front of him. For the next few weeks, things would remain quiet for the bulk of the opposing armies; the allies waiting, the French looking for food and destroying the Portuguese countryside in the process.

Masséna ordered smiths, carpenters and other associated tradesmen to be taken from the ranks and despatched to Santarém to start work on constructing vessels to cross either the river Tagus or the river Zêzere, allowing access into other regions and possibly to make contact with other French forces. This would solve Masséna's food supply problem, it was also what Wellington feared most. His strategy to starve the French army into retreat required them to have no access to other parts of Portugal. Masséna had one other significant supply problem, his army was very low on gunpowder. As well as asking Foy on his journey back through Spain to ask for powder

---

61   Horward, *Pelet*, p.232.
62   Brindle, *With Napoleon's Guns*, p.104.
63   Oman, *Peninsular War*, Vol.3, p.449.

to be sent, he also asked *Général de division* Jean Baptiste Éblé, the artillery commander in charge of work at Santarém to manufacture some.[64]

During these tense few days, Wellington watched the French activity, trying to determine what they were planning. On 15 October, he still thought the French might try another attack on his centre at Sobral. Following the recent skirmishes, Wellington had ordered immediate work to strengthen the weakest positions in the First Line. These will be described later. Also, on 15 October 1810, Wellington received disquieting news from Berkeley that the French had taken 40 boats around Santarém and this, if true was a major set-back. The report probably came from Captain John Cowan RN who Berkeley had sent upriver to collect or destroy river boats. Cowan had reported that the French 'may have taken sufficient boats to cross the Tagus.'[65] Wellington replied that:

> The loss of the boats at Santarem to be the greatest misfortune that could happen to us, and it may oblige us to change our position, and take up our second line. The French will either arm these boats, and operate upon Hill's right flank, in which case, the strength of your flotilla, and the support to be given it by larger vessels, will become an object for your consideration; or they will use them to form a bridge, and establish themselves upon the island in the Tagus [Mouchão de Alhandra], across Hill's right flank; or they will use them to form a bridge or other communication with Mortier [in Extremadura], whom they will have it in their power to draw to their support either on this side or on the other side of the river. In whichever way the boats may be used, their loss is a serious misfortune.[66]

Wellington complained about the Portuguese Government's failure to ensure that all boats were removed from the river. In the same letter, Wellington asked Berkeley as a priority to make sure that the French did not establish themselves on the small river island off Alhandra by positioning gunboats upriver. Next in priority was to secure the larger island (Mouchão) of Lezíria (Lyceria) which he believed had supplies of 'corn and cattle'. He asked Berkeley if he could get gunboats up the smaller eastern channel of the Tagus to secure the island, and also stop any French vessels approaching the Tagus estuary by this route.

Wellington then wrote immediately to Charles Stuart asking for the Portuguese government to urgently remove all resources from Lezíria. He also asked for the Alentejo province to be evacuated towards Palmela and Setúbal and for all resources to be removed to stop them falling into the hands of the enemy. Similarly, he asked for immediate action to ensure the fortresses in the Alentejo had provisions to withstand a siege, noting the Portuguese Government had neglected to do this at Óbidos, forcing it to be abandoned.[67] Finally he asked, again, for all boats to be removed to safety

---

64   Horward, *Pelet*, p.243. Éblé was unable to make any powder because he could not find supplies of sulphur and saltpetre.

65   De Toy, *Berkeley*, p.508.

66   Gurwood, *Dispatches*, Wellington to Berkeley, 16 October 1810.

67   Gurwood, *Dispatches*, Wellington to Stuart, 16 October 1810 and 18 October 1810.

on the river. His next letter was to Hill, to inform him of the situation and that he had ordered a battery for four heavy guns to be constructed on the Tagus bank at Alhandra to 'support the gun boats' and of course to attack any French vessels that tried to come down the river.[68] This battery is almost certainly what is now known as battery 1A.

On 19 October, Squire set off with Commander John Houston RN, commander of HMS *Vestal*, to reconnoitre the left bank of the Tagus. They crossed from Lezíria to Samora Correia and travelled north to opposite Santarém, returning the next day to Alhandra via the north-east tip of Lezíria. Squire reported a number of pieces of information. Firstly, on the 40 boats which Berkeley had claimed were at Santarém: 'The story of the 40 boats is a mere tale; five bullock carts with their standing poles on the sides were mistaken for 40 boats!!! At Santarem there are two large boats not yet launched.'[69]

Pelet appeared to confirm this view.[70] Berkeley was completely wrong, and his claim is not mentioned again by Wellington who must have been furious about the time and effort wasted reacting to the report. Squire's update continued:

> I found the people on the left bank completely panic struck because the Leiria Militia etc at Chamusca and other places were ordered to Setuval – as well as that very brigade of artillery which has been extremely useful in preventing the assemblage of the boats at Santarem. There is indeed a fine peasantry, numerous and willing in all towns and villages between Chamusca and Samora – but they want officers to direct and troops of the line and artillery to animate and support them. The zeal and spirit seemed universal, but the people were sadly depressed by the retreat [of the militia] yesterday.

Whilst Wellington expected that he might have to evacuate the Alentejo at some point, being forced to do it with no advance warning for the population would cause the same sort of scenes as at Coimbra. Squire noted that three of Berkeley's gunboats had arrived in the channel to the east of Lezíria, as Wellington requested, and had calmed the civilians a little. The channel was not always navigable, being 'dry at low water, [and] it is muddy and impassable'. The final piece of information that Squire provided was that the roads on Lezíria 'will be impassable for artillery after six hours rain'. This would have been good news for Wellington who was concerned that the French might establish batteries on the island. Although the French had not captured 40 boats, they were building them, so the risks had not gone away, just been put off for a few weeks. Wellington still needed to counter this threat by strengthening the defences on the Tagus and looking for ways to stop any attempt to cross the river.

Wellington was not only having to deal with the French. The issue of the 40 boats was not the only time where Berkeley's 'enthusiasm' to help and

---

68   Gurwood, *Dispatches* 1st edition only, Wellington to Hill, ¼ before 1 a.m., 16 October 1810.
69   REM: 5501-79, Squire to Fletcher, 20 October 1810.
70   Horward, *Pelet*, p.252.

challenging of procedures caused Wellington problems. We have already seen one example when Berkeley demanded extra allowances for his sailors manning the telegraphs, an allowance that had never previously been given. Berkeley also decided at this moment to raise two other matters, the handling of prisoners of war and the risk to the fleet if the French took the heights to the south of the Tagus estuary. Wellington patiently answered both but there is an element of frustration creeping into his language, 'I am perfectly aware of the strength of the ground on the left of the Tagus' he responded.[71]

Wellington was also continuing to deal with challenges from the Regency about his operations. Although the Portuguese Government had agreed to his strategy of withdrawing to the Lines and the evacuation of the population, now it was happening, every decision was being challenged and the actions delayed. Wellington felt that the Regency would make better use of their time if they concentrated on their responsibilities rather than constantly challenging his. There was also a sharpness in dealing with correspondence from home. A letter from Torrens, asked Wellington to make enquiries about a complaint from a junior officer made directly to the Secretary of War. After explaining that he was aware of the case and attaching copies of the correspondence, he noted that if an enquiry is needed then it had better start with an enquiry into his actions.

Wellington received another letter from Berkeley, dated 21 October 1810, but he did not reply until four days later. Berkeley was now challenging how boats were obtained on the Tagus for military use. Wellington's response said that requests followed the 'regulations of the service' and Berkeley 'will be able to procure copies of … these regulations at Lisbon.'[72]

Wellington continued to watch and wait. Writing to Stuart on 23 October, he said he believed the French were collecting material to make a bridge across the Tagus. He was uncertain whether it was for a retreat or to open up new foraging areas. One possibility was that the French, having built the bridge, would throw everything at the Allied position hoping to break through. If they failed, then the bridge would provide a ready escape route into a fertile region. It was because of this that he was reluctant to move any of his army to the south bank of the Tagus even though this was being requested by the Regency. The letter continued with instructions for the Portuguese government. Firstly, he confirmed the previous request to evacuate the Alentejo. Secondly, to incapacitate the mills in the region. Thirdly, to collect boats to allow three bridges to be built at Punhete, Abrantes and Vila Velha 'which might be laid down and used on the lower part of the Tagus for the passage of the army, if that mode of passage should be found preferable to that by boats.'[73]

Two days later, Wellington wrote in frustration to Stuart, complaining that the Regency, with Souza in the lead, had challenged his instructions, complaining 'since that person has been in government, I have not made one proposition … that he has not opposed.' His letter continued with complaints

---

71   Gurwood, *Dispatches*, Wellington to Berkeley, 17 October 1810.
72   Gurwood, *Dispatches*, Wellington to Berkeley, 25 October 1810.
73   Gurwood, *Dispatches*, Wellington to Stuart, 23 October 1810.

about no action being taken on desertion from the militia and the regular failure to supply workers for the Lines. The next day Wellington wrote again to Stuart on the subject of the Regency, proposing that Souza should be removed, and made it clear that the Regency had no authority on military matters. In another letter to Liverpool, Wellington said 'if Principal Souza is not removed from the Regency and even from Portugal and if the Prince Regent does not give power and authority … to the government … it is useless to pretend to carry on military operations … or to preserve this country.'[74]

Berkeley now made another offer to Wellington, to station marines and sailors on Lezíria. Wellington took five days to respond saying they 'are not necessary to keep the enemy's marauding parties in order' and asked him not to send the party.[75] The next day Wellington explained to Berkeley that he had ordered three bridges which he intended to place above Salvaterra if the army needed to cross. He said Berkeley's suggestion of crossing over Lezíria was not feasible due to the lack of a good road. Wellington wrote in frustration that: 'The Portuguese government and the Admiral are not aware of the difficulties of my situation … and they give me more trouble in writing letters upon their nonsense, and lose more of my time, than can be conceived.'[76]

On 28 October 1810, by a process that is not clear, Wellington's request to the Regency through Stuart, to collect boats for three bridges was taken up by Berkeley, Wellington commenting that 'the government ought not to have imposed on you.'[77] Wellington explained his need for three boat bridges, two to replace those destroyed at Punhete and Vila Velha and possibly a third for Abrantes. His intention was still to use the boats for the army to cross the Tagus before moving the bridges up to their final positions. In this letter, Wellington seems to backtrack on his previous statements that there was no decent road across Lezíria and left the option open for further investigation. Wellington appointed an engineer officer to liaise with the navy and report directly back to him on the preparations.[78]

On 31 October 1810, Wellington explained part of his reluctance to send troops to the left bank of the Tagus. The Portuguese government had been organising troops and operations on the left bank and Wellington was not interested in the risks associated with two forces operating independently in the same area. He wrote that *Ordenança* were being armed against his wishes and without him being consulted. He asked Beresford to 'hint to Forjaz, that as long as the government continue to carry on their operations, and to give their orders to officers on the left of the Tagus, it is impossible for us to interfere in any manner.'[79] He had mentioned the same to Berkeley as part of the reason why he was reluctant to put any troops on Lezíria.

---

74   Gurwood, *Dispatches*, first letter, Wellington to Liverpool, 27 October 1810.
75   Gurwood, *Dispatches*, Wellington to Berkeley, 26 October 1810.
76   Gurwood, *Dispatches*, Wellington to Stuart, 3 November 1810. The printed version does not mention Berkeley, the original letter did. It was up for auction in July 2020. Thanks to Rory Muir for bringing this to my attention.
77   Gurwood, *Dispatches*, Wellington to Berkeley, 29 October 1810.
78   Gurwood, *Dispatches*, Wellington to Wedekind, 28 October 1810.
79   Gurwood, *Dispatches*, Wellington to Beresford, 31 October 1810. Wellington to Berkeley, 29 & 31 October 1810.

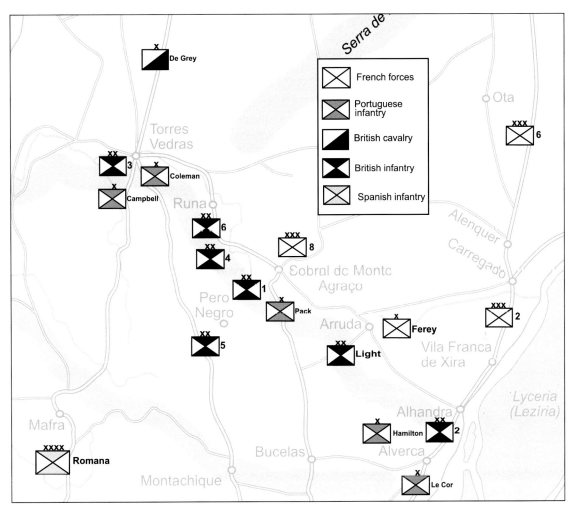

Positions October to November 1810.

Whilst Wellington's concern about potential conflicts in uncoordinated operations was understandable, it was entirely reasonable that the Portuguese authorities were making arrangements for defence of the south bank of the Tagus whilst Wellington was not. It was no good Wellington complaining when he was doing nothing. One wonders if he was stung into action by the Portuguese government and the Royal Navy taking action, whilst he seemed determined to stay north of the Tagus.

An agreement was quickly reached for these *ordenança* to operate under Fane who crossed from Lisbon to the left bank near Samora Correia on 2 November 1810. The force comprised of a brigade of Portuguese cavalry and one regiment of *caçadores*. Fane's orders were to observe and report on the French activities; 'to prevent them crossing if possible'; and to destroy their boats and bridge making equipment which had been discovered at Santarém and at Barquinha.[80]

---

80   Gurwood, *Dispatches*, Wellington to Fane, 1 November 1810.

Before this agreement had been reached, Berkeley had moved a small force across to Lezíria. It is not clear if Wellington had subsequently agreed to this move, Burgoyne commenting, 'It appears that the Admiral [Berkeley] has sent [a force] to the other side of the Tagus, the whole under Captain Houston'. The naval force had crossed on 31 October from Alhandra to Samora Correia and the following morning they moved to Salvaterra. The force was made up of 100 marines, 100 sailors and four field guns.[81] On 2 November the first two guns were mounted in an earthwork battery on the north-east corner of the island, with one more gun added on 6 November.[82] Wellington commented 'If the enemy pass the Tagus in force, the Admiral cannot defend the island of Lyceria [which was 20 kilometres long] with 100 marines and his gun boats.'[83] By this time the gunboats were operating as far up the river as Salvaterra, keeping the French away from the islands in the Tagus.[84]

Also, apparently without Wellington's knowledge, a Spanish force under Carlos de España arrived opposite Abrantes. Wellington had to quickly make arrangements for this force to be fed and for tents to be issued from the stores at Abrantes, something the governor, Lobo, was unwilling to do without orders.[85] De España had been at the crossing point at Vila Velha when Foy's strong detachment had approached on his journey back to Paris. Fearing an attempt to capture the Tagus crossing point, De España had crossed to the south bank, burnt the bridge and then retired towards Abrantes.[86] The French were aware of all this activity and Pelet commented: 'The enemy carefully guarded all the usual fordable points and opposite Santarém they placed cannon which fired on everything that showed its face. They kept a battery with a strong detachment of Portuguese infantry at Escaroupim [north of Salvaterra] facing Azambuja and numerous posts of peasants were lined up along its entire bank.'[87]

Wellington made another request to Berkeley. On 10 November he asked if he would be willing to form a force of seamen and marines to operate on the banks of the Tagus near São Julião.[88] The proposal was for the sailors to occupy fortified positions, allowing more troops to be released back to the army. Berkeley readily agreed to this and Gillmor noted on 15 November: '900 seamen and 200 marines to be landed on north side of the Tagus.'[89]

81   H.N. Edwards, 'The Diary of Lieutenant Gillmor – Portugal – 1810', *Journal for the Society for Army Historical Research*, Vol.3, No.13, p.150; De Toy, *Berkeley*, p.509; REM: 4201-68, Burgoyne Journal, 1 November 1810. De Toy said 50 sailors; Burgoyne said six guns. The present author has gone with Gillmor, as he was there.

82   De Toy wrote that Houston 'took possession of the island' on 20 October 1810 following Wellington's request of 16 October. Wellington's letter of that date makes no such request and the date claimed for occupying the island is also wrong. A number of Berkeley's claims as recorded in De Toy's thesis are difficult to reconcile with other accounts.

83   Gurwood, *Dispatches*, Wellington to Stuart, 3 Nov 1810.

84   REM: 4201-68 Burgoyne Journal, 1 November 1810; Edwards, 'Diary', p.150.

85   Gurwood, *Dispatches*, Wellington to Fane, 11 & 12 October 1810.

86   Oman, *Peninsular War*, Vol.3, p.455.

87   Horward, *Pelet*, p.261.

88   Gurwood, *Dispatches*, Wellington to Berkeley, 10 November 1810.

89   Edwards, 'Diary', p.153.

THE LINES – OCTOBER TO NOVEMBER 1810

These were in addition to the naval personnel already operating on the south bank of the Tagus. Berkeley even claimed that he had seamen and guns permanently established in Alhandra town, but this seems unlikely as they would be easily captured if the French made any advance on the position.[90]

When Wellington ordered Fane to the southern bank, he also asked Berkeley to supply some rockets as Fane 'might probably derive some advantage … in the destruction of the enemy's collection of materials for a bridge at Barquinha and Santarém.'[91] Berkeley replied questioning the effectiveness of them and Wellington, admitted that he had never seen them used, but commented that the Master General of the Ordnance would not have issued them if he thought they were useless. Wellington also noted in the same letter that he was trying the rockets as it was not possible to get the gun boats with 24-pounders higher up the river than Salvaterra. Berkeley complied, they were unloaded on 7 November and by 10 November they were opposite Santarém under the command of Captain Houston. The naval contingent had joined with a Portuguese force and moved up a number of cannon of different calibre which they used to unsuccessfully bombard the six boats visible on the river bank on 12 November 1810.[92] Fane now asked Wellington for permission to attack Santarém with the rockets to ensure the boats and supplies were destroyed. This attack will be covered later.

The day after the artillery bombardment, Gillmor noted that the French had started moving some of the boats 'towards the Zêzere' (eastwards).[93] But it wasn't only boats that were on the move as Wellington was soon to find out.

So, what had the French been doing since 14 October? The setting up of a *depôt* at Santarém has already been mentioned. Éblé's orders were to construct two flying bridges as a matter of urgency. His task was nearly impossible, there were almost no resources available for him, he described the situation to Pelet as *tout manque* (everything missing).[94] Materials had to be scavenged from buildings and tools had to be made before any building work could begin. Patrols had been sent out to reconnoitre the banks of the Tagus and the Zêzere for crossing points and boats.

Masséna, having realised the weakness of his position, had issued orders that if attacked the whole army would concentrate at Alenquer 20 kilometers to the north of the Lines.[95] The poor weather, lack of supplies, and desertion were draining his strength. Foy had been despatched to Paris and Montbrun had mounted a strong demonstration against Abrantes, crossing the Zêzere at Punhete. Even before Foy arrived in Paris, Napoleon had been pressing *Général de divsion* Jean-Baptiste Drouet's IX Corps to advance and make contact with Masséna, although Masséna would not know this until Drouet's arrival at the end of December 1810.[96] Pelet believed that if Drouet had arrived

90   Sutcliffe, *Expeditionary Warfare*, p.134. Edwards, 'Diary', p.149
91   Gurwood, *Dispatches*, Wellington to Berkeley, 1 & 3 November 1810.
92   Edwards, 'Diary', pp.151–152. Guns mentioned by Gillmor were two 12-pounders, two 6-pounders, two 3-pounders and two howitzers.
93   Edwards, 'Diary', p.153.
94   Horward, *Pelet*, p.251.
95   Horward, *Pelet*, pp.243–244.
96   Oman, *Peninsular War*, Vol.3, pp.457–459. Horward, *Pelet*, pp.259–260 fn.

Abrantes and boat bridge.
(Author's collection)

with 12–15,000 men it would have been possible to breach the Lines. Such a large reinforcement, which was unlikely, would have brought Masséna's army back to the strength he had when he set off. It is difficult to see how this could have been enough, when Wellington's army was larger, excluding the militia and *ordenança* which he could use to occupy the defensive positions.[97] Pelet continued, saying Masséna had four options. First, retire to Coimbra and occupy Porto. Second, retire to Castelo Branco. Third, cross the Tagus into the Alentejo and fourth, to remain near Santarém and temporarily keep his options open. He also recorded that Montbrun had been ordered to attempt a *coup-de-main* on Abrantes. A British officer recorded that 'On 31st October, 200 French cavalry and infantry crossed by fording the Zêzere near Punhete. Abrantes is secure against a coup de main and cannot be attacked by less than 14 or 15,000 men.'[98] Pelet disagreed stating that on their first approach, the allied bridge across the Zêzere had been destroyed and he was not able to cross. On 4 November 1810, a second approach was made by Loison who crossed the river and a reconnaissance was made around Abrantes, determining that it was too strong for a *coup-de-main*.[99]

The importance of Abrantes was fully understood by the allies. Work on improving the defences had started in 1808, long before any work started on the Lisbon defences. Engineer officers were permanently placed there to oversee this work and substantial resources were provided. In an unusual step, the senior British engineer, Captain Peter Patton had to agree that the

---

97   Horward, *Pelet*, pp.242–243.
98   BL: ADD63106 ff.13-15, Squire to Bunbury, 6 Nov 1810.
99   Horward, *Pelet*, pp.252, 257.

place was indefensible before the governor could negotiate with the French about surrender.[100]

In the meantime, the French struggled to find food in front of the Lines. By 10 November, Masséna realised that he could not remain there any longer and ordered a withdrawal to Santarém, which was more defensible and would provide access to new foraging areas. This location also allowed another possible route of retreat through Castelo Branco if the Zêzere could be bridged. This was why Masséna had moved his boats east from Santarém. Masséna, had already moved to Santarém on 29 October 1810. Despite the understanding shown by Pelet and Masséna's chief of staff, *Général de brigade* François Nicholas Fririon, the commander-in-chief was unhappy with the progress Éblé was making.[101]

The next step was for the French to make.

---

100   BL: RP5296, Beresford to Patton, 4 October 1810.
101   Horward, *Pelet*, p.261 fn.

11

Operations and Building Work – November 1810 to March 1811

Santarém was a strong position. On the right bank of the river Tagus with extensive low ground around the river that was prone to flooding on both banks. To the west was the smaller rio Maior, again on a wide plain that was prone to flooding.[1] There was a single major bridge across the rio Maior, that was exposed to defensive positions on the eastern bank. To attack would require a difficult frontal assault or a wide outflanking manoeuvre. Prior to their withdrawal to Santarém, the French had made plans for the defence of the city. They were also having some success at obtaining boats. Masséna claimed to have 42 boats and with 20 more would have enough 'to cross the Zêzere. Eventually, a bridge was established at Punhete and another was then placed [10 kilometres upstream] at Martinchel.'[2]

The first stages of the withdrawal occurred on 10 November 1810, when the corps' hospitals and commissary stores were moved. On the 13 November the bulk of the artillery was withdrawn, and the infantry retreated from 8:00 p.m. on the night of 14 November 1810. Masséna had a piece of luck with the arrival of a dense fog that hid his troops movements until the morning of 15 November. He gained 12 hours before his withdrawal was discovered.[3] The French used two primary routes in the retreat. The first used by Ney and Junot, north from Alenquer towards Alcoentre before turning east near Moinho do Cubo. Once these corps were clear, Reynier used the direct road through Cartaxo to Santarém.

Having discovered the French withdrawal, Wellington responded cautiously, not knowing what the French intentions were. He considered three possibilities; a full retreat, an attempt to move to the southern bank of the Tagus, or a relocation to improve the poor supply situation. Each of these

---

1   The river, rio Maior flows past the town of Rio Maior 30 kilometers north west of Santarém.
2   Horward, *Pelet*, p.268. No dates were given as to when this happened but its position in the text infers before the retreat to Santarém.
3   Oman, *Peninsular War*, Vol.3, p.465.

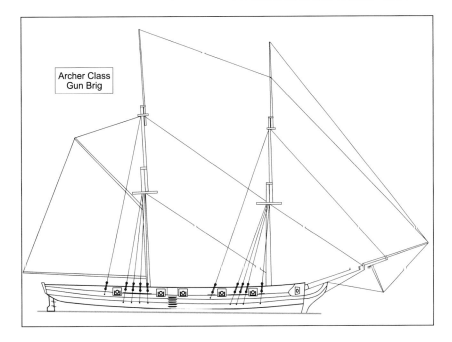

Archer Class Gun Brig.

options could require an allied advance on Abrantes. Three allied divisions moved slowly forward concentrating towards Alenquer, witnessing dead soldiers, animals and a wanton destruction of Portuguese towns and villages. Wellington ordered Fane who was already on the south bank to move up towards Abrantes. He then ordered Hill with two allied divisions to cross the Tagus at Valada (south of Cartaxo) to strengthen the forces able to resist an attempted crossing by the French.[4] The allied crossing was facilitated by Berkeley who by 18 November, arranged: 'The flotilla … to the amount of 5 or 600 [boats which were] anchored at Valada and in six hours constructed a wharf and ferried over General Hill and his division.'[5]

With the flotilla was Berkeley's deputy, Rear Admiral Sir Thomas Williams aboard HMS *Growler*, an *Archer* class gun brig. This was a substantial vessel 24 metres long, weighing 180 tons with ten 18-pounder carronades and two 18-pounder cannon.[6] Along with the smaller gun boats the Royal Navy was bringing significant firepower to support the allied advance.

There was an additional advantage from the presence of naval vessels. Wellington's correspondence twice mentioned boats for communication.[7] It would appear that boats capable of signalling were following the army upriver. This makes sense as it kept Wellington in immediate contact with his army (to Alhandra, then to the telegraphs on the Lines), and to Lisbon and Berkeley. Wellington had left a substantial force in the rear at Alenquer and on the Lines until he was certain what was happening and might have needed

---

4   2nd Division and Hamilton's Portuguese Division.

5   De Toy, *Berkeley*, p.536; Fortescue, *British Army*, Vol.7, p.549.

6   Cy Harrison, *Three Decks – Warships in the Age of Sail*, <https://threedecks.org/index.php? display_type=show_ship&id=6691>, accessed 3 March 2020.

7   Gurwood, *Dispatches*, Wellington to Lumley 21 and 22 November 1810.

to call them up quickly. On 17 November the allied advance guard came up against the French rear guard near Cartaxo but judging it too strong to attack with the available troops, they were allowed to withdraw to Santarém.

The Rocket Attack on Santarém

On 1 November, Wellington had asked Berkeley to provide some Congreve rockets for Fane to try and destroy the 'materials for a bridge at Barquinha and Santarem'[8]. After Fane failed to damage the stores at Santarém with artillery on 12 November, he asked for permission to use the rockets. He was understandably concerned about civilian damage to the town. Wellington replied on the 14 November: 'I am anxious that an attempt should be made ... whatever may be the consequence to the town ... I should be very sorry to destroy the town ... but I should never forgive myself if, having it in my power to destroy the means of passing the Tagus, I omitted to make use of it.'[9]

By the next morning, finding the French had withdrawn, but not knowing why, Wellington would have been even more determined to destroy any French bridging equipment. Crossing the Tagus or the Zêzere was now much more likely. A second letter to Fane that day was more insistent, 'You must in the first instance rocket Santarem'. Gillmor recorded that the attack was made at 7:00am on 16 November 1810. Of the 42 rockets fired, four exploded on their launchers and only four hit the town. He concluded 'I have a very poor opinion of Congreve's rockets.'[10]

For several days Wellington was not sure if the French planned a full retreat. It had started raining on 15 November and he thought the delay at Santarém might have been because of the bad weather and the poor state of the roads. However, it soon became apparent that they were not retreating further. The French settled themselves in their new locations, spread over 50 kilometres. Their line was from Alcanede to Santarém with the reserve at Tomar. There were also troops further east towards Punhete, where a bridge had been built across the Zêzere leavings options for attacking Abrantes or moving further east.[11] At this time Wellington's forces were also widely spread out over similar distances. In front of Santarém there were only two British divisions with another in close support at Alenquer. Nearly half of his forces were still on the Lines, and a British and a Portuguese division were south of the Tagus. Wellington was probably as much at risk as the French from a rapid advance.

Whilst there was now more country to search for food, the French were still hemmed in to the north, south and west; to the east was the allied held city of Abrantes and the barren central Portuguese countryside. Having looked at the options for a frontal attack or an outflanking manoeuvre,

---

8   Gurwood, *Dispatches*, Wellington to Berkeley, 1 November 1810.
9   Gurwood, *Dispatches*, Wellington to Fane, 14 November 1810.
10   De Toy, *Berkeley*, p.533. Oman, *Peninsular War*, Vol.3, p.462 gets the date wrong, saying the attack happened on 13 November. Fortescue, *British Army*, Vol.7, p.548, says 15 November.
11   Oman, *Peninsular War*, Vol.3, p.470.

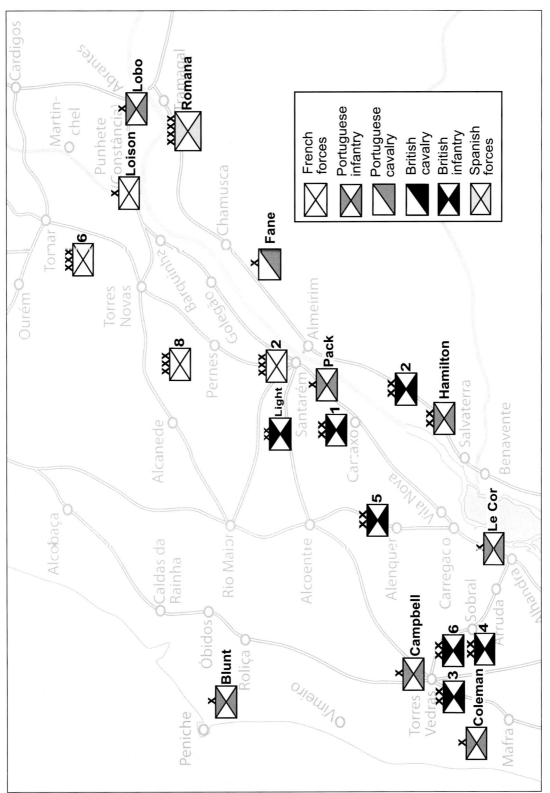

Positions of armies on 19 November 1810.

the allies knew it was there and that boat construction continued. Masséna only waited for news of the arrival of reinforcements before he made his next move. When they arrived at Espinhal on 26 December 1810, it was not the full corps he expected but a part, only 8,000 strong, which did not even replace his losses so far. To make matters worse its commander, Drouet, insisted that his command was separate and he was not under Masséna's orders. Until something changed, Masséna was not strong enough to advance and food would run out by mid-January. What Masséna did not know was that Soult, stung by criticism from Napoleon for not advancing to support the French invasion, had eventually decided to move into Estremadura and attack Badajoz, hoping this would force Wellington to despatch troops south and reduce the numbers in front of Masséna. The increased threat of the French crossing the Tagus spurred Wellington to begin defences on the south side of the estuary facing Lisbon; the Fourth Line, which will be covered later.

Lieutenant General Hill fell ill at the end of November 1810 and his subordinate Major General William Stewart commanded for a few weeks until Beresford was sent to take command of the southern corps. On 1 January 1811, Beresford inspected the position at Punhete and ordered batteries to be built opposite the mouth of the Zêzere to resist any French attempt to move the boats from their boatyard. Even though Wellington was confident that the French were contained, the artillery crews remained in the forts on the Lines. Fletcher wrote an update to Wellington:

Memorandum of the number of guns in the several districts, and of the number of artillerymen required for their service at six per gun with the number stated to be actually present.

District	Guns	Men required	Men present
1 (Torres Vedras)	128	768	482
2 (Sobral)	53	318	479
3 (Alhandra)	74	444	518
4 (Bucelas)	85	510	431
5 (Montachique)	65	390	677
6 (Mafra)	70	420	621
Total	475	2,850	3,208

N.B. In the above return, District No. 1 is considered to include the three new redoubts, the right of which is the new signal post [Forts 128–130].[19]

Over the next few weeks, the uneasy stalemate continued on the north side of the Tagus. There was little activity other than foraging and Wellington waited to see what the French would do. Drouet settled at Leiria to stretch the allied defences and to try and keep communications with Spain open. Masséna still considered crossing the Tagus.

On 30 December 1810, Soult left Seville with around 20,000 troops and moved into Spanish Extremadura. His intention was to take control of the

---

19   REM: 5501-59-18, Cartaxo, 27 December 1810.

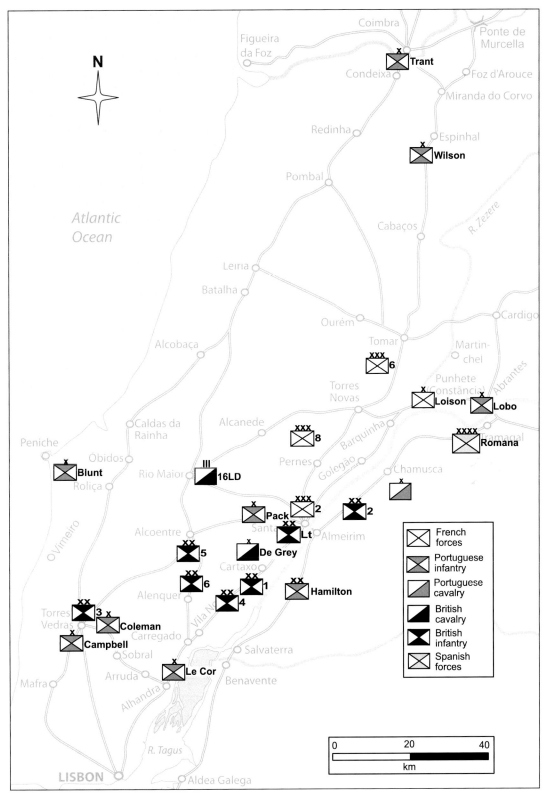

Positions of armies 1 December 1810.

Wellington decided that neither were practical. The weather made a flank march impossible, and Wellington made his opinions on a frontal attack clear in letters to his brother, Henry Wellesley 'the French have a position at Santarém, compared with which Bussaco is nothing' and Stuart 'the enemy have a position stronger than Bussaco or Sobral'.[12]

The positions of both armies at the end of November 1810 would be broadly where they would remain through the winter months.[13] Being able to move off the Lines gave the allies more opportunities to get the troops under cover through the worst of the winter.

The Armies Settle In – December 1810

Colonel Jean-Nicholas Noël described the new French position, 'The army's position between Santarém and Tomar was much better than the previous one, more concentrated and better to resist attack.'[14] Pelet agreed and added that the position 'intercepted the two principal communication routes of the area. The plain of Golegã … was still covered with growing corn.'[15] For the moment, there was food for the French army. Unfortunately, the food in the Golegã region was being sent to Lisbon and this meant there was less food reaching the city. Jones commented that the residents near Golegã thought they were safe from the French until too late and 'not one fiftieth part of the corn had been removed.'[16]

Oman was critical of Wellington's decision to move a corps under Hill to the south of the Tagus believing that Masséna was not determined to cross the river. Whilst Wellington had second thoughts about the decision when he realised the French were concentrating around Santarém it was probably still the correct choice. A crossing was still very much in Masséna's mind, although it had significant technical difficulties. Pelet described the rivers, saying the Tagus at Punhete was 300 metres wide expanding to 500 metres by Barquinha. When it flooded it would rise five metres above its normal level. The riverbanks were usually steep and difficult to access. The Zêzere was 'only' 150 metres wide at its mouth where it joined the Tagus although it was shallower and had narrowed to about 80 metres by Martinchel, 10 kilometres upstream.[17] The bridge the French had placed across the Zêzere near its mouth comprised 20 boats, all recently built, with another 35 ready to use. Éblé had promised 80 boats by the end of December 'to have bridges over the Zezere and Tagus simultaneously, as the Prince [Masséna] desired.'[18] Whilst much of the shipyard was invisible from the south bank of the river,

---

12 Gurwood, *Dispatches*, Wellington to Wellesley and to Stuart, both 21 November 1810.
13 Wyld, *Annex*, p.41.
14 Brindle, *With Napoleon's Guns*, p.108.
15 Horward, *Pelet*, p.284.
16 J.T. Jones, *Account of the War in Spain, Portugal and the South of France from 1808 to 1814 inclusive*, second edition (London: Egerton, 1821), Vol.1, p.312.
17 Rui Moura says these widths are excessive, suggesting the Tagus was 200m wide and the Zêzere 100m wide at Punhete.
18 Horward, *Pelet*, pp.300–304.

province, rather than a direct advance to support Masséna, but Wellington did not know this and feared that this force could tip the balance in front of Lisbon. These were anxious days as Wellington first tried to ensure the routes across the Guadiana river were secure and then ensuring that Beresford could retreat all the way to Almada if necessary. The news that Olivenza was being besieged mid-January and Badajoz invested at the end of the month reassured Wellington that Soult was not making a thrust towards Lisbon. Masséna remained ignorant about these operations.

On 5 February 1811, Foy arrived back at Masséna's headquarters from Paris with Napoleon's latest orders which were now six weeks old. He informed Masséna that he had ordered Mortier's V Corps from Soult's Army of the South and Lahoussaye's small Army of the Centre to advance and reinforce him, and he had to remain until they arrived. Based on this, it made sense for Masséna to delay placing a bridge across the Tagus. If a French force made it to the south bank of the Tagus, then the bridge could be built without interference. If the bridge was thrown across earlier, it could be destroyed by the enemy, and this would make it more difficult for the French forces to co-ordinate their movements. Unfortunately for Masséna, Lahoussaye had been turned back by Portuguese forces at Cardigos, and Mortier was involved in the siege of Badajoz with no orders to support Masséna. However, by this time, Masséna had decided that retreat was the only option and crossing the Tagus would move his army further away from the major source of provisions in central Spain. Following a meeting with his senior commanders, the decision was made to retreat unless a relieving force arrived. No-one expected that to happen.[20]

The first French troops withdrew on 4 March 1811, with the remainder following the next day. The Allies were aware something was happening. Jones commented on 4 March, 'Great movements observed amongst the enemy particularly near Punhete. All seemingly indicate a speedy retreat.'[21] Fortunately, luck once again assisted the French. Wellington had decided that it was time to attack the French. Allied reinforcements were due and once these landed Wellington would attack. Most of these units arrived later than expected between 4 and 6 March 1811 and Wellington was looking towards Lisbon just as the French started their retreat. Had the French delayed their retreat for a week, things could have been very different. Wellington followed the retreat closely through Leiria, Pombal and on to the Spanish border.

The Role of Food in the Outcome of the Third Invasion

One of the underlying stories of Masséna's invasion of Portugal was the availability of food and forage. Part of the allied strategy was to minimise the enemy's access to food by removing or destroying it, and also to order the evacuation of the civilian population from the areas that would be occupied by the invaders. If there was no population present, then there was no-one

---

20   Oman, *Peninsular War*, Vol.4, pp.75–81.
21   REM: 5501-59-1, Jones Diary, 4 March 1811.

from whom the French could take food. The French army would then have to advance to the Lines across a large area where there was no access to supplies. The French armies across Europe relied on being able to requisition local supplies; this was always difficult in the Peninsula where there was barely enough feed the population most years.

This story has two aspects, firstly, the French finding food and secondly, feeding the displaced Portuguese civilians.

Feeding the French

When the French invaded Portugal after the capture of Almeida in September 1810, they brought limited supplies with them. The route they followed took them through Viseu and Coimbra, where further supplies could be collected before their advance towards Lisbon. Masséna had some success, and the early days of the invasion were hampered more by bad weather than lack of food. On the route from Coimbra to Lisbon the French were able to find more supplies to increase their magazines. This should not have been possible due to the allied scorched earth policy of removing all access to food. What had gone wrong?

The first reason is understandable; the population were unhappy being asked to destroy all their possessions and flee from the French, leaving them destitute. Many tried hiding their produce and valuables, but the French soldier was very good at finding things and as the situation deteriorated they were not averse to murder and torture to get food.

The main reason, however, was a breakdown in the consensus between the allied army under Wellington and the Portuguese Regency. The strategy of retiring to the Lines in front of Lisbon and abandoning the country had been agreed with the Regency (but not unanimously) in February 1810. Wellington knew he was not strong enough to stop the larger French armies on the 1,200 kilometre long border. Once the reality of the situation arrived in summer of 1810 a furious disagreement broke out between Wellington and the Regency Council, primarily driven by Principal Souza. Whilst Wellington retained Forjaz's support, the whole strategy was now challenged with the Regency demanding that Wellington fought on the border at all risks and they then challenged the need, and details, of abandoning the countryside. This led to delays in ordering and enforcing the flight of the population. In many cases there was little, or no warning given to the civilians. Whilst the population might have been told that it would be necessary to evacuate, no-one was going to flee their home until they absolutely had to. Apart from the rich, the rest waited until it was too late.

Wellington, writing to Liverpool on 27 October 1810, said he could not estimate how long the French could stay in front of the Lines due to the failure of the Portuguese Regency to order removal of supplies. He continued, 'If Principal Souza is not removed from the Regency and even from Portugal … it is useless to pretend to carry on military operations … of which Portugal is to be the basis, or to preserve the country.' He had made a similar comment the day before to Stuart, 'if Principal Souza does not go … the country will be lost'.[22] Wellington's argument with the Regency got so bad that he more or less issued a 'he goes, or I go' ultimatum about Principal Souza. He took the very unusual step of writing directly to the Portuguese Regent in Brazil. On 30 November, he sent a draft of his letter to the Regent to Stuart for him to review:

> Having formed a plan … I went to Lisbon early in February [1810] … purposely to communicate it to the Governors of the Kingdom, whose approbation, including that of the Patriarch [Souza], it received … the allied army under my command was the only organised body existing in the Peninsula which could keep the field against the enemy … I considered that Lisbon and the Tagus were the sinews of your Royal Highness' government … and that they were essential for the allies to retain, and for the enemy to get possession of … Unfortunately, one of the gentlemen who was appointed by your Royal Highness … did not approve of the plan of operations … possibly when your Royal Highness appointed me to be the Marshal General of your armies … your highness intended that I, and not the local government, much less any individual member … should be responsible for the plan and conduct of the military operations … I could not let any individual, however respectable, to interfere in the performance of [my] duties … The Principal Souza, however, was of the opinion, that the war ought to have been [fought] … on the frontiers of Beira; that an offensive operation ought to be carried on or within the Spanish frontier; and that a general action ought to be fought, at all risks … he, by his influence over others … prevailed on the government to omit and delay … many measures recommended by me … I recommended that the people of the country should be directed to remove out of the enemy's reach … what could be useful to the enemy and rendering the mills useless … it could be carried into execution … only by being adopted at an early period … it was delayed in respect of the country between the Tagus and the Mondego till the last moment … particularly because it was contended by the Principal Souza … The influence of the Principal Souza has, in this instance been pernicious; and I leave it to your Royal Highness to determine, whether it is expedient that that gentleman should continue to be a member of the government.[23]

Stuart showed the draft letter to the council, and they were unhappy with its content. Wellington was unmoved stating that it was only proper that the council had an opportunity to refute Wellington's statements before it was sent and that until otherwise instructed, the military decisions were his to make.[24] Whilst the recriminations continued for some time, the consequences did not alter; there was more food available to the invaders than Wellington had wanted.

It is clear that the allied soldiers knew that the plan was to starve the French out. There are numerous comments on the availability of food both during the retreat to, and the occupation of, the Lines. One officer commented

22 Gurwood, *Dispatches*, Wellington to Liverpool, 27 October 1810. Note: there were several letters to Liverpool on this date. Wellington to Stuart, 26 October 1810.
23 Gurwood, *Dispatches*, Wellington to Prince Regent, Cartaxo, 30 November 1810.
24 Gurwood, *Dispatches*, Wellington to Stuart, Cartaxo, 5 December 1810.

on 2 October that supplies had been left at the convent at Batalha, just south of Leiria, 'which they beg the general to distribute, as, if not, the French will have it.' He also noted that a nearby *Quinta* had left 'large quantities of wine, corn and oil.'[25] A similar story came from the rearguard on passing through Coimbra: 'I went into one or two houses, which the people had only left in the morning. We found sheep, turkeys, geese and fowls in greatest abundance. He also noted that military supplies had been destroyed at Coimbra and Condeixa as there was no time to remove them.'[26]

Whilst it is understandable that the lack of warning would have left much food around Coimbra, it is less easy to understand why there was still food available immediately in front of the Lines.

Two different accounts from the 71st Regiment tell of finding food in Sobral on 15 October: 'to our great joy, found a large store-house full of dry fish, flour, rice and sugar.'[27] Days after arriving in the Lines, Wellington was still complaining about the situation '[T]he enemy are living upon grain found close to the lines; and they grind it into flour with the mills in our sight, which the government were repeatedly pressed to order these people to render useless.'[28] French sources told a similar story; Pelet reported finding grain at Vila Franca and Santarém and that the troops were constructing bakeries.[29] The engineer John Squire commented:

> Do not ... believe that the enemy are in want of provisions. As they arrived just at the conclusion of the harvest, I believe they are most amply supplied. From our sudden and unexpected retreat, the country was not driven. The inhabitants it is true, fled with whatever they could carry with them, but their granaries were left full of corn and their cellars filled with the wine of the recent vintage. Large herds of cattle also remained for the enemy and ... I saw an abundance of stacks of straw, Indian corn etc untouched [on the right bank of the Tagus], which convinced me that their supplies were by no means exhausted.[30]

His views were supported by John Burgoyne who noted food being left on the retreat to the Lines and the presence of 'a very large quantity of grain' at Vila Franca and 'the idea of starving the enemy out of their ground is out of the question.'[31] Squire's comment about the 'sudden and unexpected retreat' does not fit well with the view that the retreat from Coimbra was expected and well planned. It is difficult to reconcile Wellington's plan for withdrawal to the Lines, made many months before, with the actual events where many were surprised when Wellington retreated through Coimbra. Forjaz also claimed that the area in front of the Lines was not cleared of supplies as they

25   George Wrottesley, *Life and Correspondence of Field Marshall Sir John Burgoyne* (London: Richard Bentley, 1873), Vol.1, pp.115–116.

26   James Tomkinson, *Diary of a Cavalry Officer* (London: Swan Sonnenschein, 1895), p.47.

27   Hibbert, *Soldier of the 71st*; Anon, *Vicissitudes in the Life of a Scottish Soldier* (London: Colburn, 1827), p.115.

28   Gurwood, *Dispatches*, first edition only, Wellington to Berkeley, 16 October 1810.

29   Horward, *Pelet*, p.243.

30   BL: ADD63106, ff.13–15, Squire to Bunbury, 6 November 1810.

31   Wrottesley, *Burgoyne*, Vol.1, p.121, diary entry for 1 November 1810.

did not hear until early October of Wellington intention to retreat and then had no time to implement the plan![32]

Whilst food was being found in the early weeks of the stalemate in front of the Lines, when this was used up there was nothing to replace it. The French troops had to travel further to find food, and steps were being taken to make that difficult. Raiding parties operated out of Peniche and Óbidos (which had been re-occupied). Captain Fenwick, the governor of Óbidos, regularly led raiding parties made of up Portuguese militia and recruits until his death in December 1810.[33] Brigadier Blunt, the governor at Peniche also reported the actions of Portuguese groups attacking the French.[34] Colonel Wilson patrolled the area between Coimbra and Leiria; Colonel Waters, one of Wellington's exploring officers, roamed the area with cavalry detachments. These groups could not stop foraging in force, but French in small groups were regularly being attacked.

Noël recorded that initially supplies were not a problem but 'these were quickly exhausted and in order to live, recourse was had to marauding … the men gave themselves up to every sort of pillage. Noël paints a darker picture commenting that peasants were also tortured to steal money, not just food. Pelet used the words 'horrible excesses' to describe the actions of the French foragers. He continued: 'The men, full of wine, committed violent acts against the peasants they met in order to discover the hidden supplies. The peasants avenged themselves whenever they found isolated or drunk soldiers … as they left [the villages] the soldiers would set them on fire.'[35]

The seriousness of the supply situation was shown by Noël who reported visiting a position in front of Sobral and finding it abandoned, all the officers and men having dispersed to find food.[36] In early November, Richard Fletcher noted that: 'Some [French] deserters say that the men were yesterday ordered to provide themselves with two months provisions. Skilful as they are in plundering, I should conceive they cannot easily obey this order.'[37]

Pelet confirmed that there was some truth in the story, saying 'almost all of them had executed the order to make twenty-day rations of biscuit in case of a movement.'[38] The French had stayed four weeks in front of the Lines before accepting that the troops needed to retire to an area with better provisions. The situation when the French pulled back improved, but the need to forage widely remained until the retreat started in March 1811.

---

32   Francisco de la Fuente, *Dom Miguel Pereira Forjaz. His early career and role in the mobilization of the Portuguese Army and Defense of Portugal during the Peninsular war, 1807–14* (Lisboa: Tribuna, 2011), pp.184–185.

33   Gurwood, *Dispatches*, Blunt to Military Secretary, 16 October; Wellington to Liverpool, 3 November and reporting his death, Wellington to Liverpool, 15 December 1810.

34   Gurwood, *Dispatches*, Blunt to Military Secretary, 19 October 1810.

35   Howard, *Pelet*, p.309.

36   Brindle, *With Napoleon's Guns*, pp.105–106. Also, Oman, *Peninsular War*, Vol.3, p.463.

37   TNA: WO55/958 Fletcher to Morse, 10 November 1810.

38   Howard, *Pelet*, p.308.

Feeding the Portuguese Population

When the French invaded, many civilians abandoned their homes as ordered by their government, or because they had previously experienced the behaviour of French troops. The few who remained were robbed or murdered by foraging parties with little attempt to control their behaviour. This evacuation had a devastating impact on the Portuguese population, particularly in the area between the Mondego and Tagus rivers.

The number of civilians who fled to Lisbon is unclear. Estimates range from 40,000 to 300,000 with the likely number being between 100,000 to 200,000.[39] Attempts were made to disperse them across the area behind the Lines rather than concentrate them all in the city. Many thousands were transported over the Tagus for the perceived safer southern bank and regulations were introduced to stop profiteering by raising prices. One recent writer summarised:

> The influx into Lisbon of refugees, for the most part from the region between the Mondego and the Lines forced the authorities ... to radically alter the city's infrastructure, they had to find food and lodging for a mass of humanity who ... contributed to a scarcity of local provisions .... Steps were taken to prevent the usual speculation which is caused by such events; the excessive rise in the prices of staples with some success.[40]

Two edicts issued on 8 and 10 October laid down strict guidelines for the Lisbon population. The first started:

> The duties of humanity requiring that all possible assistance should be afforded to those who, abandoning their homes, have sought an asylum in the capital, against the tyranny and oppression of the enemies of this kingdom; and it being incompatible with the duties of the Police to allow these unhappy fugitives to perish, exposed to the calamity of a rainy season, I order as follows ...

It continued saying owners of empty houses could not refuse to let them at the current rate and if they did not, they would be fined, and their properties let rent-free. Poor families would also be housed in empty buildings. The second edict focussed on allowing passage to the south side of the Tagus where the same rules for accommodation were in place.[41] Howard suggested the measures had limited success in controlling prices and access to food.[42] Jones in his early history of the war wrote that 200,000 fugitives arrived in Lisbon and an additional 50,000 that 'fled to the left bank of the Tagus, long remained exposed to the weather, and a large proportion miserably perished

---

39 Cristina Clímaco, *As Linhas de Torres Vedras, Invasão e Resistência 1810–11* (Torres Vedras: CMTV, 2010), p.128fn. The main text says 400,000 the footnote 300,000, author's translation.

40 M. Monteiro (ed.), *The Lines of Torres Vedras; A Defence System to the North of Lisbon* (Lisbon: PILT, 2011), p.163.

41 Proclamations, issued at Lisbon, 8 and 10 October 1810, by Lucas de Scabra da Silva, copies published in *Cobbett's Political Register*, July to December 1810, pp.858–859.

42 Horward, *Pelet,* p.243fn.

Sopa dos Pobres em Arroios.
(BNP: Public Domain)

from hunger and disease, before relief could be administered.'[43] As the huge number of civilians started arriving in Lisbon, systems were set up to try and feed them. A soup kitchen was set up in the *Arroios* district and another near the docks for refugees arriving by boat.[44]

Even in the early weeks of the occupation of the Lines, whilst he was still in open disagreement with the Regency, the plight of the refugees was causing Wellington concern. Writing to Liverpool on 27 October he highlighted the issue that the harvest on which much of the population relied had been taken or destroyed by the French, leaving the civilians with nothing and 'there are no means whatever in this country of relieving [their distress]'. He noted that 'wealthy inhabitants of Great Britain' had previously contributed towards relieving distress 'and there never was a case in which their assistance was required in a greater degree'. He 'recommended … the inhabitants … to your Lordship's protection … and I request you to consider … the benevolent disposition of His Majesty's subjects.'[45] A subscription was taken up in London but it was 1811 before the funds were available to help the poorest restart their lives, often in the form of cattle.[46]

Leach of the 95th wrote about the terrible conditions in which many of these refugees lived and died. He noted that the British divisions arranged for 'soup made from the heads and offal of the cattle killed for the troops' to be given to the starving civilians.[47] One aspect is puzzling. Throughout the

43 Jones, *Account,* Vol.1, p.333. In the first edition of this work, published in 1818, Jones wrote that 50,000 had fled to Lisbon. This number was increased to 200,000 for the second, 1821 edition.

44 Clímaco, *Linhas*, p.128.

45 Gurwood, *Dispatches*, Wellington to Liverpool, 27 October 1810.

46 Thanks to Marcus Beresford for information on this subject including notes from BL: X.708 2695.

47 Jonathan Leach, *Captain of the 95th (Rifles)* (London: Leonour, 2005), p.112.

period the French were in front of Lines, there were constant complaints about the difficulty in getting civilians to work on the Lines. As Wellington complained in a letter to Stuart, 'It is curious that … the people are said to be starving, and we are ready to give them work, and money and bread in payment, the government … are unable to collect them for us!'[48] The pay for a labourer was 10 vintens daily, which was roughly one shilling, the same pay as a British soldier received. Deductions for a pound of biscuit daily was 3 vintens. A tradesman received 16 vintens (nearly 2 shillings daily).[49] There was potentially paid employment for thousands of civilians, with guaranteed pay and food, why were they not willing to take up this offer? This was better pay than the Portuguese regular and militia soldiers were getting at the time.

As well as civilians retiring towards Lisbon, further north, they had been ordered to cross to the north bank of the Mondego. The French foragers were roaming between Santarém up to the south side of Coimbra. This whole area was a dangerous wasteland. Pelet tried blaming the British for the French atrocities which even he called 'horrible excesses',[50] citing Wellington's scorched earth policy: 'How many [Civilians] must have died during the six months we remained in this country, maintained by food that extreme necessity forced us to wrest from them.'[51] The French way of waging war was to make the invaded country pay for it. This was the extreme consequence of such a policy.

As the French retreated a proclamation was issued by the Portuguese Regency on 25 March 1811 ordering:

> … the recording of the damage, fires and deaths caused by the last invasion … Summarizing the information that came from the parish priests, the province of the Diocese of Coimbra … opened its December 1811 report, "The bishopric of Coimbra … [which] contains 290 parishes, will only count 26 of them where the enemy did not enter". According to their calculations, 3,000 people died violently at the hands of the soldiers and as a result of the epidemic that followed, at least 35 thousand inhabitants of the diocese died.[52]

This 'epidemic' was the result of starvation, exposure to the weather, poor housing and sanitation. Another recent Portuguese analysis of the impact on civilians at Santarém reports hundreds of deaths from illness, starvation and brutality during the French occupation.[53]

---

48   Gurwood, *Dispatches*, Wellington to Stuart, 31 December 1810.
49   Thompson, *Mulcaster*, p.101. Also, Jones, *Sieges*, Vol.3, p.66.
50   Horward, *Pelet*, p.309.
51   Horward, *Pelet*, p.243.
52   Maria Antónia Lopes, 'Sofrimentos das populações na terceira invasão francesa. De Gouveia a Pombal', in P.A. Avillez (ed.), *Os Exército Português e as Comemorações dos 200 Anos da Guerra Peninsular* (Lisboa: Tribuna, 2008–2011), Vol.3, pp.299–323, author's translation.
53   Carlos Guardado da Silva, 'A vila e o concelho de Santarém sob a invasão francesa de 1810–1811', *Impactos materiais e humanos*, <https://www.academia.edu/5340183/A_vila_e_o_concelho_de_Santarém_sob_a_invasão_francesa_de_1810_1811_Impactos_materiais_e_humanos>, accessed on 24 January 2021.

Whilst the allied strategy was successful, the biggest losers in the short term were the low-income civilians who suffered hugely through the winter of 1810 and then had to try and rebuild their lives in 1811. Fortunately, the French never returned, so the rebuilding of their lives could start uninterrupted in the spring of 1811.

The arrival of the armies in October 1810, is not the end of the story of the building of the Lines. Significant new construction work continued through the winter of 1810 and into 1811.

12

Building Work on the Lines from October 1811

The decision to hold the French at the first line, does not appear to have been made until late August or early September 1810. As described above, the first work on strengthening the forward defences started in late July. Further discussions in late August led to the start of the construction of Forts 121–124 to strengthen the Calhandriz and Matos valleys. If the area from Alhandra to Sobral was secure, then the French would have to move further west to the position Wellington selected for his army between Sobral and Torres Vedras. When the allied troops arrived, work was immediately commenced to support the forts by blocking any route across the hills near Arruda, and to build field works between Sobral and Portela. John Squire described the Alhandra area on 10 October 1810:

> It consists of a ridge of heights, which commences about 600 yards from the Tagus and extends about 2½ miles in a westerly direction, where the country becomes less difficult of access. The interval between the heights of Alhandra and the Tagus is occupied by low marshy ground, across which is an entrenchment having a double ditch and since our arrival I have added an impenetrable abbatis, so that I consider our right as secure as if we were in the fortifications of Malta. … Every day adds to our strength and enables us to increase the force destined to meet the enemy in the field.

In the same letter, Squire's doubt about the viability of the defensive positions had now diminished:

> When I told you … that the lines in front of Lisbon neither could, nor ought to be defended I calculated that the enemy would not have committed the unpardonable error of invading this country with an army inferior in numbers to those who defend it. I did give him credit for greater foresight and a larger share of prudence. I conceived that he would never have attacked this country without an overwhelming force, and that an attempt to oppose his progress in this situation would have been preposterous and absurd. Now indeed in consequence of the follies of our enemy our affairs wear a most brilliant appearance and the

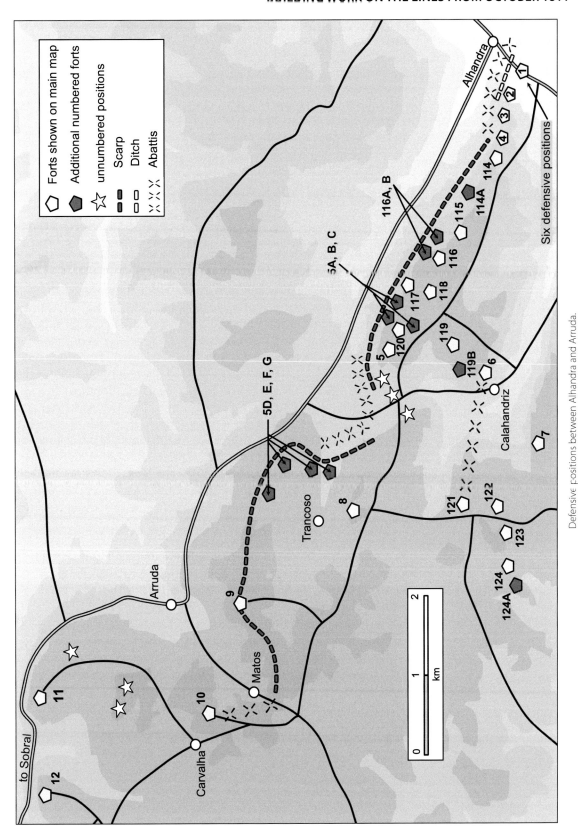

Legend:
- Forts shown on main map
- Additional numbered forts
- unnumbered positions
- Scarp
- Ditch
- Abattis

Six defensive positions

Alhandra

1
2
3
4
114
114A
115
116
116A, B
5A, B, C
117
118
119
119B
6
120
5
Calahandriz
7
121
122
123
124
124A
5D, E, F, G
Trancoso
8
9
Arruda
Matos
10
11
to Sobral
12
Carvalha

km
0   1   2

Defensive positions between Alhandra and Arruda.

179

very safety of the French Army becomes every day in my mind more and more precarious.[1]

Work continued, improving the defences from Alhandra to Arruda over the coming weeks. Wellington writing to Hill (at Alhandra) and Craufurd (at Arruda) stated the defences around Arruda were, 'necessary for securing the entry of the valley of Calhandriz [placing] a battery at the point of ground extending from redoubt No.9 to fire on the road from Arruda to Alhandra and to defend the left of the entrance of the valley of Calhandriz.'[2]

Looking at contemporary maps, there are several unnumbered defensive positions in this area. There were three between Forts 10 and 11 and three more at the north-eastern end of the Calhandriz valley. Also, there were four more at the north-western end, which became Forts 5D–G.[3] In all there were 46 defensive positions from Fort 11 to the west of Arruda, to the Tagus at Alhandra a distance of 10 kilometres. Further scarping work was carried out between the Calhandriz valley and Arruda although this took time due to the scarcity of tools.[4] Squire's description of 'impregnable' is accurate.

There were few forts in the 12 kilometres between Sobral and Torres Vedras. This was intentional as this was where the bulk of the allied forces would stand, but more defences were planned. New forts were started in October, first above Portela where initially a new signal station was built and later protected by a redoubt (128). Two further forts were built to the west (129 and 130). Although Jones' *Sieges*, suggested that these were all constructed in October 1810, they were actually built between October and December 1810.[5] On 18 November, Fletcher ordered Mulcaster to construct a new redoubt (129) after completing the signal station (128). A diagram in the letter shows a signal station only, (i.e., no fort) at 128, then the position for 129 and a mill where 130 would eventually be built.[6] It was not until 18 December that orders were given to start Fort 130, built around the mill, to command the road from Torres Vedras to Montachique.[7] Mulcaster reported his progress on 27 December 1810:

> I have this morning laid out the new mill redoubt on the Serra da Cadriceira [130] but although I have gone well into the dip it will as now traced hold only 200 men and I think will be worse if made larger as the ground falls so much from the mill [original order was for 300 men] … I shall not however begin it till I hear further from you … With regard to the weekly progress by Saturday night all the traverses in the new redoubt [129] will be finished and there only remains some trifling additions to the parapets and glacis … the ditch of the centre redoubt [129] is five feet deep and the reform of the signal post work [128] has been proceeded, but

1   BL: ADD63106, ff.11-12.
2   Gurwood, *Dispatches*, Memorandum to Hill & Craufurd, 23 October 1810.
3   TNA: MR 1-523.
4   TNA: WO55/959, Squire to [unknown], Sobral Pequeno, 8 November 1810.
5   Jones, *Sieges*, Vol.3, p.33.
6   REM: 5501-59-4, Fletcher to Mulcaster, 18 November 1810.
7   REM: 5501-59-4, Fletcher to Mulcaster, 18 December 1810. Also, Fletcher to Mulcaster, 5 January 1811, the owner of mill to be compensated.

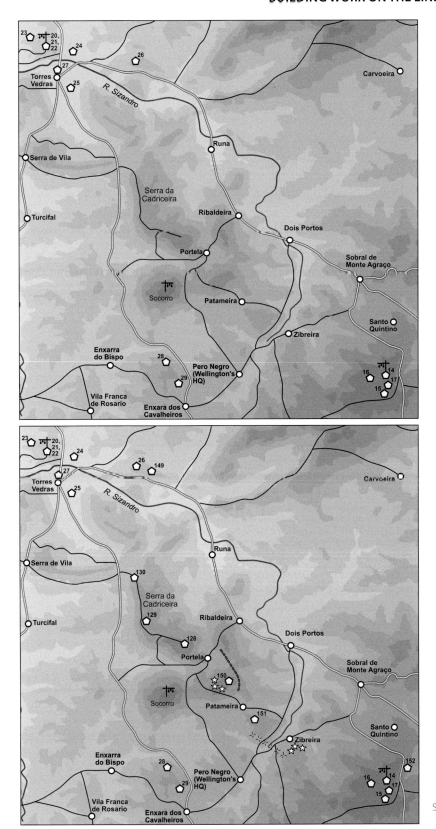

Sobral to Torres Vedras, before and after October 1810.

as it is indefensible, I keep there only a few men. I can begin work round the mill as soon as I receive your answer if it may be executed as now traced. … I request to know if the mill on the Serra da Cadriceira which is a new one of two sets of stones will receive the same compensation as those formerly dismantled at Torres Vedras and the same weekly allowance.[8]

Another contemporary map shows that Fort 150 above Patameira was completed by November 1810.[9] Also shown are additional unnumbered batteries near 150 and above Zibreira.[10] The remaining forts in this area were; 149 to command the road from Runa to Torres Vedras; 151, in the centre of the valley between Runa and Sobral (started February 1811) and 152 to the east of Sobral on the road to Bucelas (started January 1811).[11] It is not clear when 149 was started but there is one letter dated 22 March 1811 in which 'Orders [are] sent to Captain Mulcaster to construct a redoubt for 250 men and four guns on a plateau on the right of the road leading down to Ribaldeira'.[12] The size of the fort matches.

The final part of the first line was that to the west of Torres Vedras. In October 1810, Fletcher noted that:

The most vulnerable part of our present front is on the left of Torres Vedras. We have already established six guard redoubts upon this ground and are now throwing up seven [more] for forty-eight pieces of artillery … as his Lordship seems inclined to do all I have proposed to render us secure, we shall have to employ seven thousand workmen at different points at the same moment.[13]

This work had started soon after the allies entered the Lines. A request was issued for 25 portable magazines to be made, capable of holding 120 12-pounder cartridges for these forts.[14] Mulcaster had overall control of the building work. As well as the forts, orders had been given to flood the Sizandro valley by damming the river. He reported on 11 November:

The river is not swollen but the valley begins to be and is a good deal intersected by ditches which would prevent the passage of troops. We have dammed everything below Ponte do Rol; between this [place, Torres Vedras] and it are some ditches which can be done on the approach of the enemy but at present they would make the road almost impassable and it is a good deal used for the conveyance of forage and provisions for the troops on the left. Today being Sunday, added to the rain, left us destitute of ordenanças but I am assured of a great many tomorrow. But as long as such violent weather continues you know our progress must be slower. Indeed but for the emergency, on such very bad days, it is almost better they should not come as they expend the money without much advancing the work.

---

8   REM: 5501-59-18, Mulcaster to Fletcher, 27 December 1810.
9   REM: 4201-152-2.
10   Sousa Lobo, *Defesa*, p.241, calls these 150a-c; TNA: MR1-930-1 and MR1-930-6.
11   REM: 5501-59-1, 18 January and 13 February 1811.
12   REM: 5501-59-1, Jones to Mulcaster 22 March 1811.
13   TNA: WO55/958, Fletcher to Morse, 26 October 1810.
14   AHM: PT-AHM-DIV-1-14-020-06, Fletcher to Forjaz, 29 October 1810.

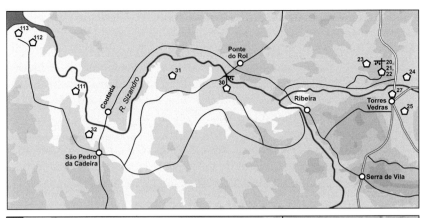

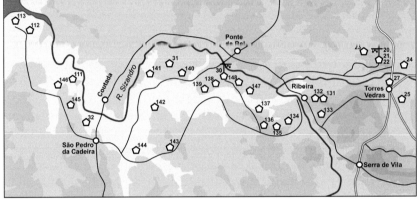

Defences to west of Torres
Vedras; before and after
October 1810.

I have cut some of the sides of the drains as you mentioned but as yet only one is
full which has caused a small inundation. Their great use will be in preventing the
water running off after the great rains.[15]

The rain was not only filling the rivers. Reports of water damage to the forts
were growing and would continue throughout the winter. Work continued to
the west of Torres Vedras for the next two months and by early January 1811,
14 forts, numbers 131–144, had been added although Jones wrote that they
were not completed until the Spring of 1811.[16] A further four, 145–148, were
completed over the next few months making a total on 18 new forts and 24
in total over 12 kilometres.[17]

There were no more forts built on the second line after the allied army
arrived, but there was one other major piece of work. In December 1810,
orders were given to create an abatis at the western end of the Line from the
coast at Ribamar to Murgeira near Mafra a distance of 15 kilometres. This
complemented the additional work at the western end of the first Line.[18]

From the day the allied army arrived at the Lines, there were problems
with damage caused by rain. The earthwork defences were not capable of

15   REM: 5501-59-18, Mulcaster to Fletcher, 11 November 1810.
16   REM: 5501-59-18, table listing forts dated 6 January 1811; Jones, *Sieges*, Vol.3, p.40.
17   REM: 5501-59-4, Fletcher to Mulcaster, 7 January 1811.
18   REM: 4601-86, Ross to Dalrymple, 14 December 1810.

surviving a Portuguese winter. The first mention by Wellington of facing the forts in stone was in early December when Wellington suggested that this should be done at Fort 11 near Arruda.[19] Many more would be faced through 1810 and 1811. There were heavy rains again at the beginning of February 1811 and substantial damage was done, which required the constant attention of the engineers and workmen.[20] The complaints about the lack of workmen never went away through the whole period of the construction and maintenance of the Lines.

The withdrawal of the French from in front of the Lines in November 1810, whilst not stopping the work on the Lines, led to additional work nearer the new French positions. On 27 November, orders were issued to mine four bridges at Vila Nova (da Rainha) and Carregado, making any future French advance on the Lines more difficult.[21] Towards the end of December, the bridge between Vale (de Santarém) and Santarém was mined as was another three kilometres upriver. The mines at Vale were refreshed on 18 February 1811. An attempt was also made to dam the Rio Maior at Santa Anna with casks, but this was abandoned.[22]

Soult's advance from Seville in January 1811 raised the concern of a second French front developing on the south side of the Tagus. Beresford's position watching for any attempt by Masséna to cross the Tagus was now threatened from the rear. If Soult advanced towards Abrantes or made a thrust directly towards Lisbon, Beresford could be cut off. The weather that hampered Soult's advance also threatened Beresford's retreat. The rain had swollen the Rio Sorraia near Benavente, blocking the road on the southern bank of the Tagus.[23] A bridge of 16 boats was thrown across the river to ensure the allied forces on the left bank had a route back to the Tagus estuary at Almada.[24] In the end this was not required as Soult advanced no further than Badajoz.

Wellington now started fortifying positions to further restrict the French movements. In late January, defensive positions for five batteries were started at Alcoentre. Walls were strengthened, and dams were constructed to raise the river level. Fletcher and Jones were there most of the time from mid-January to mid-February. The allies also had an advanced picket in Rio Maior with the nearest French troops being around Alcanede.[25] Wellington now had a defensive line running from Cartaxo on the Tagus to Rio Maior. French activity around Santarém was carefully monitored.

Fletcher reported in early February that there was 'still several thousands of workmen employed' in building work.[26] Wellington was taking no risks

---

19   REM: 5501-59-4, Chapman to Archer, 9 December 1810. Mulcaster had mentioned stone facing for the scarps as early as March 1810.
20   REM: 5501-59-1, 1-6 February 1811.
21   REM: 5501-59-4, Fletcher to ?, 27 November 1810.
22   REM: 5501-59-1, entries 25-30 December 1810 and 16-18 & 28 February 1811. Probably Santana, south-east of Cartaxo.
23   See Mark S. Thompson, *Albuera – The Fatal Hill* (Sunderland: Amazon CreateSpace, 2014), pp.10–22 for a description of Soult's operations. Wellington called the river, Zatas, Beresford called it the Sor.
24   REM: 5501-59-1, 18, 20 & 27 January 1811.
25   REM: 5501-59-1, diary entries from 21 January to 22 February 1811.
26   TNA: WO55/958, Fletcher to. Morse, 2 February 1811.

and continued to improve the defences. The last numbered forts had been started in January and February and by the time of Masséna's retreat in March 1811, the initial construction work on the Lines was complete. There was still much to do. Through 1811, many of the forts were stone faced to provide better protection from the weather, rather than the enemy. Repairs due to weather related damage would continue until the end of the war,

With the retreat of Masséna in March 1811, the immediate risk to the allies reduced and Wellington ordered the militia and *ordenança* on the Lines to be stood down and sent home, although they had to remain 'ready to return at the shortest notice.'[27] Also, steps were quickly taken to reduce the huge cost of the transports stationed in the Tagus estuary. On 20 March 1811, Wellington told Berkeley he had been instructed to send most of the shipping home, keeping the best – for 3,000 troops and 300 horses – and the hospital ships. Most of the regimental baggage would be consolidated in a small number of ships and the ordnance stores, with the exception of the siege train, were to be unloaded and stored in São Julião. The disagreements with Principal Souza and the unrest in Lisbon were still on Wellington's mind. Wellington felt that since 'some members of it [the Regency Council] have taken pains to inflame the mind of the people against us ... I should not now think anything safe in Lisbon in case the British government ... withdraw their army.' He reported that he had ordered four jetties to be built at São Julião and asked Berkeley to give his opinion of the best 'place for them.'[28] Captain Charles Holloway RE was initially put in charge of the work and applied to Forjaz for tools, workmen and a Portuguese engineer with hydraulics experience. Work continued there for over a year. In July 1811, Holloway complained that some of his workmen were being called up for military service and asked for them to be exempted.[29] A permanent superintendent of jetties was appointed to manage the loading and unloading. These jetties remained in use for the rest of the war.

The Defences to the South of the Tagus Estuary

There is one final area to look at, the 'fourth line'. Wellington had recognised from his first arrival in 1808 that enemy possession of the south bank could endanger any shipping anchored in the estuary. Writing to the Duke of Richmond, Lord Lieutenant of Ireland, before returning to the Peninsula in 1809, he said: 'I have no doubt that Lisbon, may be, and will be, defended; and I have long determined to fortify the heights of Almada, so as to be able to hold them with a small body of men, as the first step I should take on my arrival.'[30]

It is surprising that having recognised the risk of the left bank falling into French hands and having said he would fortify them immediately; he then

---

27   Gurwood, *Dispatches*, Wellington to Beresford, 19 March 1811.

28   Gurwood, *Dispatches*, Wellington to Berkeley, 20 March 1810.

29   AHM: PT-AHM-DIV-1-14-163-22, Holloway to Forjaz, 29 March, 11 April & 3 July 1811.

30   Gurwood, *Dispatches*, Wellington to Richmond, 14 April 1809.

did nothing for 20 months. Whilst the risk was understood, it was probably not worth the effort until there was a real chance that the French could approach the area.[31]

Rear Admiral Berkeley also raised the risk in March 1810 and suggested that a defensive line could be prepared between Coina and the Lagoon of Albufeira on the Atlantic coast, providing a defensive position away from the banks of the Tagus. Wellington asked Fletcher to investigate, and the proposal was rejected as 'difficult to occupy with advantage.'[32] This area was looked at again in November 1810 as one of three possible solutions to defending the southern bank of the river.[33] Goldfinch also investigated the line from Aldeia Galega (now called Montijo) through Moita, Palmela to Setúbal and other defensive positions further east towards Pinheiro. Whilst the riverbanks were difficult 'no natural impediments are to be found between the Tagus and Palmella [and] Setuval.'[34] The solution chosen was to fortify the banks of the Tagus between Almada and Trafaria. Goldfinch had also been asked to investigate this area in early November and was chased to complete his report on 16 November 1810. The report must have been submitted before the end of the month as John Burgoyne noted on 1 December:

> A project has been given in by Goldfinch for taking up the ground on the left bank of the Tagus from opposite Lisbon at Almada to near the sea at Trafaria, a distance of 4 miles, the ground not being naturally difficult the proposal is to make 35 redoubts on the most commanding spots and intrench villages and buildings, which works will require a garrison of 11,000.[35]

As well as the 35 redoubts, Goldfinch recommended strengthening another 25 buildings requiring 197 guns, 10,750 troops and a reserve of 4,000 troops.[36] Wellington made a personal reconnaissance on 6 December and like Goldfinch's proposal for the defences of the city boundaries, his proposal was cut back. Jones said that the reduced defences required 7,500 men and 86 guns but did not specify the number of forts.[37] Sousa Lobo wrote that 21 were completed, and the maps in his book and Jones' show the same 21 forts. Sousa Lobo stated that only Forts 1–7 were started in 1810 with the last fort not being completed until 1812.[38] This appears to be confirmed by Jones who recorded that Wellington put a temporary halt on building work in November 1811 when 17 had been constructed. The final four forts were in the centre and in advance of the previous constructions.[39]

The work on the south bank was plagued by the same resource issues as the work to the north. Goldfinch had been told to request manpower

---

31   For his views see Gurwood, *Dispatches*, Wellington to Berkeley, 17 October 1810.
32   Gurwood, *Dispatches*, Wellington to Berkeley 6 & 8 March 1810.
33   REM: 5501-79, Goldfinch to Fletcher, 19 November 1810.
34   REM: 5501-59-4, Goldfinch to Fletcher, 9 & 12 November 1810.
35   REM: 4201-68, Journal entry for 1 December 1810.
36   Jones, *Sieges*, Vol.3, p.101. Original REM 5501-59-16.
37   Jones, *Sieges*, Vol.3, p.39. see also p.100 for original proposal.
38   Sousa Lobo, *Defesa*, p.201.
39   REM: 5501-59-2, 11 November 1811.

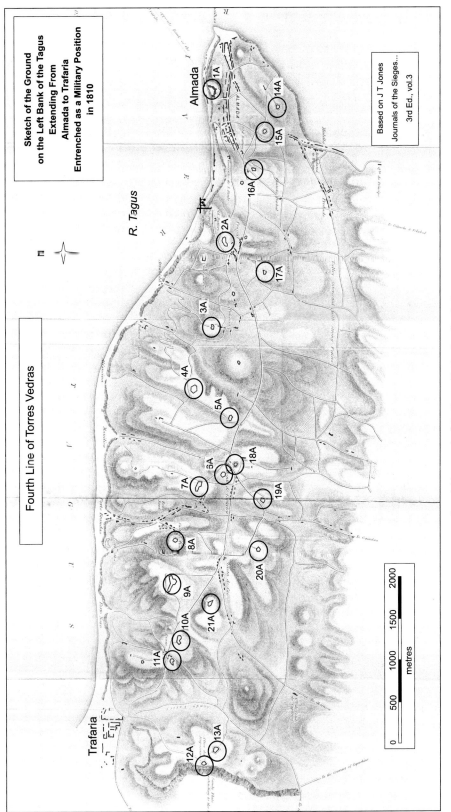

Sketch of the Ground
on the Left Bank of the Tagus
Extending From
Almada to Trafaria
Entrenched as a Military Position
in 1810

Fourth Line of Torres Vedras

R. Tagus

Almada

Trafaria

Based on J T Jones
Journals of the Sieges...
3rd Ed., vol.3

metres

0   500   1000   1500   2000

Fourth Line, south of the Tagus. (Author's collection)

from the governor of Setúbal and workmen were diverted from around São Julião to assist.[40] He fell out with the *Juiz de Fora* (senior magistrate and head of town council) at Almada and made a formal complaint against him. By mid-December he was having difficulty finding food for the Portuguese workers.[41] Civilians were being forced to work to expand the workforce. A letter complained that the methods used by the intendant of police to obtain labour were unsuitable.[42] On 20 December, Fletcher wrote to all his senior engineer officers informing them that posters had been put up advertising for local labour. As previously mentioned, the rates of pay on offer were better than soldiers were being paid and should have been attractive to the displaced people behind the Lines, particularly as food was also being offered. Ten days later, Goldfinch reported that the labour situation had eased, perhaps through more workers volunteering. Portuguese engineers and artificers from British line regiments were also used on the works.[43]

At the end of January 1811, Goldfinch was once again reporting labour shortages but work on Fort 11A was commencing, so progress was being made.[44] Goldfinch wrote directly to the Portuguese Minister of War, Dom Miguel Forjaz:

> Since your excellency's communication of the suspension of the coercive measures previously pursued by the police of Lisbon for the purpose of supplying these works with labourers from the unfortunate refugees who were there without employ, I have not ceased endeavouring to substitute other means. I cannot however say that I have been successful. My last expedient was sending two ordenança serjeants well acquainted with the nature of the work here, to endeavour to persuade these people, who certainly must be very numerous to join voluntarily, promising the serjeants a certain sum for each good workman they might bring ... This plan has not procured, after a fortnight, 20 men and I fear will not answer.[45]

Forjaz clearly suggested another solution as Goldfinch wrote again: 'I beg leave to acquaint your excellency that Captain Morera [Francisco Pedro d'Arbués Moreira] of the Portuguese engineers has this day arrived here and has taken upon himself the superintendence of the supply of workmen from the ordenanças, agreeable to the arrangement proposed by your excellency.'[46]

In April 1811, more extreme measures were being considered to provide manpower:

---

40 REM: 550159-4, Fletcher to Goldfinch, 12 December 1810; Fletcher to Wedekind, 13 December 1810.
41 REM: 5501-59-4, Fletcher to Goldfinch, 15 & 17 December 1810.
42 REM: 5501-59-4, Fletcher to Goldfinch, 20 December 1810.
43 REM 5501-59-4, Fletcher to Goldfinch, 17, 26 & 31 December 1810.
44 REM 5501-59-4, Fletcher to Goldfinch, 28 & 30 January 1811.
45 AHM: PT-AHM-DIV-1-14-172-39, Goldfinch to Forjaz, 10 February 1811.
46 AHM: PT-AHM-DIV-1-14-172-39, Goldfinch to Forjaz, 17 February 1811.

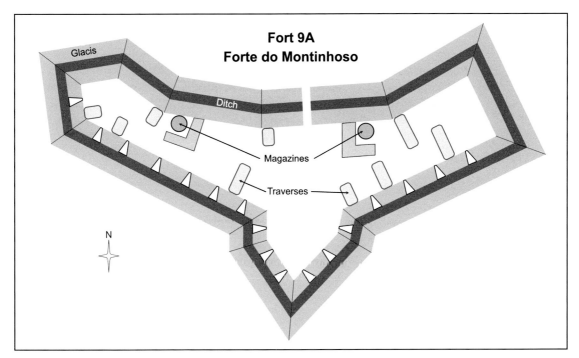

Fort 9A, Montinhoso, fourth line.

with regard to your excellency's suggestion, concerning the employment of French prisoners, in lieu of the ordenanças, for the completion of these works, after mature consideration, I feel persuaded that the plan would not answer. I am well aware of the advantages proposed and pointed out by your excellency … [but] during the day … very considerable guards would be required, as the prisoners would be scattered on the whole extent of the line in ten or twelve different works. It would not be possible to employ prisoners alone in any part, the consequence of intermixing them with the peasantry might be very serious and I think certainly would be the means of preventing much good being done with either party.[47]

Goldfinch remained in charge of the building work for most of 1811 and 1812. On 30 December 1811, he received orders to start construction of three new redoubts.[48] In July 1812 an order was given to prepare a covered way near Almada, by raising the side of a road. For this task Goldfinch told Forjaz that French prisoners could be used as the group could be kept together to complete the work.[49] This work continued to the end of the year.

In addition to this defensive line, the defences at Setúbal and Palmela were improved. Whilst Setúbal was not expected to be the main embarkation point for the British army, Wellington saw that it could have a supplemental role for the evacuation of the Portuguese government, civilians or soldiers. Peniche, which also had its defences improved, was also earmarked for this

---

47 AHM: PT-AHM-DIV-1-14-172-39, Goldfinch to Forjaz, 17 April 1811.
48 REM: 5501-59-4, Fletcher to Goldfinch, 30 December 1811.
49 AHM: PT-AHM-DIV-1-14-060-122, Goldfinch to Forjaz, 17 August 1812; TNA: WO55/981, Goldfinch to Fletcher, 10 October 1812.

role as well as being a staging point for attacks against French foragers during the occupation of the Lines.

It can be seen that the idea that work on the lines ended when they were occupied is not correct. Improvements continued for two more years. Wellington could not be sure that another invasion would not be ordered. If it was, the French army would have been stronger than Masséna's and so the defences would also need to be stronger. The fact that maintenance work continued to the end of the war suggests strongly that Wellington thought he might need them again. As it happened, he did not.

13

Conclusion – The significance of the Lines of Torres Vedras to the Peninsular and Napoleonic Wars

The Lines of Torres Vedras are very much at the fringe of Napoleonic history. They were so far from the main events in central Europe that their significance is still overlooked. The Lines were never attacked, and static defences do not have the appeal of pitched battles. However, the Lines played a critical role in Wellington's Peninsular strategy and gave him a secure base from where he could wage his war against the more numerous French. His campaigns eventually led to their eviction from the Iberian Peninsula in 1813 and ultimately contributed to the defeat of Napoleon.

The French had only one real chance to evict the British from the Iberian Peninsula, and that was in 1810. The British army was small, the Portuguese army small and untried. In future years, both would be larger and more experienced. Had the French tried again they would have had to bring more than 100,000 troops, and probably would still have failed. The main reason for the failure of the French invasion was Napoleon not introducing a single chain of command in the Iberian Peninsula that should have made eviction of the British the priority. There was nothing else in the Peninsula that could not have been postponed until this objective was achieved. Without the British presence, the Iberian Peninsula would probably have been lost. That is not to say the British army achieved the victory alone, but they probably tipped the balance in favour of their Iberian allies. The presence of the British army also meant that the British government continued to provide large amounts of money and materials to support the fight against Napoleon in the Peninsula.

It would be many years before Portuguese civilians recovered from the effects of the third invasion. However, their fate would probably have been worse if Portugal had become a poor, distant province under the control of the French empire. Even without becoming a French vassal, Portugal and

Spain would never recover economically, losing all their South American colonies within 10 years of the end of the Napoleonic wars.

Today, there are still around 100 forts in existence in varying states of preservation and restoration. The six local municipalities take care of them and signage and information are now easily accessible. There are several interpretation centres on the Lines where visitors can find out more about them. Most importantly, the Lines are now protected as national monuments. Their construction is now marked by the official, Lines of Torres Vedras Day, on 20 October, the day that Wellington wrote his memorandum to Lieutenant Colonel Richard Fletcher RE.

I will leave the final quote to a serving soldier, Colonel Jonathan Cresswell RA:

> The one thing that stood out … was deterrence. The line was so powerful that the French did not commit to attack it. This is a major gunnery consideration – creating a matrix that overcomes the adversary without firing a shot. This was a triumph of gunnery and military engineering.[1]

The work of several thousand Portuguese militia and civilians commanded by a small number of engineers, built a static defence of over 150 forts and 600 guns that Napoleon's most capable marshal did not dare attack.

---

1   Contained in email to the present author dated, 23 September 2020.

Appendix I

Memorandum for Lieutenant Colonel Fletcher, Commanding Royal Engineer

Lisbon 20 October 1809.

In the existing relative state of the Allied and French armies in the Peninsula, it does not appear probable that the enemy have it in their power to make an attack upon Portugal. They must wait for their reinforcements; and as the arrival of these may be expected, it remains to be considered what plan of defence shall be adopted for this country.

The great object in Portugal is the possession of Lisbon and the Tagus, and all our measures must be directed to this object. There is another also connected with that first object, to which we must likewise attend, viz., the embarkation of the British troops in case of reverse.

In whatever season the enemy may enter Portugal, he will probably make his attack by two distinct lines, the one north, the other south of the Tagus; and the system of defence to be adopted must be founded upon this general basis.

In the winter season the river Tagus will be full and will be a barrier to the enemy's enterprises with his left attack, not very difficult to be secured. In the summer season, however, the Tagus being fordable in many places between Abrantes and Salvaterra, and even lower than Salvaterra, care must be taken that the enemy does not, by his attack directed from the south of the Tagus, and by the passage of that river, cut off from Lisbon the British army engaged in operations to the northward of the Tagus.

The object of the allies should be to oblige the enemy as much as possible to make his attack with concentrated corps. They should stand in every position which the country could afford, such a length of time as would enable the people of the country to evacuate the towns and villages, carrying with them or destroying all articles of provisions and carriages, not necessary for the allied army; each corps taking care to preserve its communication with the others, and its relative distance from the point of junction.

In whatever season the enemy's attack may be made, the whole allied army, after providing for the garrisons of Elvas, Almeida, Abrantes, and Valença, should be divided into three corps, to be posted as follows: one corps to be in Beira; another in Alentejo; and the third, consisting of the Lusitanian Legion, eight battalions of caçadores, and two of militia, in the mountains of Castello Branco.

In the winter, the corps in Beira should consist of two thirds of the whole numbers of the operating army. In the summer, the corps in Beira, and Alentejo should be nearly of equal numbers.

I shall point out in another memorandum the plan of operations to be adopted by the corps north and south of the Tagus in the winter months.

In the summer, it is probable, as I have above stated, that the enemy will make his attack in two principal corps, and that he will also push one through the mountains of Castello Branco and Abrantes. His object will be, by means of his corps south of the Tagus, to turn the positions which might be taken up in his front on the north of that river; to cut off from Lisbon the corps opposed to him; and to destroy it by an attack in front and rear at the same time. This can be avoided only by the retreat of the right centre, and left of the allies, and their junction at a point at which, from the state of the river, they cannot be turned by the passage of the Tagus by the enemy's left.

The first point of defence which presents itself below that at which the Tagus ceases to be fordable is the river of Castanheira, and here the army should be posted as follows:- 10,000 men, including all the cavalry, in the plain between the Tagus and the hills; 5,000 infantry on the left of the plain; and the remainder of the army, with the exception of the following detachments, on the height in front, and on the right of Cadafoes [Cadafais].

In order to prevent the enemy from turning, by their left the positions which the allies may take up for the defence of the high road to Lisbon by the Tagus, Torres Vedras should be occupied by a corps of 5,000 men; the height in the rear of Sobral de Monte Agraço by 4,000 men; and Arruda by 2,000 men.

There should be a small corps on the height east by south of the height of Sobral, to prevent the enemy from marching from Sobral to Arruda; and there should be another small corps on the height of Ajuda, between Sobral and Bucellas.

In case the enemy should succeed in forcing the corps at Torres Vedras, or Sobral de Monte Agraço, or Arruda; if the first, it must fall back gradually to Cabeça de Montachique, occupying every defensible point on the road: if the second, it must fall back upon Bucellas, destroying the road after the height of Ajuda: if the third, it must fall back upon Alhandra, disputing the road particularly at a point one league in front of that town.

In case any one of these three positions should be forced, the army must fall back from its position as before pointed out, and must occupy one as follows:

5,000 men, principally light infantry, on the hill behind Alhandra; the main body of the army on the Serra de Serves, with its right on that part of the Serra which is near the Cazal de Portella, and is immediately above the road which crosses the Serra from Bucellas to Alverca; and its left extending to the pass of Bucellas. The entrance of the pass of Bucellas to be occupied by the troops retired from Sobral de Monte Agraço, etc., and Cabeça de Montachique, by the corps retired from Torres Vedras.

In order to strengthen these several positions, it is necessary that different works should be constructed immediately, and that arrangements and preparations should made for the construction of others.

Accordingly, I beg Colonel Fletcher, as soon as possible, to review these several positions.

1st.	He will examine particularly the effect of damming up the mouth of the Castanheira river; how far it will render that river a barrier, and to what extent it will fill.
2nd.	He will calculate the labor [sic] required for that work, and the time it will take, as well as the means of destroying the bridge over the river, and of constructing such redoubts as might be necessary on the plain, and on the hill on the left of the road, effectually to defend the plain. He will state particularly what means should be prepared for these works. He will also consider of the means and time required, and the effect which might be produced by sloping [Jones and RE copy says scarping] the banks of the river.
3rd.	He will make the same calculations for the works to be executed on the hill in front, and on the right of Cadafoes, particularly on the left of that hill, to shut the entry of the valley of Cadafoes.
4th.	He will examine and report upon the means of making a good road of communication from the plain across the hills into the valley of Cadafoes, and to the left of the proposed position, and calculate the time and labor it will take.
5th.	He will examine the road from Otta by Abregada [Abrigada. Jones also writes incorrectly; Abringola], Labrugeira to Merciana [sic Merceana], and thence to Torres Vedras; and also from Merciana to Sobral de Monte Agraço. He will also examine and report upon the road from Alemquer [Alenquer] to Sobral de Monte Agraço.
6th.	He will entrench a post at Torres Vedras for 5,000 men. He will examine the road from Torres Vedras to Cabeça de Montachique; and fix upon the spots, [at] which to break [it] up, might stop or delay the enemy; and if there should be advantageous ground at such spots, he will entrench a position for 400 [Jones says 4,000 men, which is wrong] men to cover the retreat of the corps from Torres Vedras.
7th.	He will examine the position at Cabeça de Montachique, and determine upon its line of defence, and upon the works to be constructed for its defence, by a corps of 5,000 men; of which he will estimate the time and the labor
8th.	He will entrench a position for 4,000 men on the two heights which command the road from Sobral de Monte Agraço to Bucellas.
9th.	He will entrench a position for 400 men on the height of Ajuda, between Sobral and Bucellas, to cover the retreat of the corps from Sobral to Bucellas; and he will calculate the means and the time it will take to destroy the road at that spot.

10th.   He will construct a redoubt for 200 men and three guns at the windmill on the height of Sobral de Monte Agraço, which guns will bear upon the road from Sobral to Arruda.

11th.   He will ascertain the points at which, and the means by which, the road from Sobral to Arruda can be destroyed.

12th.   He will ascertain the labor and time required to entrench a position which he will fix upon for 2,000 men to defend the road coming out of Arruda towards Villa Franca and Alhandra, and he will fix upon the spot at which the road from Arruda to Alhandra can be destroyed with advantage.

13th.   He will construct a redoubt on the hill which commands the road from Arruda, about one league in front of Alhandra.

14th.   He will examine the estuaries [Jones and RE say little rivers] at Alhandra, and see whether, by damming them up at the mouths, he could increase the difficulties of a passage by that place; and he will ascertain the time and labor and means which this work will require.

15th.   He will fix upon the spots and ascertain the time and labor required to construct redoubts upon the hill of Alhandra on the right, to prevent the passage of the enemy by the high road; and on the left, and in the rear, to prevent by their fire the occupation of the mountains towards Alverca.

16th.   He will determine upon the works to be constructed on the right of the position upon the Serra de Serves, as above pointed out, to prevent the enemy from forcing that point; and he will calculate the means and the time required to execute them. He will likewise examine the pass of Bucellas, and fix upon the works to be constructed for its defence, and calculate the means, time, and labor required for the execution.

17th.   He will calculate the means, time, and labor required to construct a work upon the hill upon which the windmill stands, at the southern entrance at the pass of Bucellas.

18th.   He will fix upon spots on which signal posts can be erected upon these hills, to communicate from one part of the position to the other.

19th.   It is very desirable that we should have an accurate plan of the ground.

20th.   Examine the island in the river opposite to Alhandra and fix upon the spot, and calculate the means and time required to construct batteries upon it to play upon the approach to Alhandra.

21st.   Examine the effect of damming up the river which runs by Loures; and calculate the time and means required to break up the bridge at Loures.

Wellington.[1]

---

1   Taken from: Gurwood, *Dispatches*, 20 October 1809; Royal Engineers Museum, 5501-91-1 (copy in two different hands. I believe the first six pages are by Fletcher, the rest in another hand); Jones, *Sieges*, Vol.3, pp.117–119. Note: There are minor differences between the versions.

Appendix II

Complete List of Forts to Defend Lisbon

This information comes from various published and unpublished sources including Jones, *Sieges,* pp.64–101 and tables in REM 5501-59-18 (There are two slightly different tables of forts in the file). The table format below is for the seven district layout rather than the earlier six district layout as many later forts did not exist when the six district layout was established.

Contemporary plans of the defences identified that some forts had more than one component which were physically separate. These are identified with a letter suffix, e.g. 5A. It is not possible to positively identify the number of soldiers and guns in each of these defensive positions. Some were meant to temporarily hold field pieces.

Comparison of District on Lines of Torres Vedras			
Six Districts	**Location**	**Seven Districts**	**Location**
First Line		First Line	
1	Sea to Torres Vedras	1	Alhandra to Arruda
2	Sobral to Calhandriz	2	Arruda to Sobral
3	Calhandriz to Alhandra	3	Sobral to Runa
		4	Runa to sea
Second Line		Second Line	
4	Tagus to Bucelas	5	Tagus to Bucelas
5	Bucelas to Mafra	6	Bucelas to Mafra
6	Mafra to the Sea	7	Mafra to the Sea

WELLINGTON AND THE LINES OF TORRES VEDRAS

Line	Fort	Fort Name	District	Men	Guns				
					24-pdr	12-pdr	9-pdr	6-pdr	Howitzer
1	1A	Bateria do Tejo (for 4 guns)	1 Alhandra	1,000		4	3	6	
1	1B	Entrincheiramento (for 2 guns)	1 Alhandra						
1	1C	Bateria da Estrada (for 1 gun)	1 Alhandra						
1	1D	Bateria da Estrada (for 2 guns)	1 Alhandra						
1	1E	Bateria da Estrada Real (for 7 guns)	1 Alhandra						
1	1F	Bateria da Subida (for 2 guns)	1 Alhandra						
1	2	Bateria do Conde	1 Alhandra	800		2			
1	3	Reduto da Boa Vista	1 Alhandra	200		2			
1	4	Bateria de São Fernando	1 Alhandra				2		
1	5	Reduto Serra do Formoso	1 Alhandra	120			3		
1	5A	Bateria das Antas (for 2 guns)	1 Alhandra						
1	5B	Bateria 1a de Alfarge (for 2 guns)	1 Alhandra						
1	5C	Bateria 2a de Alfarge (for 3 guns)	1 Alhandra						
1	5D	Bateria 1a do Bulhaco (for 2 guns)	1 Alhandra						
1	5E	Bateria 2a do Bulhaco (for 2 guns)	1 Alhandra						
1	5F	Bateria 1a da Serra do Pinheiro (for 2 guns)	1 Alhandra						
1	5G	Bateria 2a da Serra do Pinheiro (for 1 gun)	1 Alhandra						
1	6	Bateria dos Melros	1 Alhandra			2			
1	7	Forte do Calhandriz	1 Alhandra	200		3			
		Valley of Calhandriz [between forts 6 and 121] is closed by a line of intrenchments and abatis, not numbered, thrown up when the army occupied the Lines [REM5501-59-18]					11	1	
1	8	Forte de Trancoso	1 Alhandra	200		3			
1	9	Forte do Casal do Cego	1 Alhandra	280			3		
1	10	Forte da Carvalha	1 Alhandra	400		2	1		
1	11	Forte do Moinho do Céu	1 Alhandra	300		4			
1	12	Forte do Passo	2 Sobral	120			3		
1	13	Forte da Caneira	2 Sobral	120		2			
1	14	Forte do Alqueidão	2 Sobral	1,590		14	6	4	1
1	15	Forte do Machado	2 Sobral	460		3	3	1	
1	16	Forte do Trinta	2 Sobral	250		1	2		1
1	17	Forte do Simplício	2 Sobral	300				7	1
2	18	Forte da Ajuda Grande	5 Bucelas	300		4			
2	19	Forte da Ajuda Pequeno	5 Bucelas	200			3		
1	20	Forte de S. Vicente	4 Torres Vedras	470		5		2	1
1	21	Forte de S. Vicente (REM:5501-59-18 different tables say 6 or 4)	4 Torres Vedras	270		2	4/6		1
1	22	Forte de S. Vicente	4 Torres Vedras	380		5		3	1
1	20-22	Defence of curtain wall (South 150, North 90, North-East 360: REM 5501-59-18)	4 Torres Vedras	600					
1	23	Reduto dos Olheiros	4 Torres Vedras	180			4	3	
1	24	Reduto da Forca	4 Torres Vedras	300			7		
1	25	Forte de São João	4 Torres Vedras	200			2		
1	26	Forte da Ordasqueira	4 Torres Vedras	300			3		
1	27	Castelo de Torres Vedras	4 Torres Vedras	500		5			
2	28	Forte Pequeno da Enxara	3 Portela	270		3			

Line	Fort	Fort Name	District	Men	Guns 24-pdr	12-pdr	9-pdr	6-pdr	Howitzer
2	29	Forte Grande da Enxara	3 Portela	280			4		
1	30	Reduto do Grilo	4 Torres Vedras	340		3	1		
1	31	Reduto da Alquiteira	4 Torres Vedras	370			3		
1	32	Forte do Formigal	4 Torres Vedras	260		3	1		
2	33	Forte do Salgado	5 Bucelas	300		4			
2	34	Forte do Curral	5 Bucelas	200			3		
2	35	Reduto da Quintela Pequeno	5 Bucelas	120			4		
2	36	Reduto da Quintela Grande	5 Bucelas	370		9			
2	37	Forte da Abrunheira	5 Bucelas	50			3		
2	38	Forte da Casa	5 Bucelas	340			5		
2	39	Forte da Quintela Reentrante	5 Bucelas	340		5	3		
2	40	Forte da Aguieira	5 Bucelas	150					
2	41	Reduto da Portela Grande	5 Bucelas	240		5			
2	42	Reduto da Portela Pequeno	5 Bucelas	350		6			
2	43	Bateria do Vizo	5 Bucelas			4			
2	44	Bateria da Cachada	5 Bucelas				2		
2	45	Bateria dos Penedos	5 Bucelas			3			
2	46	Bateria das Oliveiras	5 Bucelas				2		
2	47	Bateria dos Galvões	5 Bucelas			3			
2	48	Forte do Tojal	5 Bucelas	200		2			
2	49	Forte do Picoto	6 Montachique			2			
2	50	Reduto do Quadradinho	6 Montachique	160			2		
2	51	Forte do Freixial	6 Montachique	300		4			
2	52	Forte do Capitão	6 Montachique	190			3		
2	53	Forte da Presinheira	6 Montachique	230			2		
2	54	Forte do Moinho (for 0 guns)	6 Montachique	210					
2	55	Forte do Vale	6 Montachique	150		3			
2	56	Forte do Permouro	7 Mafra	150		2			
2	57	Forte do Mosqueiro	6 Montachique	270		3			
2	58	Forte do Carrascal	6 Montachique	310			3		
2	59	Forte do Moinho da Carambela	6 Montachique	260		4			
2	60	Reduto da Achada 1	6 Montachique	150			2		
2	61	Reduto da Achada 2	6 Montachique	190			2		
2	62	Forte do Alto do Cheira	6 Montachique	390		3			
2	63	Forte do Casal da Serra	6 Montachique	280			3		
2	64	Forte do Canto do Muro da Tapada	6 Montachique	210			3		
2	65	Forte de Santa Maria	6 Montachique	270		3			
2	66	Forte da Feira	6 Montachique	350		4			
2	67	Forte do Cabeço Gordo	6 Montachique	120			2		
2	68	Forte do Matoutinho	6 Montachique	260		4			
2	69	Forte da Quinta do Fidalgo	6 Montachique	240		4			
2	70	Forte da Quinta do Estrangeiro	6 Montachique	240		4	2		
2	71	Forte da Portela	6 Montachique	240			4		
2	72	Forte da Estrada	6 Montachique	130			2		
2	73	Forte da Coutada	6 Montachique	340		3			
2	74	Forte do Casal da Pedra	7 Mafra	190			2		
2	75	Forte da Milhariça	7 Mafra	70			2		
2	76	Forte do Sonível	7 Mafra	390		4			
2	77	Forte do Juncal	7 Mafra	380		4			
2	78	Forte do Telhadouro	7 Mafra	110		2	1		

Line	Fort	Fort Name	District	Men	Guns 24-pdr	12-pdr	9-pdr	6-pdr	Howitzer
2	79	Forte do Gio	7 Mafra	270		3			
2	80	Forte da Quinta da Boa Viagem	7 Mafra	310		3			
2	81	Forte da Serra de Chipre	7 Mafra	280			3		
2	82	Forte da Patarata	7 Mafra	210		2	2		
2	83	Forte do Meio	7 Mafra	240			3		
2	84	Forte do Curral do Linho	7 Mafra	290		3			
2	85	Forte do Areeiro	7 Mafra	290		3			
2	86	Forte de Nossa Senhora da Paz	7 Mafra	280		3			
2	87	Forte do Pinheiro	7 Mafra	340		3			
2	88	Forte do Cabeço do Neto	7 Mafra	200		3			
2	89	Forte do Moxarro	7 Mafra	310		3			
2	90	Forte de Penegache	7 Mafra	230		3			
2	91	Forte da Alagoa	7 Mafra	200		3			
2	92	Forte do Picoto	7 Mafra	180		3			
2	93	Forte de Marvão	7 Mafra	330		3			
2	94	Forte de Ribamar	7 Mafra	320		2			
2	95	Forte do Zambujal	7 Mafra	250		2			
2	96	Forte da Carvoeira	7 Mafra	280		3			
2	97	Forte de São Julião	7 Mafra	350		2			
3	98	Forte do Algueirão	Third Line – São Julião	1,340	20			6	
3	99	Bataria do Arieiro	Third Line – São Julião	70		6			
3	100	Bataria da Estrada	Third Line – São Julião	50		6			
3	101	Reduto 1o da Medrosa	Third Line – São Julião	250		10			
3	102	Reduto 2o da Medrosa	Third Line – São Julião	260		8			
3	103	Reduto 1o das Antas	Third Line – São Julião	130			3		
3	104	Reduto 2o das Antas	Third Line – São Julião	100			2		
3	105	Reduto 3o das Antas (REM:5501-59-18 says 4 guns)	Third Line – São Julião	170			4/2?		
3	106	Reduto da Lomba	Third Line – São Julião	320		6			
3	107	Reduto da Quinta Nova	Third Line – São Julião	800		6			
3	108	Reduto do Junqueiro	Third Line – São Julião	360		6			
3	109	Reduto da Figueirinha	Third Line – São Julião	500			7		1
3	110	Fortified line from Fort 103 to coastline at Forte das Mais. (REM:5501-59-18 does not list guns, but it seems likely)	Third Line – São Julião	1,000			3		
1	111	Forte do Passo	4 Torres Vedras	250		5			
1	112	Forte das Gentias	4 Torres Vedras	220		4			
1	113	Bataria da Foz	4 Torres Vedras	50		2			
1	114	Forte 1o de Subserra (REM:5501-59-18 does not list 6-pdr)	1 Alhandra	100			2	1?	

Line	Fort	Fort Name	District	Men	Guns				
					24-pdr	12-pdr	9-pdr	6-pdr	Howitzer
1	114A	Bateria Nova de Subserra (for 2 guns)	1 Alhandra						
1	115	Forte 2o de Subserra	1 Alhandra	100			2		
1	116	Forte 3o de Subserra	1 Alhandra	100			5		
1	116A	Bateria Anexa ao Forte 3o de Subserra / Forte 4o de Subserra (See note 1 below)	1 Alhandra						
1	116B	Bateria do Casal da Entrega (for 4 guns)	1 Alhandra						
1	117	Reduto Novo da Costa da Freiria	1 Alhandra	150					
1	118	Forte dos Sinais	1 Alhandra	400		8			
1	119	Reduto dos Dois Moinhos	1 Alhandra	350		6			
1	119A	See Note 2 below table.							
1	119B	Forte da Subida da Serra (for 2 guns)	1 Alhandra						
1	120	Forte Novo do Formoso	1 Alhandra	130		2			
1	121	Forte 1o do Calhandriz	1 Alhandra	250			3	1	
1	122	Forte 2o do Calhandriz	1 Alhandra	300		3			
1	123	Forte 3o do Calhandriz (REM:5501-59-18 does not list 6-pdr)	1 Alhandra	300		3	1		
1	124	Forte 4o do Calhandriz	6 Montachique	350		3	1		
1	124A	Bateria do Calhandriz (for 2 guns)	6 Montachique						
1	125	Forte da Serra de Arpim	6 Montachique	250		4			
2	126	Forte Novo do Cabo	5 Bucelas	188		2			
2	127	Forte do Moinho	5 Bucelas	154					
1	128	Forte da Archeira	3 Portela	500		6			
1	129	Forte da Feiteira	3 Portela	350		6			
1	130	Forte do Catefica	3 Portela	200			5		
1	131	Bateria da Cruz	4 Torres Vedras	90		4			
1	132	Bateria dos Palheiros	4 Torres Vedras	150		6			
1	133	Bateria dos Pedrulhos	4 Torres Vedras	120			4		
1	134	Bateria do Outeiro da Prata	4 Torres Vedras	110		4			
1	135	Bateria da Carrasqueira	4 Torres Vedras	160			4		
1	136	Bateria da Milharosa	4 Torres Vedras	150		4			
1	137	Bateria do Outeiro da França	4 Torres Vedras	100		4			
1	138	Bateria do Pombal	4 Torres Vedras	100				2	
1	139	Bateria da Bordinheira	4 Torres Vedras	160		4			
1	140	Bateria do Outeiro do Monte	4 Torres Vedras	120		4			
1	141	Bateria do Mogo	4 Torres Vedras	180		4			
1	142	Bateria do Bonabal	4 Torres Vedras	150		4			
1	143	Forte da Galpeira	4 Torres Vedras	150			4		
1	144	Bateria das Mouguelas	4 Torres Vedras	130		4			
1	145	Forte de Belmonte	4 Torres Vedras	250			4		
1	146	Forte de Bececarias	4 Torres Vedras	250			6		
1	147	Bateria da Ponte do Rol I	4 Torres Vedras	0					
1	148	Bateria da Ponte do Rol II	4 Torres Vedras	0					
1	149	Forte Novo da Ordasqueira	4 Torres Vedras	250		4	2		
1	150	Bateria da Ribaldeira (Missing from tables in Jones, Sieges)	3 Portela	250		4	2		
1	151	Reduto da Patameira	3 Portela	300					
1	152	Forte Novo	2 Sobral	250		4	2		

Note 1: There is some confusion on the numbering of Forts 116 and 117. On one contemporary Portuguese plan, Fort 117 is clearly shown as an annex on the side of Fort 116 and called *4o de Subserra*. Modern interpretations show this work as 116A, *Bateria Anexa ao Forte 3o de Subserra*, which makes sense as Fort 116 is *3o de Subserra*. Jones, *Sieges*, Vol. 3, p.94, describes Fort 117 as a *fleche*, i.e. a minor defensive position which supports the attachment to Fort 116. Many modern interpretations show Fort 117 as being a square redoubt, *Reduto Novo da Costa da Freiria*. Another contemporary map (TNA:MR1-523) shows this large square fort but no number is recorded against it. It is likely that at some point the large square fort is numbered 117 and the fleche was renumbered to 116A.

Note 2: There is no evidence this fort existed, other than there is a 119B.

Fourth Line (see map in Chapter 12)

Fort	Fort Name	Fort	Fort Name
1A	Castelo de Almada	12A	Forte Raposeira Grande
2A	Forte Pragal	13A	Forte Raposeira Pequeno
3A	Palença	14A	Forte Margueira
4A	Forte Raposo	15A	Forte Alorna
5A	Reduto Bicheiro / Bixeiro	16A	Forte São Sebastião
6A	Forte Prior	17A	Forte Armeiro-Mor
7A	Reduto Granja	18A	Forte Melo
8A	Castelo Picão	19A	Reduto Pombal
9A	Forte Montinhoso	20A	Reduto Piçolos
10A	Forte Guedes	21A	Forte Pêra
11A	Forte Morfacem		

Note: Most of the information in this table comes from Sousa Lobo, *Defesa*, pp.163–172. Jones' *Sieges*, is very superficial on the subject, including using the table of forts in the original larger proposal, not the final agreed set. Jones was never involved in the building work on the fourth line. The present author has been unable to find a complete breakdown of the men and guns in the forts on the fourth Line.

Lisbon City Defences (see map in Chapter 3)

Fort No.	Name	Fort No.	Name
1L	Forte da Cruz da Pedra	17L	Bateria de S. Sebastião
2L	Bateria de Manique	18L	Bateria da Quinta do Seabra
3L	Bateria dos Apóstolos	19L	Bateria 1a do Louriçal
4L	Bateria de São João	20L	Bateria 2a do Louriçal
5L	Bateria de Penha de França	21L	Forte do Alto da Atalia
6L	Bateria dos Sete Castelos	22L	Forte de Campolide
7L	Bateria da Quinta dos Águias	23L	Bateria do Alto de Campolide
8L	Bateria do Alto do Pina	24L	Bateroa do Águas Livres
9L	Bateria Quinta dos Ciprestres	25L	Bateria do Alto do Carvalhão
10L	Bateria de Arroios	26L	Bateria de Poisos
11L	Forte do Alto de Arroios	27L	Bateria de Seta Moinhos
12L	Forte do Barão de Manique	28L	Bateria 1a dos Paulistas
13L	Reduto do Castilho	29L	Bateria 2a dos Paulistas
14L	Bateria do Feliciano	30L	Bateria dos Prazeres
15L	Bateris das Picoas	31L	Bateria da Ponte de Alcântara
16L	Bateria da Cova da Onça	32L	Bateria do Livramento
1N	Reduto de Estevão Pinto		

Note: The numbering of the defences is as used by Sousa Lobo. Positions of forts 29-32 are estimated, based on their names. The contemporary maps by Fava also show another defence near fort 21L, called Reduto de Estevão Pinto. It is marked as 1N in above table and is marked on the map in chapter 3.

Map based on Sousa Lobo, *Defesa*, pp.174–183; BD: 2301-2-16-22-2 & 2235-2-16-22 (Fava maps); TNA: MPH1-152.

Bibliography

Archival Sources

Arquivo Central Da Marinha (ACM)
    1305-12: Ciera Code book
Arquivo Histórico Militar (AHM)
    AHM:PT-AHM-DIV-1 (various)
    AHM:PT-AHM-DIV-3 (various)
Bibliotechas da Defesa (BD)
    2235-2-16-22: plan of Lisbon
    2301-2-16-22: plan of Lisbon
    3935-2-16-22: plan of Lisbon
Royal Engineers Museum (REM)
    2001-149-2: Report on defence of Lisbon
    4201-68: Burgoyne Journals
    4201-152-2: Map
    4501-86: Letters from Ross to Dalrymple
    4601-57-1: Emmet Journal
    4601-74: Engineer Letters
    5501-59-1,2,3: J.T. Jones' Journals from 1810–12
    5501-59-4: Fletcher's Letter book, November 1810–February 1811
    5501-59-5: Fletcher's Letter book, October 1811–October 1812
    4501-86-4: Letters from Captain George Ross to Sir Hew Dalrymple
    5501-59-8: Letters of Fletcher and Jones related to Torres Vedras
    5501-59-15: Goldfinch on defence of Lisbon
    5501-59-18: Letters on Lines of Torres Vedras
    5501-79: Letters
    5501-91-1: Memorandum on building Lines
    5501-123: H.D. Jones letters
British Library (BL)
    ADD39201: Mackenzie diary
    ADD41961-3: Pasley papers
    ADD63106: Letters of John Squire RE to Sir Henry Bunbury,1810–1812.
    RP5296: Beresford correspondence.
National Army Museum
    2004-05-26: Military Engineering in the Peninsular War 1808-1814. A Digest of References by
        Maj. J.T. Hancock.
National Archives (TNA)
    ADM1/4333: Naval allowances.
    MPH1-152; Planta da Defesa da Lisboa, February 1809 by *Tenente Coronel* Olivera
    MR1-523: Maps of Lines of Torres Vedras.
    MR1-930: Maps of Lines of Torres Vedras.
    WO55/958: Engineer papers 1798–1811.
    WO55/959: Engineer papers 1812–1846.
    WO55/978: RE Letters 1809.

WO55/979: RE Letters 1810.
WO55/980: RE Letters 1811.
WO55/1561: Various reports.
Wellington Archives, Southampton University (WP)
    WP9/4/1/3-4: Two (different) Popham code books

Published Sources

Books – Primary Sources

Bamford, Andrew (ed.), *With Wellington Outposts. The Peninsular War Letters of John Vandeleur* (Barnsley: Frontline, 2015)

Brindle, Rosemary (ed.), *With Napoleon's Guns. The Military Memoirs of an Officer of the First Empire. Colonel Jean-Nicholas Noël* (Barnsley: Frontline, 2016)

Brown, Stephen (ed.), *The Autobiography, or Narrative of a Soldier. The Peninsular War Memoirs of William Brown of the 45th Foot* (Solihull: Helion, 2017)

Gurwood, J. (ed.), *The Dispatches of the Duke of Wellington*, New and Enlarged Edition (London: John Murray, 1852)

Hibbert, Christopher, *A Soldier of the 71st* (London: Leo Cooper, 1975)

Jones, J.T.J., *Account of the War in Spain, Portugal and the South of France from 1808 to 1814 inclusive*, Second Edition (London: Egerton, 1821)

Jones J.T.J., *Journal of the Sieges Carried out by the Army Under the Duke of Wellington*, 3rd Edition (London: John Weale, 1846)

Jones, J.T.J., *Memoranda Relative to the Lines Thrown Up to Cover Lisbon in 1810* (London: Private circulation, 1829)

Muir, Rory (ed.), *At Wellington's Right Hand* (London: Sutton Publishing, 2003)

Neves Costa, José Maria das, *Memoria militar respectiva ao terreno ao norte de Lisboa* (Lisboa: Revistas das Sciencias Militares, 1888)

Popham, Home, *Telegraphic Signals or Marine Vocabulary* (London: Egerton, 1803)

Shore, Henry (ed.), *An Engineer Officer under Wellington in the Peninsula* (Cambridge: Ken Trotman, 2005)

Tomkinson, James, *Diary of a Cavalry Officer in the Peninsular and Waterloo Campaigns* (London: Swan Sonnenschein, 1895)

Thompson, Mark S. (ed.), *The Peninsular War Diary of Edmund Mulcaster RE,* (Sunderland: Amazon CreateSpace, 2015)

Thompson, W.F.K., *An Ensign in the Peninsular War* (London: Michael Joseph, 1981)

Vane, C.W., Lord Londonderry (ed.), *Correspondence, Despatches and other Papers of Viscount Castlereagh, Second Marquess of Londonderry, Edited by his Brother, Charles William Vane, Marquess of Londonderry*, Second Series (London: Shoberl, 1851)

Wellington, 2nd Duke of (ed.), *The Supplementary Despatches of the Duke of Wellington* (London: John Murray, 1858–1872)

Books – Secondary Sources

Avillez, P.A (ed.), *Os Exército Português e as Comemorações dos 200 Anos da Guerra Peninsular* (Lisboa: Tribuna, 2008–2011)

Ayres, Christovam Ayres de Magalhães Sepúlveda, *História Organica e politica do Exercito Portuguez* (Lisbon: Imprensa Nacional, 1910)

Bamford, Andrew (ed.), *Command and Leadership, 1721–1815* (Warwick: Helion, 2019)

Berkeley, Alice (ed.), *New Lights on the Peninsular War* (Lisbon: British Historical Society of Portugal, 1991)

Boscawen, Hugh, *The Origins of the Flat-Bottomed Landing Craft 1757–1758* (London: National Army Museum, 1985)

Burnham, R., & McGuigan, R., *British Army Against Napoleon, Facts, Lists, and Trivia* (Barnsley: Frontline, 2010)

Burnham, R., *Wellington's Light Division in the Peninsular War. The Formation, Campaigns and Battles of Wellington's Fighting Force: 1810* (Barnsley: Pen & Sword, 2020)

Butler, Arthur (trans.), *The Memoirs of Baron Thiebault* (Felling: Worley, 1994)

Chartrand, René, *Fuentes de Oñoro, Wellington's Liberation of Portugal* (Oxford: Osprey, 2002)

Clímaco, Cristina, *As Linhas de Torres Vedras, Invasão e Resistência 1810–11* (Torres Vedras: CMTV, 2010)

Fletcher, Ian, *The Lines of Torres Vedras, 1809–11* (London: Osprey, 2003)

Fortescue, J., *History of the British Army* (London: Macmillan, 1899–1930)

Fuente, Francisco de la, *Dom Miguel Pereira Forjaz. His early career and role in the mobilization of the Portuguese Army and Defense of Portugal during the Peninsular war, 1807–1814* (Lisboa: Tribuna, 2011)

Grehan, John, *The Lines of Torres Vedras* (Staplehurst: Spellmount, 2000)

Havard, Robert, *Wellington's Welsh General* (London: Aurum, 1993)

Holtzmann, G.J., & Pehrson, B., *The Early History of Data Networks* (California: IEEE, 1995)

Horward, Donald (ed.), *The French Campaign in Portugal. An Account by Jean Jaques Pelet* (Minneapolis: University of Minnesota, 1973)

Leach, J., *Captain of the 95th (Rifles)* (London: Leonour, 2005)

Lobo, Francisco de Sousa, *A Defesa de Lisboa 1809–1814* (Lisboa: Tribuna, 2015)

Maurice, J.F., *The Diary of Sir John Moore* (London: Arnold, 1904)

Melícias, André Filipe Vítor, *As Linhas de Torres Vedras, Construção e Impactos Locais* (Torres Vedras: CMTV, 2008)

Monteiro, M. (ed.), *The Lines of Torres Vedras; A Defence System to the North of Lisbon* (Lisbon: PILT, 2011)

Napier, W.F.P., *History of the War in the Peninsula and in the South of France from the Year 1807 to the Year 1814* (London: T & W Boone, 1828–1834)

Norris, A.H., & Bremner, R.W., *The Lines of Torres Vedras. The First Three Lines and Fortifications South of the Tagus* (Lisbon: British Historical Society of Portugal, 1980)

Oman, C.W.C., *History of the Peninsular War* (Oxford: Clarendon Press, 1902–1930)

Raeuber, Charles, *Les Renseignements La Reconnaissance et Les Transmissions Militaires du Temp de Napoleon l'exemple de la Troisième invasion du Portugal 1810* (Lisboa: Commissão Portuguesa de História Militar, 1993)

Rocha, Artur, *Guerra Peninsular. Forte de Alqueidão. Arqueologia e História* (Lisboa: CILT, 2015)

Sidney, Edwin, *The Life of Lord Hill GCB, Late Commander of the Forces* (London: John Murray, 1845)

Da Silva, Carlos Guardado (ed.), *A Vida Quotidiana nas Linhas de Torres Vedras* (Torres Vedras: CMTV, 2010)

Soriano, Simão José da Luz, *História da Guerra Civil e do Estabelecimento do Governo Parlamentar em Portugal* (Lisboa: Imprensa Nacional, 1893)

Sutcliffe, Robert, *British Expeditionary Warfare and the Defeat of Napoleon, 1793–1815* (Woodbridge: Boydell & Brewer, 2016)

Thompson, Mark S., *Wellington's Engineers* (Barnsley: Pen & Sword, 2015)

Thompson, Mark S., *Wellington's Favourite Engineer. The Making of a Field Marshal: John Fox Burgoyne in the Napoleonic Wars, 1798–1815* (Warwick: Helion, 2020)

Thompson, Mark S., *Albuera – The Fatal Hill, The Allied Campaign under Beresford in Southern Spain in 1811*, 2nd Edition (Sunderland: Amazon CreateSpace, 2014).

Verner, W. (ed.), *Major George Simmons. A British Rifleman* (London: Greenhill, 1986)

Vincente, A., *Le Génie Français au Portugal Sous L'Empire* (Lisbonne: Estado-Maior do Exército, 1984)

Ward, S.G.P., *Wellington's Headquarters* (Oxford: Oxford University Press, 1957)

White, Kenton, *The Key to Lisbon. The Third French Invasion of Portugal 1810–11* (Warwick: Helion, 2019)

Wrottesley, G.W., *Life and Correspondence of Field Marshall Sir John Burgoyne* (London: Richard Bentley, 1873)

Wyld, James, (ed.), *Memoir annexed to an Atlas containing Plans of the Principal Battles, Sieges and Affairs in which the British Troops were Engaged During the War in the Spanish Peninsula and the South of France* (London: Wyld, 1841)

Theses

De Toy, Brian, *Wellington's Admiral: The life and career of George Berkeley, 1753–1818* (PhD Thesis, Florida State University, 1997)

Periodicals

Cobbett's Political Register, July to December 1810, pp.858–859.

Gazeta de Lisboa, no. 50, 13 December 1808.

Journals

Chartrand, R., 'Wireless Communications in the Peninsula: Portuguese Telegraph Corps in Wellington's Army', *Journal of the Society for Army Historical Research*, Vol. 78, No. 315, pp.220–221

Edwards H.N., 'The Diary of Lieutenant Gillmor – Portugal – 1810', *Journal for the Society for Army Historical Research*, Vol. 3, No.13, pp.148–161

Geraldo, José Custódio Madaleno, 'José Maria Das Neves Costa e as Linhas de Torres Vedras', *Revista Militar*, No. 2495, December 2009, pp.1–23

Luna, Sousa & Leal, 'Telegrafia visual na Guerra Peninsular. 1807–14', *Boletim Cultural 2008* (Mafra: CMM, 2008), pp.67–141.

Henry Shore, 'An Engineer Officer in the Peninsula', *Royal Engineers Journal*, Vol.16, No.3, September 1912, p.171

Thompson, Mark S., 'The Portuguese Telegraph System in 1810', *Fortress Study Group, Casemate*, No.104, September 2015, pp.18–22

Thompson, Mark S., 'The Lines of Torres Vedras 1809–14', *The Royal Engineers Journal*, Vol. 132, No.1, April 2018, pp.43–49

Online Sources

Da Silva, Carlos Guardado 'A vila e o concelho de Santarém sob a invasao francesa de 1810-1811, Impactos materiais e humanos', <https://www.academia.edu/5340183/A_vila_e_o_concelho_de_Santarém_sob_a_invasão_francesa_de_1810_1811_Impactos_materiais_e_humanos>, accessed 24 January 2021.

Viera, José Manuel, 'Abrantes Militar 1810 Capitulo V', <https://coisasdeabrantes.blogspot.com/2017/06/>, accessed 3 November 2020

Gaudêncio, M. & Grey, A., 'The Peninsular Journal of Major General John Randoll Mackenzie', <https://www.napoleon-series.org/research/biographies/GreatBritain/Mackenzie/MackenzieJohnRandol.html>, accessed 3 November 2020

Cy Harrison, *Three Decks – Warships in the Age of Sail*, <https://threedecks.org/>, accessed 3 November 2020

Conference Papers

Rua, Helena, 'Historical and Territorial Analysis. A Contribution to the Study of the Defence of the City of Lisbon: The Peninsular Wars', *Computer Applications to Archaeology* (CAA), 2009, Williamsburg, USA.

Unpublished Sources

Capitão de Fragata Rui Sá Leal, research on the construction of the Lines and the proposals of Neves Costa